I BOUGHT A STAR

I BOUGHT A STAR

by

THOMAS FIRBANK

AUTHOR OF
"I BOUGHT A MOUNTAIN"

Come away, come away,
  Hark to the summons!
Come in your war array,
  Gentles and commons.

Come from deep glen, and
  From mountain so rocky.

SIR WALTER SCOTT
Pibroch of Donuil Dhu

GEORGE G. HARRAP & CO. LTD
LONDON SYDNEY TORONTO BOMBAY

First published 1951
by George G. Harrap & Co. Ltd
182 High Holborn, London, W.C.1
Reprinted 1951

Dewey Decimal classification: 940·548142

Composed in Baskerville type and printed by Western Printing Services Ltd, Bristol
Made in Great Britain

PREFACE

SOME ten years ago I wrote a book about my Welsh upland farm. Events had already separated me from my farm when I joined the Army in 1939. Most of my companions were then, like me, civilians in uniform groping for military adequacy. It was not surprising that they achieved competence quickly, for, just as in the owner of a pot of geraniums one finds the farmer, so beneath the civilized lick of paint the primitive fighter is discovered. Farming and fighting are very old occupations, and are instinct in all of us. Men plough and sow their peaceful seeds, but just as readily, like Jason, they yoke together the wild bulls and plant dragons' teeth.

Perhaps it will be many centuries before one small boy forbears to punch another, and before his father ceases to resort to arms. When this time of goodwill comes the qualities of selflessness, comradeship, and courage will be robbed of a powerful stimulant. To that extent war serves a good purpose.

Most of the farming year is but a preparation for the spectacular few days of reaping what has been sown. So in war the time of training is long, and the fulfilment of action brief. This, therefore, is not a war book saturated with the blood and touched with the glory which so few of us Servicemen had the opportunity to see or earn. It is the story of one of the millions of civilians who were caught up in the machine of Service tradition and fashioned to its ends.

T.F.

CHAGFORD, DEVON
May 1, 1951

CONTENTS

CHAPTER I

STORM ON MONT SAINT-JUSTIN

FAR below on the mountain path a small black figure was toiling upward. I speculated on this unusual event, as I ate my honey and croissants, and drank more coffee. At that early hour the summit of Saint-Justin, floating silent on a sea of vapour, was detached from the world beneath, and even the sparse life of the five valleys which radiated from its foot was hidden. The climbing manikin was an intrusion in that enchanted cloudland, as it moved like a fly against the vast backcloth of Pyrenean peaks. Away beyond, the Pic du Midi du Bigorre was lazily unveiling itself like a waking woman, and beyond its bulk lay Spain.

Even at so great a distance the small black figure was ponderous in its movements. It was not, therefore, little Jacqueline. The satchel of little Jacqueline was my universal provider, and she mounted to my eminence two or three times a week. But her progress was always like that of a dragonfly as she darted from side to side of the track in her pursuit of lizards and giant grasshoppers. Her father, the good Monsieur Casavant, owned the café in the village at the foot of Mont Saint-Justin, where the Col du Tourmalet began its long climb into the Pyrenees. Once, in a frenzy of enterprise, M. Casavant had thought to build a summer hostel on the tip of conical Saint-Justin, but during the labours of construction, complicated by the steepness of the mule-track, landslides, and the dimming of the flame of ambition, the building had shed its aspirations, and had stayed in a state of arrested development as a square stone shed. Earlier in the summer of 1939 I had rented the shelter at a few francs a week, and had remained in possession through the hot July and August days. On this, the first day of September, I was even wondering whether to remain into the winter, and whether if I did I should be too often cut off by snow and storm. But these speculations were now disturbed by the portentous small black figure so slowly crawling upward to my dwelling.

With the clarity of mental vision conferred by a high place, I already knew quite well that my visitor would bring me no good news, and my mind revolted against a disruption of the peace I had found at Saint-Justin.

I had come there by devious routes.

Until the spring of 1939 I had for seven years been farming on a mountain in North Wales. Esmé, who had married me at the start of my venture, had been as young as I. Both of us had had in full measure the intolerance of youth. Both of us, true enough, loved Dyffryn and its crags and waterfalls, but we loved for different reasons. Esmé, a woman, valued its security, the comfort we had made, the prosperous future to which we could look forward. I, a man, had loved Dyffryn for its wildness and its hardness. It had been an adventure, this carving of a tiny kingdom out of rock and heather, and the struggle against wind and geography had been, in a way, hard. I knew our natural adversaries in that outlandish place were subdued, not conquered, but their strength and weakness was now known, and disposition against the enemy would in future be routine. During the pre-Munich year I was often reminded of the most terrible saying of Jesus: "If the salt have lost its savour, wherewith shall it be salted?"

To me, joy is in the building. Anticipation is a spur, realization an anticlimax. A restlessness came on me. There were other worlds to conquer, other songs to sing, strange customs to be learned among races still unknown to me, new philosophies to hear expounded. The boundaries of my kingdom closed and became the walls of a prison. The salt lost its savour.

If Esmé and I had been a little older, a little less obstinate, a little less preoccupied with our own views on life, we might have adjusted our outlook, and, by each giving way on a few points, this crisis in our affairs might have been tided over. To add fuel to the flames of unrest came rumours of march and countermarch, of dark pagan hordes surging through the sombre alleys of the Germanic forests. One tenet to which I clung, and which had been inspired by my rough life at Dyffryn, was the right of the individual to work out his own salvation or damnation. It was clear that Nazidom meant to subordinate men to the will of the State, and a corrupt State at that. It was easy for me to persuade myself that it was my duty to resist this 'ism,' though really I thought of war as a means to escape my problems, just as traditionally a discontented boy has always run away to sea.

But Neville Chamberlain returned from Munich with his scrap of Gothic script, and the ferrule of the Ministerial umbrella arrested for a while the onset of war. Most homes in Britain were affected by the strain of that uneasy twelve months. At Dyffryn the gap widened between Esmé and me, until neither of us could bridge it.

My mind cast back again over the summer which was now merging into the crisp mountain autumn. I had found Saint-Justin by chance during aimless wanderings with Arabella and a tent. Arabella stood behind the Casavants' café, far below. She was the old and faithful Bentley which was my only link with what had gone before. To keep her in the style to which she had become accustomed, I had been denying myself any luxuries, and was the better for it. Dyffryn still needed all the money that was produced by its rough pastures, and I could not expect to maintain myself away from the place without crippling the finances of the farm. Therefore I was now forced to build my fortunes anew. When a man has no material assets he must turn to the abstract. Dyffryn had taught me a crude philosophy, for whose moral I was still groping, but the tale was not uninteresting.

I had begun, therefore, to write the story of Dyffryn. The title of the book came to me at once: *I bought a Mountain.*[1] But there was irony in the name, for I still believe the mountain possessed me, and not I the mountain.

[1] Harrap, 1940.

And so at Saint-Justin I needed little. A few francs sufficed for food and shelter; Arabella cost me nothing when out to grass on the patch behind the café—and I was rich in time to write my book, and to disentangle my mental twists in the writing. But, if time was my only wealth, then I was to be robbed of it. A plump figure, red of face, and muffled in black garments, surmounted the ledge on which I was finishing my breakfast. The climber was Madame Casavant herself on an unheard-of pilgrimage!

Madame sank on to a wooden bench. Between the gasps by which her lungs sought to regain their even functioning, the lady coughed forth the bombshells which shattered my placidity.

"M'sieu! The route is formidable! There are five years since I am here! The Boche will be upon us! You must fly! A little of the coffee, m'sieu, and a thousand thanks. M'sieu le patron est mobilisé. That is good, for such a thing cannot continue. My son Henri is *mobilisé* four times during the past year, and under such conditions a business cannot survive. My son Henri was born in Paris during the Great War, and a shell of Big Bertha upset his cradle. Now he is a man, and he stands again against the Boche. M'sieu! You must depart in the old green automobile before the petrol is refused to you.

"Thank you, m'sieu. Some honey and a croissant. The English in the valley are already departed some days. M'sieu! The Army of France and the cruisers of the English will prevail once more against the Boche. There must this time be a terrible reckoning, for the Boche is not human. His threats and wars ruin our businesses."

I reflected that the forbears of these English cruisers had stood between Spain and world domination, and, later, Napoleon's burning star had been doused in the waters of La Manche.

In my fastness I had been secure against the alarums and excursions of that turbulent summer. The backwash of rumour had scarcely lapped against my remote peak, and the approach of the tidal wave of war was almost unheralded. My finances allowed me to live quietly, but not to undertake without warning the journey to England. I explained this difficulty to Madame, who assured me that all would be well, and that any sum which I owed her could be sent from Britain. It was the first day of the new month, so that I was in her debt for thirty-one days of food and lodging.

I had very little gear to pack, though Madame herself had to take one of my rucksacks which had come up on mule-back.

It was not until the steady rhythm of the descent had set my mind free once more that I realized fully how I was caught in the machine of circumstance. It seemed to me then, as now, that man can never determine his own end. Blind, groping creature, the jigsaw of his affairs is ever upset before he can put in the last piece, and the picture of his destiny never becomes whole before the giant elbow of events shatters his labour.

My mind was filled with bitter thoughts as we descended from the peace of Saint-Justin to the brawling world below. Madame must have sensed this, for she said in consolation:

"Cousin Annette has washed your short drawers for you."

We came at length to the café. All was excitement, almost *en fête*, in the village. Most of the men of military age were a little drunk, which is an event out of the ordinary in France. M. Casavant himself came out to greet me, bearing a glass of Izarra Verte, that potent nectar distilled in certain Pyrenean villages. Le Patron was dressed in the faded blue of the First German War poilu. Moth had tattered his jacket, and the three top buttons of his trousers could not fulfil their function. He brandished the Izarra at me, and I took it to save waste.

"I go to fight for France, m'sieu!" cried Casavant, and added inconsequentially, "Long live the King of England! I report at Pau at midday."

Another glass of Izarra appeared as by magic in Le Patron's hand, and we toasted one another. I pointed out that it was now eleven o'clock, and Pau fifty miles away.

"It does not signify. The Boche shall not stop me," said Casavant, and we toasted the Republic.

Madame came forth, bringing with her another glass and

the bottle. We toasted the King of England, the French Army, and the English fleet. Little Jacqueline came up shyly with a *pâté* to stay my hunger on the road north, and hid her face in my jacket when I gave her the few francs I could spare. It was all very affecting. We toasted Jacqueline, and as the admiration became more personal at this gesture, salutations were given to me, to Le Patron, to Madame, and, for some reason, to the good General Georges.

Madame was now seated sleepily on a bench, while Le Patron and I reclined on the running-board of Arabella, who took on a tipsy list to be in keeping.

Midday had come and gone when Le Patron leapt to his feet, with a hand on Arabella for security. He flourished one of the empty bottles as though it were a sword, cried in a great voice, "Forward!" And tumbled into the front seat of the car.

I looked back as we accelerated down the steep street of the mountain village. Madame was sitting on the bench still, her head against the wall. Little Jacqueline was sobbing. The sun shone full on the summit of Saint-Justin, and somewhere in the hocus-pocus of my sentiments was a real sadness.

Le Patron slumbered as we sped through the hills to Luz. Here activity was intensified. Mules were led into the square to have ear-tags affixed against the day of requisition. Military numbers were being stencilled on the doors of private cars in readiness for them to be *mobilisé*, like the mules. Everywhere men in crumpled uniforms were taking leave of wives and children. Tears and wine intermingled under the awnings of the cafés, and, amid the confusion, Le Patron awoke to recognize an acquaintance, who carried a rusty *chassepot*.

The three of us proposed few toasts, but drank silently in a spirit of condemnation. An official came up to slap a number on Arabella, and proposed to requisition her there and then. Le Patron and his friend assaulted the official, but desisted when they learned that the man had a brother *mobilisé* who had reported that morning at Pau. We gave the official some wine, and presently assisted him into the car. Le Patron's friend entered to keep the official company, and the four of us rushed on towards Pau.

Pau was a hive of military industry. Horse-drawn guns and caissons were unlimbered along every boulevard. Aimless bands of troops wandered to and fro, and there was confused shouting. Le Patron, together with his friend and the official appendage, professed a desire to sleep, and we noticed that inside many shop-windows straw was littered deep in the display space. The three of them entered a modiste's together, and presently reappeared in the window to make a last bow before slumber. We mouthed ineffectively at one another through the glass; then the trio sank abruptly into the straw, and fell instantly asleep. I returned to Arabella, to urge her on the long road to Tours. The Pyrenees gleamed golden in the afternoon sunshine as we turned our back on them.

Arabella well proved the power of breed that day. I spared her not at all. We travelled as if in a race, using the gears, skidding the corners, wafting the dusty miles behind us as a sirocco sweeps the desert. Once we travelled seventy miles in sixty minutes, but the fat rumble of the old lady's exhaust never faltered, nor did she put a wheel wrong on the corners. Nevertheless, it was dark as we stormed at last into Tours, and Arabella's brilliant eyes raised shrill cries from the denizens of the blacked-out city. I was very tired, and took the first room to be found in a tiny inn. I remember that the lavatory was entered through the kitchen, and was knee-deep in coke. I slept that night in a room above an alley-way, with Arabella dozing beneath my window.

Tours in daylight was a mælstrom, and nearly every man was in uniform. I decided to reach Dieppe that night, but took time for an early apéritif. I was sitting on the pavement outside a café sipping my Rossi sec, with Arabella against the curb a few feet away, when a resplendent *capitaine* accosted me.

"M'sieu is English?"

I am Canadian, but did not quibble.

"That is by the grace of the good God, then!" exclaimed my *capitaine*, his piety a little marred by a patent monstrous hangover. "I will be ever in your debt if you will take possession of my niece."

I did not know whether to be surprised or gratified at this proposition, but tempered any discourtesy by explaining my hurry to depart.

"But m'sieu must take my niece with him in the grand sporting automobile. I too love the sport, and my niece is of my mind."

The story of the doctor's niece pieced itself together slowly. The doctor's sister had married an Englishman, and had died of Anglophobia shortly after giving birth to Marie. The child had been brought up by her father's two maiden sisters, who lived in an ivy-clad house in the dim, religious shadows of a cathedral close. This visit to France had been the only escape of the poor girl from the suffocation of the landscape water-colours, the muslin curtains, and the Crown Derby in the Boule cabinets. I was loath to return the bird to her cage, but the doctor was insistent.

"The Government will move to Tours," exclaimed my friend, in a stage whisper. "Then will come the aeroplanes of the Boche, and *Pouf! Pouf! Boum!*" He ordered Rossi sec for three, declared that he would return in two minutes with his niece, and strode away.

I debated with myself whether to empty all three glasses and escape, but curiosity prevailed, though I little wanted the burden of a cloister-bred novice on my journey. And, even as I decided to wait, the doctor reappeared with the girl. No maiden aunt had dressed that girl. Her crimson frock was from no store in an English Cathedral town, but in its daring simplicity murmured a seductive "Place Vendôme." She wore no hat, and her jet-black hair hung in silken skeins about her shoulders. She was long in the leg, and moved with the awkward grace of a filly. She stared at me with eyes of so deep and vivid a blue that I blinked.

"My niece, Marie," introduced the doctor.

Time was passing, and the road ahead was long. I helped Marie into the Bentley, and the doctor put her small case among my luggage in the *tonneau*. The doctor leaned over to me and, above the rumble of Arabella's exhaust, whispered, "Elle est vierge!"

I replied "Bon!" for it was the first remark that entered my head, but whether it was apt or not I do not know.

Arabella moved that day as if the devil was stabbing his trident at her back tyres. The roads were crowded with small detachments of troops on foot, with convoys of artillery and supplies, and, as we travelled farther, with the first tide of those who were evacuating themselves from the north. These refugee vehicles were laden with large families of large people, the cracks between their swelling bodies plugged with children. Mattresses were strapped on roofs and bonnets, and perambulators swayed on the luggage-grids. Accidents were two a penny, and once we passed a Citröen wedged in the fork of a tree, a man's height above the ground. Marie was interested, and a little excited. At first she had been aloof, curled up in a corner of the front seat. Later she had moved close to me, and her perfume competed successfully with Arabella's robust smell of hot oil. Before we stopped for a late lunch my charge's hand was lightly resting on my arm, and her slim form was relaxed to the thrill of speed.

We ate at a wayside café, and drank cognac at three-halfpence a glass. Marie's excitement grew as she watched the world whirl past our roadside table. She likened the scene to a disturbed antheap. After the cognac her accent became deliciously French when she spoke English, and her speech impossibly quick when she spoke French.

Marie wished to escape from Close confinement, and she felt that she had only to wave a tricolour and to tag on to the end of a passing column in order to be free. She was probably right, but I was determined to set her on the road to her aunts, if only that she might say good-bye to them before she spread her wings.

We hurried north again over bridges guarded by soldiers, past factories about which stood anti-aircraft guns, through villages in whose squares were grouping the men of France, quick to defend the threatened sanctity of their soil. We saw a nation arising in anger, resolute to stamp out the ever-recurring plague of Germanism. A year later I thought again of the surging manhood of that old and great country, and it was bitter to picture the long columns shuffling on to slavery, sold by the band of traitors who had usurped leadership.

But Marie and I were not clairvoyant. She felt that the upheaval would bring down the walls of her prison, and I, that the uncertainty of my future was solved for me. Thus we were both happy.

We came to Dieppe in the twilight, and I left Marie and Arabella at an hotel while I sought information about boats. When I returned I was able to tell Marie that we could embark by midnight. The minx sighed, nestled up to me, and murmured, "Must we leave so soon?"

A crusading spirit must have been strong in me, or there would have been one Vestal the less in France that night, for Marie's dark beauty and dainty freshness would have tempted any but a self-canonized saint. We drove Arabella through the crowded streets to the quay, and my heart misgave me as I saw the many scores of other cars awaiting shipment. However, to fret would not have assured Arabella of a passage, so Marie and I entered a café for drink and food. It was a rough place, not patronized by the English tourists, who mostly flock to those replicas of their own national establishments which the Continentals erect specially for them. Some workmen in overalls were at a table, and I pricked up my ears when one said, "There will not be a place for more than a dozen automobiles on the Packet."

I whispered to Marie, and we speedily fell into talk with the workmen. Presently, I said, "I suppose only a few cars will get across to-night."

"It is true, m'sieu. I work the crane, and I know. Calais is for the military only, and Boulogne too, so that very many English are now at Dieppe. Also it is likely that Dieppe will be closed to civilians after to-night. The war may commence at any moment, m'sieu; then will come the aeroplanes of the Boche, and *Pouf!*"

We plied our new acquaintances with drink, and it was obvious that Marie's charm was equally intoxicating to them. The guardian of the crane may have been flattered at our interest in him; at any rate, he forestalled the

object of my diplomacy by asking, "You have an automobile, m'sieu?"

Marie and I exclaimed simultaneously that we had, and added many reasons why Arabella's return to England was a necessity if the downfall of the Boche was to be ensured.

"Show me!" exclaimed my friend.

We all stumbled out on to the dark quay, and I indicated the Bentley among the many cars. The crane-driver gave directions to his companions, who turned out to be the men who fix the slings to the wheels; then he vanished into the little cabin of his crane. Three minutes later a huge hook hovered over the press of cars. Owners materialized out of the night, shouting, beseeching. The hook wavered uncertainly a moment under the alcoholic control of its master, then swooped down on Arabella. The familiars made deft motions with ropes, and Arabella rose gently into the air, swung seaward, and alighted on the foredeck of our steamer.

We sailed at one o'clock on the morning of September 3, and headed for Newhaven without lights. Marie and I sat in the back seat of Arabella, and each of us expressed noble sentiments. Marie intended to return to her aunts in order to snap her fingers before she joined one of the women's services which would without doubt be formed. I told of my broken life, and of an ambition to die unhonoured and unsung on some obscure foreign field. Marie wept openly until we both fell asleep.

Newhaven was grim in the early morning light. We lingered not at all, and drove for London. There were uniforms to be seen about the countryside, though the activity was negligible compared to France. I noticed that few vital points, bridges and the like, were under guard, but that haystacks for some reason were heavily defended. Possibly high-ranking officers were asleep on them.

Marie and I parted after a buffet breakfast at King's Cross. The child looked very beautiful and very pathetic as the train drew slowly out of the grime of the station. I never saw or heard of her again.

I drove sadly towards Piccadilly and wondered to whom

I should offer my services. There was excitement round the statue of Eros. "War!" cried the passers-by. War had been formally declared on Germany. I parked Arabella in a side-street, and even as I slipped out the air-raid sirens gave their first wail. There was urgent warning in the sound, almost panic. People looked at the sky, and all recalled Hitler's threats and Goering's air fleets. Here, they felt, was the Wellsian war so often prophesied. Swift destruction would come while the air was still trembling with the echo of the warning. The crowds melted from the streets. The traffic pulled in to the kerb and was left unattended.

I did not know London well, but remembered that the Regent Palace Hotel had a grill-room deep below ground. Many others had bethought themselves of the grill-room, and a seat was difficult to find. As we sat and waited for the thud of the bombs I noticed near by a sparsely built, grey-haired Englishman with the stamp of the Empire-builder on him. I envied his calmness amid that chattering, apprehensive throng, as he quietly read his Sunday newspaper. But was he English? The print seemed odd. Then I saw that he held his paper upside down.

The tale of the next few days is one of humiliation. The first Army Recruiting Office was a little harassed. They asked a few irrelevant questions. Was I a Territorial? Was I on the Reserve? Was I due to be conscripted? I explained that I had been a farmer, and that the Army had not previously come within my scope. I told them my age.

"Run away and plough," they said wearily. "If you are twenty-nine we don't want you yet. We'll let you know soon enough when we're ready for you."

I was not unduly depressed at this rebuff. There were other markets in which to hawk myself. But the story was ever the same. Day succeeded day, and my envy of each humble recruit grew until frustrated chivalry threatened to choke me.

A knowledge of small-boat sailing did not qualify me for the Navy. My age barred me in those days from the operational jobs in the Royal Air Force. The Auxiliary Fire Service had no fires for me. Scotland Yard did not wish an extra special

constable. I could not find even a solitary windmill at which to tilt.

One morning I bethought me of a cousin who was a regular soldier, and a distinguished officer of his Majesty's Ironside Regiment of Foot Guards. I thought that perhaps the family name and my own height might mitigate the revulsion which I now expected at my interviews. The address of the Regimental Headquarters was in the telephone directory, and I supposed that there would somewhere be a sergeant whose good graces would allow me to collect a battle-dress and creep quietly into a barrack-room. My knowledge of Service procedure was not extensive.

Two enormous sentries guarded the entrance to the Regimental offices. They were point device, and I felt slovenly at once. I probably was.

"I've come to see some one about joining up," I said.

"Have you an appointment, sir?" they asked.

The "sir" pulled me up sharply. I realized at once that a Cockney or North Country accent would have been a better passport to the omnipotent sergeant on whom I had set my heart.

"No——" I began.

"That'll be all right, sir," cut in one of the immaculate giants. "The Orderly Room is up the stairs. Ask for the Regimental Adjutant, sir," he added, possibly sensing my ignorance.

I climbed a stairway with a heavy heart, for I was sure that no Olympian officer would bother himself with my lowly affairs. My vaulting ambition had o'erleaped itself.

Many clerks were busy in the Orderly Room. I stood a moment until a benign, bald-headed one attended to me.

"Do you wish to see the Regimental Adjutant, sir?"

I did not wish it, but said, "Yes!"

The bald one disappeared into a small office, and a moment later a captain came out. The captain's belt and shoes appeared to be made of patent leather. His brasswork gave out rays of light. His trouser-creases would have sharpened a pencil. He was very affable. He knew my cousin, and immediately took an interest in the story of my pilgrimage from one recruiting office to the next. At last he said, "Well, you'd better see the Lieutenant-Colonel. But I don't know if we can get you a commission right away. Hang on for a minute."

And he vanished back into his office.

I was stunned by this reception. My aspirations had never soared higher than private soldier, and would towards the end have been contented with A.F.S. or special constable.

After a short wait the Regimental Adjutant opened his door and beckoned me inside.

Each regiment of the Brigade of Guards is commanded by an officer known as the Regimental Lieutenant-Colonel. He is, to confuse the ignorant, a full colonel. He deals largely with matters of policy affecting the battalions of his regiment, which are commanded by genuine lieutenant-colonels. My own Commanding Officer, as I was prepared to regard him, was as charming as his Adjutant.

Almost at once, somehow, the talk turned to agriculture. Perhaps Wessex Saddlebacks were a catalyst, for the interview never became formal, and it was only as if prompted by an afterthought that the Lieutenant-Colonel drew a proforma towards him, and himself filled in the personal particulars demanded of me.

Before dismissing me the Lieutenant-Colonel gave me a chit in which he stated that he was prepared to accept me as a potential officer to be trained in the ranks at the Guards Depot, Caterham. This passport was to gain me a hearing at the Recruiting Office.

It was lunch-time, and I did not expect to find the recruiting officer at his desk. Flushed with good fortune, I called on a City friend to pass the time, and we fed on beer and lobster at one of those City restaurants where the beer has a gravity suited to its environment. We lunched well, and at great length.

It was mid-afternoon when I arrived at the Recruiting Office. I proffered the Lieutenant-Colonel's chit, and was ordered into a large draughty room where I was told to strip. Eight doctors sat at eight tables, each practising curious indignities on the succession of leaping, hopping, coughing creatures who passed them by, shepherded by white-smocked orderlies. I in my turn performed my evolutions, and none of the doctors faulted me.

The final scene of this drama, which had resembled nothing so much as a voodoo smelling-out, took place behind a screen. A white-robed attendant handed me a tall, conical glass beaker, as I pranced breathless into this quiet haven.

"We wish to test a sample," he said. "Hurry, please."

My exertions among the medicine-men without had taken effect on a bladder distended by quantities of the best City ale. I was much relieved to oblige the acolyte, but it was immediately apparent that my beaker was a paltry receptacle. Once the flood of my incontinence was loosed, there was no withholding.

"Another beaker!" I cried in anguish, as I snatched a chalice in the nick of time from a startled fellow-disciple.

"Again," I cried. "And again! And again!"

The shrouded novices ran to my bidding. The high-priests deserted their tables to watch this monstrous ceremonial. The chain of examination was broken as all beakers were diverted to my purpose.

At any rate, I was passed A1.

Since I was a volunteer, I was sworn in, and even the gabbled formula in a dusty cubbyhole of an office was not robbed of its ancient dignity.

They told me I would soon receive a summons to report at the Guards Depot. I little thought that I should wait six months for my notice. Then they paid me, for some reason, four and sixpence. I went out and spent it on more beer.

CHAPTER II

GUARDSMAN

I ARRIVED outside the iron gates of the Guards Depot early on a bleak afternoon in mid-March 1940. The bus which had brought me rocketed away towards Croydon, anxious to be gone from those grim precincts. The Guard on the gate did not molest me as I crept within, but the eyes of one immobile sentry took in my civilian clothes, my suitcase, and my air of trepidation.

"You poor bloody fool!" said the sentry. "Wait till they get their hands on you!" And he licked his lips sadistically. The statue did all this without making a move or a sound. I suppose I was feeling highly strung.

The Orderly Room gave me a chit on which was typed my name, number, and the words 'Roberts 1.'

"Across the Square," said a clerk. "Move!" I was part-way across that asphalt Sahara when a bellow arrested my progress. A distant figure semaphored me towards it. I found a Company Sergeant-Major awaiting me. He was black of jowl and moustache, with scarlet cheeks. His colouring gave him the appearance of a toy soldier, except that he was about eighteen stone in weight.

"You idle, dozy man, you!" boomed the puppet familiarly. "You walk round the Square here! Understand?"

"Yes," I answered.

"Yes, sir!" corrected the figure. Unfortunately, I took this for an Americanism.

"Yes, sir?" I queried, puzzled.

"Don't sauce me, you horrible man, you!" roared the figure. "Go on! Go away!"

I skirted the sacrosanct ground of the Square until I reached a great dreary building of grey stone. There were two stories, with two barrack-rooms in each story. Over the door was writ 'Roberts.' I felt that the inscription from above the Hell-gate in Dante might have been aptly substituted. Above the entrance to the left-hand barrack-room was the figure 1. I went inside.

The room was long and narrow. There were windows and a fireplace in one long wall, and windows in the other. One wall had thirteen beds along it, and the other had twelve. Each bed was three feet long; at its foot was a square wooden box; at its head were two hooks and a shelf. Piled on every bed were three sections of mattress, known as biscuits, and four blankets. All the windows were open exactly half and half, so that there was a strong March wind gusting through the room. The fire was unlit, because troops did not in those days feel the cold until after 1600 hours on weekdays, or 1400 hours on Sundays.

There was still an hour to run before the latest time to report, and some beds were untenanted. I silently sat on one, and followed the example of the other subdued civilian figures in the room by unpacking my suitcase. On examination I discovered that my three-foot bed was telescopic, and I felt comforted.

Presently we pilgrims began a hushed discourse. I found that most of my companions were much younger than myself, and had in most cases joined up direct from the university. I compared ages with my neighbour on the next bed, whose visage was more mature than most, and found that he was twenty-nine too, but a few months younger than I. As to the rest of our companions, most of them were aged between nineteen and twenty-two. But, despite their youth, my new comrades knew far more about matters military than I did. Probably this was because they came from soldiering families which had for generations sent representatives to the Brigade of Guards. From the chatter round me, and from my elderly bed-neighbour, whose name was Ambrose Winston, I learned that Roberts 1 would house the twenty-four members of the

Brigade Squad. The Brigade Squad was made up of potential officer candidates for the five Regiments of the Brigade of Guards. Ambrose Winston told me that we should have two months' training as Guardsmen before going, if successful, to Sandhurst; that we should be chased from morning till night by ferocious sergeants; that the food would be appalling; that he was even then hungry; and that, as a barrister, he intended to stand up for his rights. He considered, furthermore, that it was an absurdity to try to convert a man of his shape into a Guardsman. His shape was certainly odd. He was elliptical, tapering north from a wide circumference at the equator to a pointed skull, and south to small pointed feet.

Many of my fellows knew one another. This was natural since they were much of an age, and since they had obviously had the same social life. My own life had been so different that I had at first few points of contact. At eighteen years of age my first spasm of restlessness had come upon me, and I had left the university to sail to Canada in search of I knew not what. When I was twenty-one I had returned to buy my farm in Wales, and, since my domestic debacle, I had lived like a tramp up and down Europe. Furthermore, I was now penniless, a battered, aged pauper among the brightly gilded youth. This was a cynical conceit which much pleased me at the time.

Amid these reflections a stalwart Guardsman strode in to the barrack-room. He was a big man even among Guardsmen, and he had a big, red, bland face. He was so immaculately turned out that it was difficult to believe that he wore a standard battle-dress. His boots were of black patent-leather.

"I'm Trained Soldier Shillitoe," he announced. "That will be my bed in the corner." He paused while an earl removed some silk pyjamas and a suitcase from the bed indicated.

"I'm here to teach you to be Guardsmen," went on Trained Soldier Shillitoe. "Nor I don't fancy the bloody job, neither. Anyway, you'd better learn how we make our beds."

This was the first of many demonstrations given us by that admirable man, whose sole function was to teach us in meticulous detail how to live in a barrack-room.

"Is this right?" asked one earnest young man, when he had extended his bed, placed the biscuits so, and folded the blankets so.

"'Trained Soldier,' I am to you," roared Shillitoe. "No! Does it bloody look right?"

"No, it doesn't," agreed the young man. "I mean, No, Trained Soldier!"

"Well, watch again," said Shillitoe, and with infinite patience he showed us for the tenth time how to obtain the most warmth from four Army blankets.

The whole squad was present by now, and we sat on our made-down beds eyeing one another, afraid to smoke because of the beautiful floor. At this psychological moment a sergeant marched through the door. The peak of his cap touched his nose, and he avoided obstacles by a sixth sense. He, like Trained Soldier Shillitoe, wore an issue battle-dress as if it had been made in Savile Row, together with black patent-leather boots.

The sergeant was a smaller man than Shillitoe. The peak of his cap hid the upper part of his face, but such as was visible was youthful and pleasant. He wore a neat black moustache.

"I'm Lance-Sergeant Smartly, instructor of the Brigade Squad," recited the newcomer. "We'll get to know each other in a day or two. My job is to teach you all I know about drill and discipline and a few other things in two months. I can do it, if you can take it. What you learn here will be your foundation always. Remember, once a Guardsman always a Guardsman. Any questions?"

Bathos was introduced by Ambrose Winston, who said, "Yes. When do we eat?"

Lance-Sergeant Smartly eyed him for a moment with the peak of his cap, and answered, in the tones of a nurse to a badly behaved child, "Stand to attention when you talk to a non-commissioned officer, and call me 'Sergeant.'"

My neighbour stood up and said, "When do we eat, Sergeant?"

Sergeant Smartly winced at the position of attention, let it pass for the moment, and then gave the whole room a talk on routine, reveille, lights-out, meal-times, Naafi hours, and parades. He impressed us all with an air of infallibility, with self-confidence without cocksureness, and, above all, with inherent decency.

Here's a nice mild man, we thought. He'll check our faults, but he'll do it in the right way.

The durbar was interrupted by the sudden entry of a recruit who had evidently strayed in absent-mindedly while making for the opposite barrack-room. He stopped short over the threshold, and exclaimed, "Sorry, Sarge! Wrong room!"

Lance-Sergeant Smartly whipped round on him like a viper. His moustache quivered with emotion, and his hands clenched until the knuckles showed white. He took on greater stature, then let out a bellow which frightened all of us. The recruit reeled back and put a hand on the doorpost to steady himself. This was my first experience of the power of the human voice.

"Don't call me 'Sarge,' you horrible, idle, dozy man, you! Come here! Double! Double, I said! Turn your wrists in, when you stand to attention! Now, what do you call me? Sergeant, yes! What are you doing in here? Came in without thinking? Well, think! Or I'll put you in the Guard Room. Now, get out! Double!"

We were all a little taken aback by what seemed undue ferocity, but we soon learned that traffic between barrack-rooms leads to pilfering. Lance-Sergeant Smartly turned back to us, his colour normal, the visible part of his face composed, his figure relaxed like a passive ramrod, and said, in a voice as mild as a southern breeze, "The Trained Soldier will take you over to Supper. After to-night you'll march to meals."

We were marched everywhere in that barracks. We were marched to meals, to the barber's shop, to the Quartermaster's stores, to the Medical Officer, to church, to pay. Never did the peak of Lance-Sergeant Smartly's cap lose sight of us for an instant. We soon learned to march in nondescript denim overalls to a sanitary fatigue as though on King's Guard in red tunics. When our squad had become attuned the Sergeant played on us as Yehudi Menuhin plays on a violin. He would improvise a dirge, as we moved in the slow march, turned to left and to right and about, halted and stepped out once more. Bored with this, the maestro would break us into quick time. Ambrose Winston called this "bags of left-right." To and fro we would swoop on the key-board of the Square, but always under the iron control of Lance-Sergeant Smartly's voice, and never out of view of his peak.

"Swing your left arm straight, Buckingham! Arms must swing straight from front to rear. No left hooks here. Heels! Heels! Heels! I want to hear those heels. Don't watch your boots, Winston—nobody's going to pinch 'em——"

"They're pinching me," *sotto voce* from Winston.

"Throw your chest out, Barclay. Don't keep all your wind in your stomach. Squad will retire! A-bout turn! One! Two! Three and lead on! Squ-a-a-d halt! Stand a-at ease! Sta-and easy! Pay attention! What we're going on with now, is Turnings on the March in Quick Time. I will demonstrate!" And so it went on, until we found ourselves eating and even shaving to subconscious numbers.

Meals we found no relaxation. The Depot was an overfilled reservoir, waiting to replace overseas casualties which as yet had not happened. We sat twelve to a table, elbows to ribs. We took it in turns to collect the pans of unsavoury food from the overworked kitchens. For the first week most of the Brigade Squad dieted delicately, until the unwonted exercise chased away any gastronomic inhibitions. Ambrose Winston was ravenous from the first. I suppose that he had many corners to fill in his ungainly frame. During the early days he was in the habit of gobbling his own food, before leaning solicitously across to his neighbour.

"Don't you care for fat, old boy? Rotten luck!"

And he would spear dreadful lumps of flesh from the plates of his neighbours with the deftness of a Norse harpooner.

The Picquet Officer for the day visited all meals, accompanied by the Sergeant in Waiting, who called the clamouring pack to attention. We sat bolt upright, silent, arms to our sides, food frozen in our mouths.

"Any complaints?" would call the Picquet Officer.

No man would move, save perhaps to swallow nervously a gobbet of gristle. As well to answer a similar query from God by saying that the manna was stale. But this system was not so autocratic as it sounds. A messing committee on which recruits were represented met fortnightly to discuss the feeding. I sat on the committee myself, and soon understood that the many faults were by reason of Army expansion and strained facilities.

This method of calling for complaints quickly changed. Under peace-time conditions grounds for complaint were rare in the Brigade. In war-time, however, there was frequently reason to criticize the food. This was soon realized, and the Picquet Officer would not have the dining-hall called to attention, but would move quietly from table to table to give individuals full opportunity to speak their minds.

Our first working day in the barracks is a blurred memory, for the speed of events left us all breathless, physically and mentally. After breakfast Lance-Sergeant Smartly gave us enough drill instruction to ensure that we were controllable, then he marched us, an untidy juggernaut of a squad, by back ways to the Quartermaster's stores. Contrary to what I had learned from the newspapers to expect, clothing was issued to us with care. We were given time to stroll up and down in our boots. The fit of our battle-dress was minutely inspected by the peak of Lance-Sergeant Smartly's cap. Our pants, woollen, long, were the right circumference. The Quartermaster's minions had unusual difficulty with the Brigade Squad. There is a minimum height for Guardsmen Other Ranks, and clothing is not held, naturally enough, to fit men below that minimum. But for officers in the Brigade there is no height-limit, and some of our squad were very small indeed. From some secret source even these small ones were equipped with imperturbable efficiency.

Self-conscious in our khaki, we were whipped from the stores to the barber's shop. Four shearers dealt with the twenty-four of us in eighteen minutes. A Guardsman may wear his hair as he likes under his cap. His private locks may legitimately be curled into a coif, but the hair that shows must be only stubble. Our barbers that grim day carried out orders to the letter, with electric clippers. I felt like an Indian brave, left as I was with but a scalp-lock.

Like part-manufactured articles on a conveyor belt, Lance-Sergeant Smartly propelled us farther on the endless round, and we found ourselves stark naked in a draughty hut, where sleet blew in through the windows, which were set half and half. In order to keep warm we pranced like dervishes before the Medical Officer, who sat inscrutable as a Rufai chieftain. It appeared that we were all healthy and free from the viler diseases. I myself was in great fear lest the Caid should discover that I had a damaged knee. I had occupied myself during the interval between enlisting and call-up by writing and by judo. I had completed *I Bought a Mountain* without suffering author's cramp, but at the judo I had sustained a wrenched knee which still troubled me extremely. However, my grimaces of pain must have been attributed to some nervous affliction, and I, with the others, was allowed to cover my nakedness and to proceed to the Dental Centre.

A white-coated explorer probed the innermost secrets of our mouths. His pungent remarks were entered cabalistically upon a chart, and I am still haunted by mine, whose diagrammatic molars leer up at me each time I see my documents.

We were tired and subdued when we returned at last to the bleak haven of our barrack-room, measured, weighed, clipped, examined, and already anonymous in uniform. Gone were the double-breasted worsteds by which we had identified each other. Gone were the elegant hair-styles of West End days. Even the top-knot left to us was concealed by an abominable side-hat. This grievous article was to become a penance. We had hoped to be put in blinkers like Lance-Sergeant Smartly, but blindness was denied to us for the first two months. On drill we shed our Field Service caps the length of the square. Each movement shook a fresh crop to the ground, as a gust of wind strips the leaves from an autumn tree. These sartorial misconceptions have had a grave effect on Service morale. No man who wears one can feel other than a fool. Dress a man like a clown and in a while he will change his name to Grock.

However, we were given little time for reflection that evening, as we grinned sardonically at one another's garb. Lance-Sergeant Smartly broke in upon our mannequin show. He carried with him one of his pairs of black patent-leather boots, which he set down reverently in the centre of the polished floor.

"Pay attention!" he said. "This is a pair of boots. I want to see yours the same. You will have a shining parade from 1800 hours to 2000 hours nightly. No one will move from his bed. You may talk but not smoke. You won't find two hours enough to shine, but lights aren't out till ten. After ten you can lock yourselves in the lavatories with the lights on. If the Sergeant in Waiting catches you, say the food's upset you."

We looked long at the squad instructor's boots. Trained Soldier Shillitoe joined the solemn group.

"Them boots was the same once as what yours is," he said. "What you got to do is to hot up a spoon handle and burn the grease out of the leather. Then you rub 'em for a few days with the handle of a toothbrush. We call that boning 'em. After that they're right for spit and polish."

I went back to my bed and sat looking at my two pairs of dull, ugly footgear. The leather was grained, and was greasy to the touch. Sadly I reached for a spoon and went over to the fire. We talked boots from then on. We dreamed of our boots. In a crowd we protected our toe-caps as though they were fetishes. And, indeed, our nightly tribute of travail to our boots, as we sat serious and intent upon our beds, must have given us the air of an erotic sect. Lance-Sergeant Smartly quickly knew each individual boot of each of the two pairs of every one of us. During the meticulous inspections which he gave us at the start of every parade he would comment intimately on the state of our footwear.

"Connelly! That left toe-cap's not up to what it was last week. Put your other boots on for the drill parade this afternoon. And mind you work on the uppers of that other pair in the lunch break. Remember what I told you about them yesterday?"

Or it might be:

"Those heels are improving, Barclay! Keep it up!"

Lance-Sergeant Smartly had the gift of rare praise. His good word became as treasured as a Mention in Dispatches. I never knew him to use a superlative, perhaps because with us he never had the occasion, but rather, I suspect, because he knew that nothing was so good that it might not be bettered. But he well understood the value of praise, and did not demoralize us with unrelieved criticism.

Drill and what was known as turn-out were inseparable at the Depot. The backs of belt-brasses were polished, and we even learned to buckle our belts without dimming the metal with finger-prints. The woodwork of our rifles shone like the barrack-room floor. Our trousers were laid nightly under our biscuits, the creases damped with a shaving-brush, and our battle-dress blouses were folded under the pillow. In later years I was to learn the value of what some units describe as eyewash. I learned that the attention to detail which is essential in the field cannot be picked up in a moment. It is a falsely facile policy to say, "We won't bother in barracks, it will be all right on the day."

Fighting ability is in direct proportion to the morale of a unit, and the morale of a unit is the aggregate of the spirit of each individual in it. The individual gains his fighting spirit by confidence in himself. He must think that he is smarter, more alert, better versed in his weapons than his comrades. When every man in a unit feels this, woe to the enemy.

I once asked a racing motorist why he sand-papered and polished the axles, brake-rods, and other unseen parts of his car. He answered, "If the metal is spotlessly clean I can see at once if there is a flaw."

Besides turn-out, we learned care of equipment. A Commanding Officer has limited power to write off lost or damaged equipment if he thinks fit, and to charge the loss against the public. We quickly found out that a write-off was very rare in the Brigade, and we cost the nation little. Loss or damage was relentlessly probed, until in nearly all cases an individual was found rightly to bear the blame and the cost. And it was not considered sufficient merely to punish the man financially, for man-hours were needed in some factory to replace the article, and the war-effort was retarded by repetition of work. So the culprit was punished in addition to a stoppage of pay. Those units which had been well-grounded in care of arms and equipment were the units which were found fit to fight the rear-guard actions on the Continent in May and early in June 1940, and which came out to the boats carrying with them as much equipment as they took in. In fact, many of them helped themselves from the litter along the dusty roads, and came home as walking arsenals.

The other lesson which we learned in full measure was prompt and exact obedience to orders. I began to draw a parallel between drill and the geometry of my schooldays. I remember once remonstrating with a master who had adversely criticized some novel amendments which I had made to the theorem of Pythagoras.

"Sir," I had said coldly, "I can take no interest in geometry, because I will never need it."

"You may one day find that you will be required to use trained thought," replied the master pointedly. "You do not deny the value of exercise for your muscles. You must regard geometry as a mental P.T."

Of course, he was right. People use cross-word puzzles for just that purpose. Now, drill exercises and strengthens those qualities which are most required in battle—namely, alertness and implicit and immediate obedience. These qualities, if previously unexercised, do not manifest themselves on the Day. Under the stress of the fear and fatigue of modern battle it is the subconscious which directs a man. The requirements of a good soldier must be implanted in the subliminal mind. Our subconscious was ploughed, planted, and frequently harrowed by Lance-Sergeant Smartly, and Trained Soldier Shillitoe fertilized such parts as lay fallow when we thought to idle in the barrack-room.

In the first few days of the War, when I was touting my unwanted services about the Recruiting Offices of London, I had tried at first to enter those units where drill was not a *sine qua non*. During the months of waiting, after my embarrassing entry into the Regiment, I had frequent nightmares about drill. I, the awkward member of the school OTC, the individualist who turned my own way and who kept my own step, was to become a precise cog in the most precise machine which the armies of the world have known. I had been haunted by visions of my self-determined meanderings upon some immense Square. But my fears were groundless. As some skilled craftsman bends unwonted material to his will, so Lance-Sergeant Smartly breathed confidence upon us all, and with consummate artistry fashioned us into the tool he wished. We began to like drill. Our mental processes were stimulated by terror of failure, and by desire to please. Success, and a word of praise, added fuel to the kindling flame of ambition.

During the early few days when we had all been new boys together, fearful of the future, and as suspicious of our superiors as a timid dog of the boot of his master, we had whispered to one another tales of sadism we had heard about the Depot. Had we known it, our superiors were too busy to take time off for sadism, and, in their adherence to the rules of soldiering, would have considered unfairness to be grossly improper.

There was, however, one P.T. instructor whose parades were a test to the point of destruction, and whose demands upon us were close to brutality. Lance-Sergeant Smartly was aware of the character of his fellow-instructor, and gave up his spare time during these periods so that he might encourage us by his silent presence in the gymnasium. But, although he sympathized with us, he was horrified one day to overhear some one say that he would refuse to perform some of the wilder excesses.

"Refuse?" he repeated, incredulous. "Refuse? A Guardsman can't refuse. If you're told to do something you think illegal or unfair you bloody do it. Then you complain, if you want to. But refuse? Good God, no! Do what you're told first, complain second. Refuse? Good God!" He then marched out of the room, to hide his emotion.

This was one of the most valuable lessons a soldier could

learn, and epitomized the essence of discipline in relation to the individual: "Obey first. Complain second, if you must."

The Army is a peaceful haven for a man who has been in civilian difficulties. He is fed and housed, and his mind is kept occupied for him. For my first few weeks as a recruit there was no time to worry about domestic problems, but, although the tempo of training increased, the ability to keep pace grew even faster, so that after a while there was some leisure to plague one. I used some of this spare time to set arrangements in train to end my marriage, for Lance-Sergeant Smartly had taught us that there must be tidiness in all things.

We recruits were at last allowed to walk out, and, after inspection by the corporal of the guard, paraded our military smartness in public. However, even when abroad in Caterham or Croydon there could be little relaxation, for the permanent staff of the Depot were to be found everywhere, and, if we thought that now we were off parade, they proved us wrong. Thus, when walking out we took care to keep our hands out of our pockets, not to lean against lamp-posts, to see that our buttons were done up and that our side-hats had the point one inch above the right eyebrow. Above all, we took care to salute anything that looked like an officer, and Ambrose once swore that he had saluted a dummy in the window of a multiple tailor.

Lance-Sergeant Smartly had explained to us the significance of the salute, and had told us that there was no need to dodge into doorways to avoid making the courtesy. The salute, we had learned, even from a private to a field-marshal, is nothing but the acknowledgment of one comrade in arms to another, and it is in ordinary good manners that the junior makes the first move. However, had unseen eyes caught us in a breach of manners, none of us felt that to state we were boors would have been a defence against neglect of custom. The good sergeant further told us that the motion of the arm was a reminder of the days when a warrior raised his visor to disclose himself as friend.

Even the Eyes Right or Eyes Left had an ancient significance. There was once a time when a serf must not raise his eyes to the face of a freeman. But lowly Service ranks are instructed to look straight into the eyes of the superior they acknowledge, in order to emphasize the comradeship of arms. Too often they revert to serfdom, and glare sullenly at his boots.

I often accompanied friends, particularly Ambrose Winston, on gormandizing expeditions. I had to be rather careful of my expenditure, for my affairs were still in a muddle, and I had to rely to an extent on my Guardsman's pay. We received fourteen shillings a week, of which two shillings were retained in a credit from which the Treasury might be reimbursed for lost or damaged equipment. The balance of twelve shillings would have been adequate for the evening a week which we were able to spend outside barracks had we visited the meaner hostelries only. Many of the Brigade Squad would have enjoyed this new tap-room view of life. Unfortunately, some of the more snug bars, and those favoured with the most attractive feminine service, were earmarked by unwritten law for non-commissioned officers. Several times we were turned into the street without beer or ceremony. Even Ambrose, a barrister, did not argue with these fierce-visaged and loud-voiced upholders of feudalism, and was prepared to let his case go by default. As a result, we were forced into hotels, as distinct from public houses. Here entertainment was more expensive and less amusing, for as rough soldiers we had to be careful not to offend.

Our eight weeks drew to a close. To the layman the only significant part of our training might have been the hour on the twenty-five-yards range, when we each fired five rounds with a Service rifle. But we, our eyes now opened, realized that every waking minute of our apprenticeship had had its lesson. The principles hammered into us were those which formed the foundation of military knowledge, and without them any superficial dexterity would have been as unbalanced as an edifice built on shifting sands.

Most of us, I think, knew how great had been the achievement of Lance-Sergeant Smartly in fashioning a smooth-running machine from the diverse scrap-heap of material which we had so recently been. It is not to decry the Sergeant's successful efforts to say that the material was pliable. I admired the members of our squad almost as much as I did our instructor, for most of them were very young, and had been uprooted from gilded surroundings. Few of them had roughed it in their short lives. Their willing adaptability sprang from the tradition of service to which their class has for so long been dedicated.

On the evening of our last day we had arranged to take Trained Soldier Shillitoe out with us. After all, we felt, he had done much to train us during the past two months, and if he was ashamed to be seen with us it was a reflection on his own instruction. I realized that the evening would be long and dangerous, and before walking out went to pay my last respects to Lance-Sergeant Smartly.

I knocked on the door of a bunk on which a card, pinned geometrically in the centre of the top panel, bore the legend 'Lance-Sergeant Smartly, Ironside Guards.' A voice replied, and I entered. A figure in shirt-sleeves lay on the bed, feet up on the foot-rail. The recumbent man wore no gaiters, and his bootlaces were undone. He was smoking a cigarette, and was reading from a paper-backed sixpenny novel. I looked hard, and I looked again. It was as if one saw on the dome of St Paul's a neon-sign advertising stout. It was as if the Speaker of the House were to enter the Chamber on roller-skates singing a collegiate song. The attitude, the undress, the occupation were so frivolous as to be quite incongruous in the paragon I had come to see. Furthermore, I was not sure that I was seeing the right man, for the figure on the bed was hatless. On a table, like a discarded toupee, lay a hat whose peak, more vertical than the vertical, could only belong to Lance-Sergeant Smartly. It was borne upon my reeling senses that this was indeed our immaculate instructor.

Sergeant Smartly looked up from his novelette and grinned, as if he realized my bewilderment. He heard me out as I made my speech of thanks, then, as I turned to go, still shaken to my marrow, he said:

"One more lesson! Don't forget how to relax."

CHAPTER III

ACADEMY FOR YOUNG GENTLEMEN

I REPORTED to Sandhurst in May 1940, wearing a Guardsman's cap which I had bought from an old soldier for three shillings and sixpence. As I drove up the well-kept drive and alighted from my taxi before the stately entrance it was difficult not to slip into an attitude of mind more suitable to a country house-party than a warrior's nursery. I was directed to a room of my own, bare and monastic though it was, as befitted the cell of a devotee of Mars. At the Depot we had all craved escape from the public life of our barrack-room. But now I, at any rate, felt at a loss without the familiar noises and irritating mannerisms of others. Shut up alone, with no herd instinct to guide me, I felt a panic lest I should be missing a parade or duty. I left my door open in order to hear the better should my fellow-anchorites stampede to some military ritual. Thus presently I saw Ambrose Winston insert himself into the room across the passage.

"Hallo, Ambrose!" I called.

"Hallo, Thomas! What's the scoff like?" replied he.

"I haven't eaten yet," I answered.

"I stopped for a snack in Camberley," Ambrose said. "But I reckon it's close on tea-time. Let's go and look."

Together we explored. It was quickly obvious that the amenities of the College were those of a good Officers' Mess, and that we would here have the opportunity to regain any refinements of behaviour which we had lost at the Depot. We saw the other members of the Brigade Squad, for we were all in one of the two Guards companies, and we greeted each other rather smugly, as might angels who, after a tumble into the Pit, had scrambled back to Paradise.

Later, in my room, I was visited by my servant, and felt that I had begun to soldier indeed. Gunter was a dried-up, despondent little man, and his only conversation stemmed from a memory stored with melancholy anecdotes of the peccadilloes of his former young gentlemen. At that very moment the Allied armies were washing back before the German tide, among them the small, hard core of British, who were such an unconscionable time a-dying. None of the British leaders were heroes to Gunter, who had valeted them, but he must have sent them away with clean buttons and equipment, for they undoubtedly now showed a martial spirit inculcated by some one.

After a few days we cadets from the Depot began to feel unhappy. The social amenities of the College did not compensate for a system of military training which had, we felt instinctively, gone awry. At the Depot the known routine had been immutable. The penances and terrors, the small rewards and relaxations, could be forecast as surely as the glide of the stars in their silent courses. At Sandhurst the horoscope was constantly upset by the rush of comets which swam into our ken unheralded. Outside the Company Office was a simple blackboard on an easel. On this some necromancer chalked the changes in our programme, and again the changes in the changed programme. Our daily greeting to one another became, not "Good morning," but "Haven't you seen? It's all been altered."

We learned to watch that board like stockbrokers on 'Change on a panicky morning. On its orders depended a lightning switch into other equipment, the need quickly to learn up a lesson which had come upon us before its time, or even, perhaps, the wrecking of such little personal arrangements as were still open to us—a prearranged telephone call to a wife, a visit to Camberley, or a rest in one's room.

Throughout the early years of the War, when the soldier was paid two shillings a day, his time was the Army's throughout waking and sleeping hours. If there were periods in the day or night when he could not be used, these intervals were given to him to spend as a privilege. They were given with an ill grace, and the grudging gift was quite likely to be snatched away before it could be enjoyed. Much of the blame for this bad man-management rested with the more wooden type of Regular soldier to whom ranks junior to himself were inanimate pieces to be moved without consideration, since to consider them sometimes called for more work or deeper thought. At any rate, a human approach to the problems of the individual would have violated the System. The System said that the soldier was entitled to nothing beyond the letter of King's Regulations, and that his superiors were there to see that he got it.

No Service unit can function as a soviet, with each individual exercising the right of self-determination. In war such a state would lead to self-destruction. The individual must sink much of his ego in order to enable the Service machine to run smoothly, for a machine becomes rough when its parts are eccentric. But the personal and human touch which can reach a soldier from above is a fine lubricant, and builds up stores of the only satisfactory motive power in battle: morale. Also, any amateur psychologist—which means anyone with common sense—could have seen that Britain was building a citizen army, and that the rigid system of the days of annual manœuvres and the Tidworth Tattoo would not readily suit the civilians in uniform, who were to do the bulk of the fighting in a war of movement and junior initiative. Little by little the progressive Regular soldier ousted those other Regulars whose minds were still buried in the trenches of Flanders. Moving up behind these enlightened professionals came the best of the civilian soldiers. After a while the blend of traditional but adapted experience and of good all-round civilian brains under a Service cap began to colour the man-management of the Army. By the war's end it is probable that the human relationships were better in the British forces than at any time in the history of our army or of any other army.

But this Golden Age dawned later.

My first shock at Sandhurst was the loss of my Guardsman's cap. One and all, we were again crowned with the folly of a side-hat. I felt that I had made no progress when I set the thing upon my head, the front point one inch above the right eyebrow. I never mastered the trick of putting the article on so that it projected horizontally from the side of the head, like fungus on a tree-trunk.

The hat was now garnished with a broad white band, which indicated that the wearer was being schooled for the King's Commission. We were marked men. We were neither officer, non-commissioned officer, nor good red-coat. We were suspect by the private soldier, who thought that in us he saw growing a rod for his back; by the non-commissioned officer we were mildly despised, as a nurse is faintly contemptuous of a backward child; and by the officer we were patronized. We were like the Undead of *Dracula*. There was no place reserved for us in heaven or in hell. We had now to restrain ourselves among private soldiers and to efface ourselves among officers.

But, as it happened, social occasions became less and less frequent as Hitler ranged to and fro on the far side of the moat which lapped the walls of our embattled island. The instruction, such as it was, began to take second place to many rôles which the gentlemen cadets were called upon to fulfil in defence of the country. There was an anti-parachute rôle, a Passive Air Defence rôle, a period during which we dug slit-trenches to defend Reading against the panzers, and there was a scheme whereby the Academy would man road-blocks and certain selected houses from which to stem the expected horde.

The theoretical instruction with which these activities interfered was no great loss. There was at least one platoon commander who read our lessons to us straight from the pamphlets. This was something which the least literate lord among us could have done for himself. It became a cruel sport to glue together two pages of this instructor's book. He would turn both over, and continue unchecked. A more skilled pastime was to lure the poor chap away from his desk and his manuals, as a fugitive might be enticed from sanctuary, and to pose a sudden question.

But presently a thin trickle of instructors appeared who had seen service in Norway or in France. We admired these heroes who had been shot at, and had fired back, for such was our respect for the fighting qualities of the German that we looked upon any man who had baited him as pre-Christians must have worshipped Daniel.

We recognized, too, the authentic touch. The citizens of Reading would have slept less soundly had they heard the comments of our new mentors on the defences we had dug on sites chosen by our earlier instructors. Inexperienced as we were, we could not fail to see the force of their teaching, as they explained the German reaction to this and to that: how he would use his mortars; how a roadside ditch and a hedge of pretty English hawthorn would not incommode a panzer; and, above all, that The Front, the magic name of 1914–18, had no front. For we learned that the Germans prodded and probed and feinted until the weak link in the chain of defence was found, and, having found it, that they rallied to the point with all their strength till the link snapped and they were through, harrying and destroying, cutting communications, dribbling on and through with fine opportunism, like a good pack of Rugby forwards with the ball at their feet. To the conventional British teachers these tactics may have been football, but they were certainly not cricket.

It is true that tactical conceptions were in a state of flux, and that the traditional Sandhurst teachings were outdated overnight. And yet an inquiring mind did not have to look so very far back in history to see that the art of war had completed a cycle, and that there was in the German method a close resemblance to the usages of Genghis Khan and Timur the Lame.

But tactics cannot be successful without the discipline which is the shield of the soldier, and which tempers his weapon. This at least was taught at the Academy. Great stress was laid on turn-out for guard, and deportment during the tour of duty.

We learned the age-old "Halt! Who goes there?" with which British sentries have startled the celestial shadows of China, the cold, clear nights of the Himalaya, the darkness of the Indian plains and the African veldt, and the frozen stillness of North America. We learned, too, that when a group approaches a sentry he must take no chance of being rushed. Accordingly, he follows up his "Halt!" with "Advance one and be recognized!" and again, "Advance one!" until all are passed.

One serious-minded student was guarding some shrubs on the main drive, and was afflicted, no doubt, with that tautening of the nerves which comes to all sentries when their comrades sleep, and only they keep vigil. A scuffle of gravel caused him to throw forward his rifle and call his challenge. There was no reply, and the ominous silence closed about him.

"Halt! Or I fire!" cried the sentry, reaching the second stage of his ritual.

And again: "Halt! Or I fire!" The young man's eyes were strained towards a spot in the middle distance, and he was startled when something rubbed gently against his ankles. He stepped back and clubbed his rifle, intent on pulverizing the first hostile parachutist to descend upon this green and pleasant land. He desisted with some regret as a small, drowsy voice from near his feet said:

"It's only Ambrose."

It was unfortunate that Captain Blundell-Hollinshead-Blundell was duty officer that evening, for he had a genius for materializing at the wrong time, and did so now.

Ambrose Winston, nestling coyly at the feet of the sentry, was awakened from his dream of pies and wine recently consumed in Camberley, and was instead forced to contemplate the reduction of his figure by several extra drills.

A little later in the course Ambrose was himself on sentry. In the still, small hours his thoughts were raised from his stomach to his duty as steps approached.

"Halt!" cried Ambrose. "Who goes there?"

"Duty officer. Captain Blundell-Hollinshead-Blundell."

"Ha!" said Ambrose. "Advance *one* and be recognized!"

Many old-style battles had been won upon the greensward before the Academy. The demonstrations given here of fire orders, patrols, range-finding, and the other subjects in which a junior leader must be versed were carefully laid on.

"Gentlemen!" would come the measured tones of the Quartermaster Sergeant Instructor over the public address system. "We are now going to demonstrate to you a reconnaissance patrol crossing a wire obstacle at night, firstly the wrong way, and secondly the right way. You will notice in the 'wrong way' that the patrol-leader is smoking a cigarette which would be visible for a considerable distance, and that he is allowing the five members of his patrol to talk loudly among themselves. You will hear the magazines, sling swivels, and piling swivels of the rifles clinking on metal. You will notice that one member of the patrol has a cough. You will also imagine to yourselves how the white faces and polished brasswork of the patrol would reflect the moonlight, or even starlight. Now, gentlemen, please observe!"

On this a Fred Karno outfit would issue from some bushes with much chatter and clatter, and would buffoon their way forward until impaled upon a barbed-wire fence. Whereupon some alert concealed German would blast them with blank and leave their limp bodies draped over the obstacle.

"And now, gentlemen," would ooze the unctuous tones, "we will see the 'right way.' You will notice that rifles are carried at the trail for instant action. The patrol-leader is a little way in front of his men, and a getaway man follows at a discreet distance to the rear. Should the worst happen it is his rôle to return to tell the tale. . . ."

Sotto voce from Ambrose Winston:

"I knew there'd be something I could do."

"Further, gentlemen, you will notice that faces are blackened, stocking caps are worn, and all brasswork is dull. Magazines fit snugly, and piling swivels are bound tight with string. Observe, gentlemen!"

The gentlemen duly observed a troop of nigger minstrels armed, not with banjos, but with rifles, who sunk silently from the undergrowth and made their blind way towards the erection of wire.

"Ave atque vale!" murmured Ambrose, with surprising classical aptness. But no! He was wrong. At a distance of a few feet the patrol-leader saw in front of him the wire, and sank silently to the ground. The patrol followed suit, each man alternately disposed to watch the right or left flank. The getaway man covered the spectators to rear of him with a menacing muzzle. The patrol-leader crawled like a rubber-bellied lizard to the wire, examined it, and beckoned up his prostrate Number Two. Number Two held the wire in both hands, and the patrol-leader took out his cutters and snipped between the hands.

"You will note," said the QMSI, "that the patrol-leader has called up his Number Two to hold the wire so that the severed ends will not fly back and thus indicate to the enemy that something is afoot. . . ."

However, the alert German had heard the snick of the wire-cutters, and he fired a shot. The infallible patrol-leader flung a thunderflash into a patch of long grass, where it lay spluttering for a suitable interval before going off with a bang. Whereupon a field-grey figure wearing a steel helmet staggered to his feet, clutched at his throat, and pitched forward motionless, to the plaudits of the onlookers.

"Got the bastard!" ejaculated a spectator, quite carried away by this Grand Guignol.

"Having disposed of the enemy standing patrol," the QMSI summed up, "the reconnaissance patrol continues to its objective."

"After waking the whole bloody area," breathed a voice down my neck. I turned to see the soldierly figure, rigid with scorn, of Tiger Badcock, a ranker of the Ironside Guards who had served in France, and was taking a commission in a Northern regiment.

We raw cadets had many discussions with our more experienced comrades, such as Badcock. We felt that, even when we were taught efficiently, we were often taught the wrong lessons, and that for our own sakes we should be wise to fill in the wide gaps in our instruction.

Badcock agreed that discipline and alertness were demanded at the College, and that training in these qualities was a prerequisite. It was, then, he maintained, the greater pity that when the foundation was correct the edifice should be jerry-built. He instanced a man in France, detailed to stop the panzers with an anti-tank rifle, who, faithful to his Bisley instructors, laid his groundsheet in the middle of the road, placed the butt of the gun on the forward edge of the sheet, with a clip of ammunition beside it, and lay down to wait.

"He didn't have to wait long," said Badcock, and added, "poor bastard."

Badcock, and those like him, maintained that it was useless to train on a lawn to fight Germans. He said that the German was familiar with his weapons to an extent where he could fire an assortment of them with speed and accuracy from any unexpected and unorthodox position, and he pointed out that fire-power won battles.

At Sandhurst our course shot twice on the range, being allowed to fire fifteen rounds with the Bren gun on the second occasion. We received the impression that the use of grenades and mortars was dangerous in practice, and that these weapons were to be reserved for emergencies of life or death.

There came a September night when I was lying on my bed, enjoyably contemplating nothing. My senses were drawn back from limbo by the sound of church bells. I experienced at once the instinctive reaction of the soldier. This was not "Invasion is here!" but "Does it take me?"

My servant Gunter put an end to hopeful doubts. He stuck his leathery face round my door, and said, more brightly than I had heard him speak before, "Well! They're 'ere."

"Where?" I asked.

"By the Bull and Butcher, I reckon. You'd better 'urry. It takes you."

I jumped up and scrabbled for equipment. Gunter might have experienced a score of invasions, for, calmly and with method, he fitted me up, and as an afterthought handed me my rifle.

"You might as well have it with you," he remarked, without sarcasm.

He jerked his head eastward.

"London's burning," he said. And I felt an urge to continue the roundelay with an absurd "Fetch the engine!"

"Reckon they'll be there by morning," added Gunter, "and they can put the fire out theirselves."

All this time he had worn an air of triumphant gloom, like a vindicated Cassandra.

"Reckon it'll finish the War, any'ow," he went on, with unusual loquacity. I felt that I should reprimand him for his defeatism, but he forestalled my words by going on "We can't get at 'Itler in Yurrup, but now the bloody fool's come over 'ere 'e's arst for it. Wait till the Navy gets at 'is barges with them new flame-throwers. Wait till them 'underds of new tanks come out of Savernake Forest——" I could not wait for more revelations of high strategy, but fled to join my platoon, fortified with the knowledge that Gunter was confident.

As we marched out of the Academy grounds towards the road-block where, like so many Canutes, we were to attempt to stem the flooding tide, we saw a glow in the sky above London. It seemed that the real war was upon us at last.

Ambrose and I had our appointed place in the jig-saw of national defence, for with an anti-tank rifle we were to be one of the rocks against which the tide of attack would crumble. Unfortunately, it looked at first as if we should be unable to fit ourselves into our place, since the shop in which we were to site our rifle was locked. My mind began a jingle.

"For want of a key, the road-block was lost. For want of a road-block, Camberley was lost. For want of Camberley . . ."

When it seemed that at any moment the widespread structure of the nation's security must disintegrate into ruin, Ambrose, inspired by the shades of a score of warrior ancestors, kicked the door, and said, "Let's bust it in!"

We gazed at each other, then at the door with a wild surmise. The inhibitions of correct English upbringing were sloughed from us as a wolf is said to shed its sheep-skin. It was our first taste of the licence of battle, and we found it more satisfactory than smashing crockery at a fun-fair. A heavy iron picket post lay on a waste patch beside the shop. I picked it up and menaced the door. Ambrose licked his lips. As I swung back to deal my blow for St George and England the door opened and a sleepy male voice said, "What was it?"

I arrested the iron bar within inches of the apparition's skull. Instinctively I glanced about me for a policeman, but none was there to demand what went on. Between us we explained how the safety of our beloved soil depended upon us siting an anti-tank rifle at an upper window. Our host did not appear to think this request unusual, for he invited us in without hesitation, locked the door carefully, and led the way through a passage stacked with boxes of brussels sprouts, and up the stairs to a landing. Our guide, who was a very silent person, raised an inquiring eyebrow in the direction of the landing window. We nodded; he nodded.

As we were placing the rifle the man reappeared with two chairs. We were evidently meant to fight in conditions of some luxury. Five minutes later he came back with a tray on which were four cups of tea. He offered us each a cup, said "Good night," and retreated with the other two into what must have been his conjugal bower. There was a brief murmur of voices before our friend's head showed round the bedroom door.

"Make much noise?" he asked, projecting his eyebrow at the rifle. "Wife's got a headache."

"Don't know," I said. "Never fired it."

He considered this statement for a moment in silence, then withdrew his eyebrow and head, shutting his bedroom door gently behind him.

As for Ambrose and me, resolved as we were to sell our lives dearly, to be faithful unto death like a Roman sentry whom I had once seen roasting in a burning sentry-box in Madame Tussaud's, we remained a while keyed up with selfless devotion. Out in the darkness we heard from time to time those little unexplained movements made by men in ambush, as the other members of our platoon changed their position, relieved bladders, or became frankly bored. With the chill of the dead hours of early morning our enthusiasm died away. No man can be a martyr when the faggots are too damp to take fire.

At first light an officer emerged from a bush and blew a whistle. As if sprung from dragon's teeth, our bedraggled platoon arose out of the ground, and fell in limply on the road.

The battle of Camberley was never fought, and, when I look back upon our dispositions, I think it was a fortunate omission.

"Better go," said Ambrose. "Must be time for breakfast."

"Yes," I answered.

We lifted our anti-tank rifle, now metamorphosed from the sword of Gabriel to cold metal, and crept down the stairs, and past the sprouts. We unlocked the door, and outside Ambrose hesitated a moment to give it a last look. So must his ancestors with Richard Lionheart have stared at the walls of Jerusalem.

Of course, the Germans did not come. Many reasons are advanced why not. I think that Hitler, the mystic, was hypnotized by the impregnable British tradition. He was a gambler, but he dare not stake his gains against a history of undefeat. On our side, our traditional leading class had seen too many Continental upstarts exposed for them to believe that this latest would succeed in domination. As for the country's rank and file, they could not take seriously a teetotal, non-smoking vegetarian of suspect sexual habits.

With measured steps we approached the end of our course. Candidates for the regiments of the Brigade of Guards were sure of their destinations, provided their reports were good, for they had already been conditionally accepted by their respective regimental lieutenant-colonels, and the postings branch of the War Office would not interfere. But the other pilgrims among us were by no means certain of reaching their Mecca.

Tiger Badcock had bought trews with which to grace the Scots regiment of his choice.

"Bet they post me to a Home Counties mob," he said. "You can't buck the System."

They did better. They sent him to a West Country regiment. However, to compensate, his chum from Somerset was sent to the Durham Light Infantry. A Service unit defies the laws of mathematics, in that it can be greater than the sum of the individuals who are its parts. Eight hundred Loamshire men, serving all together in a Loamshire battalion, each bring to their unit a touch of territorial pride which in the aggregate builds a pillar to uphold morale. Dispersed, this individual pride becomes merely a cause for argument. Much morale is squandered, therefore, by unimaginative posting.

Certain regiments and corps have no particular territorial affinity, but it is noticeable that the best of these set up in its place a fanatical pride in the regimental name. The effect is the same.

This gregarious cockiness is rooted in the history of man. No doubt each troop of primitive baboons thought that their own stamping-ground produced a better type of monkey.

The course ended. Most of us went away in battle-dress, garnished now with an officer's lowest badge of rank. I went to London to spend my few days' leave before I was due to report to the Ironside Guards Holding Battalion, at Portland Barracks on the fringe of Regent's Park. As directed, I went first to my tailors to order two uniforms and a pair of plus fours, whose use later became apparent. I then went to my publishers to find out whether I should be able to pay for these clothes. They were very nice to me, for *I Bought a Mountain* was recently published, and had been well received. I could now look forward to modest affluence until my still complicated affairs were unravelled.

Inspired by good fortune, I continued my round to my hatters. On the discreet counter I flung my abominable side-hat. The thing flipped once and lay still, as if it had been an animate monstrosity deprived suddenly of the head on which it must batten in order to live.

The hatter took an order for my blue service dress cap, and fitted me immediately with the khaki field service cap. They produced for me the cap badge, a small silver star. The star was several centuries older than I, and so much wiser. Many brave men had added their mite of glory to the small emblem. I put on my cap, and went out. But I could no longer feel that my actions were my own affair, for the star seemed to me to have an individuality of its own, which reminded the wearer always of the qualities it symbolized.

CHAPTER IV

ENSIGN

MOST old-style military barracks have about them the air of a well-kept slum. The messes are like mission huts, the barrack-rooms like tenements.

Everywhere for the objective eye to see are examples of man trying to triumph over environment. Flowers stand in stiff rows, their planting supervised by some horticulturally minded warrant-officer. But their blooms are timid, afraid to expose themselves fully to an atmosphere vibrant with shouted orders and tramping boots. Paint is liberally used, but the authorities are blind to the brighter colours, so that its only merit is its freshness.

The mural decoration of the interiors follows a pattern, too. The Officers' Mess hangs etchings of long-dead and over-dressed generals. The Sergeants' Mess, a more practical body, favours under-dressed women of no rank at all. The men's barrack-rooms willy-nilly show charts of the internal organs of the Bren gun, and the dining-halls are scrolled with battle-honours.

Portland Barracks, which housed the Ironside Holding Battalion, which I was to join on completion of my leave, was typical of all such ancient monuments. I had sent my kit by taxi, and walked up to report. The bricks of the high surrounding wall were to the imagination rubbed smooth as water-worn boulders by the stalwart backs of those generations of Guardsmen who had required support during their timeless good-night kisses.

A sentry was at the gate. At my approach he went into motion as if my shadow had activated a hidden device—up to attention; pace forward; slope arms; salute with the fingers of the right hand on the small of the butt. The smack of flesh on wood made me jump, although I had been taught myself to smack with the loudest of them.

"Go on! Hit it till you bleed!" had instructed Lance-Sergeant Smartly.

But this was the first time that I had been at the receiving end. I jumped as if I and not the rifle had been struck, looked quickly round to see who was being saluted so that I might also pay the compliment, saw that it was indeed I who was the recipient, and marched into barracks saluting to the left for the regulation six paces with a smartness which must have gratified the sentry. It takes a long time for an officer to learn to return a salute in a manner which is nonchalant and yet military. Some merely acknowledge a salute, which is wrong, since the recognition of one comrade in arms by another is a mutual affair, with the junior making the first move out of ordinary good manners. Others try to outdo the junior rank in smartness. This also is usually wrong, since the junior has more recently had instruction in the art, and is considerably better at it. I soon noticed that the officers of the Brigade had a fine flair for returning salutes with a kind of aloof camaraderie poised on a knife-edge between Grand Seigneur and back-slapping. This flair takes several generations to acquire.

I had to run the gauntlet of salutes from the barrack gate to the Orderly Room. Previously I had been one of the many saluting the few; now I was one of the few saluted by the many. The work was some forty times harder. In those few yards I received the 'Eyes Right' from fatigue parties who were being marched about their duties, and from a Guardsman who was carrying a bucket of tea; salutes from Guardsmen on their way out of barracks, or moving briskly on unguessed errands. A party at work repairing with tarmac a rough patch on the Square were called to attention by their corporal, who saluted, and then stood frozen with his men until I remembered to say, "Carry on, please!"

And finally, with a slow, majestic briskness impossible to imitate, the vast figure of the Regimental Sergeant-Major ploughed through the teeming throng, as some battleship speeding unhurried undulates with regal pomp past a convoy of tramps. Everybody rocked in his wake. I was startled to see this super-dreadnought move with the speed of an M.T.B. to salute a human posterior which protruded from the door of a parked car. The legs which supported the posterior ended in brown boots, and were therefore of officer type. Next moment I received the formidable salute which rebounded off the unconscious stern. The flash of the compliment flourished at me the blazon of the Royal Arms. The eyes which looked unwinking into mine took in my boots, with particular attention to the studs and to polish on the heels, the blanco on my gaiters, the inside of my belt brasses, the chin-strap of my cap, and whether my star was put in the right way up.

I slid into the Orderly Room like a ball-player making first base.

A door was marked "Adjutant." I knocked, and entered.

A voice said, "Always treat the Orderly Room as a parade ground, and salute when you come in. You're Tom Firbank, aren't you?" went on the voice.

I admitted this, and expected the crime to be noted in writing. But the Adjutant got up from his desk and said, "I'll ring for the Picquet Officer to take my place, and we'll go over for tea."

The Picquet Officer, when he had saluted, startled me by saying to the Adjutant, "Go at the double, Bill; the buns are nearly finished."

To me it was as if an acolyte had spat in the eye of the High Priest.

It was some days before I found the key to behaviour in an Ironside Mess. Once found, all was easy, for the simple rule was to treat the Mess as a club. In fact, the Mess was less formal than a club, for in some venerable institutions a newly joined member might well address the most decayed inmates as 'sir' in order to gain their toleration. But in the Mess everyone save the Commanding Officer was hailed by his Christian name or his nickname. Only the Commanding Officer on his lonely eminence was given the title of respect. One of the bravest things I ever did was to test this usage upon the second-in-command, a bemedalled, grizzled major, named Badger Benson. The nickname was apt, for he was short, stocky, and of fierce aspect. His head grew straight out of his shoulders, and was capped with grey stubble. He came and sat next to me at breakfast one morning. Over his grapefruit he cocked a bloodshot eye at me.

"Those abroad men were over here in their flying-machines last night," he asserted.

"Yes," I answered. "I had to get a tube back to barracks. All the taxis had packed up."

Badger ruminated on this news until well into his porridge.

"What's it like?" he asked suddenly.

I was a little at a loss, and said so.

"The tube!" said Badger impatiently.

I explained briefly how the Underground system worked, and he seemed quite interested.

"It's rather pathetic now," I added, "because all sorts of people sleep down in the stations. Some are in bunks, but most of them just lie on the platform."

"What the devil do they want to sleep there for?" demanded Badger angrily.

I pointed out that many had had their homes bombed, and others went down for shelter.

Badger thought a bit, then muttered, "Poor things! Poor things! Must go and have a look at 'em one night."

It was during the kidneys that the trouble came. An ensign as junior as myself came in, helped himself to cereal, and sat down a little nervously. He caught Badger's eye upon him, flinched, and exclaimed defensively, "Good morning, Sir John."

"Don't call me 'Sir John'!" shouted Badger. "You're not a bloody butler!"

"No, sir!" agreed the ensign.

Badger swelled in size, and for an interminable moment there was silence. Then he regained control and said, in a very quiet voice, "Be silent, and eat your breakfast."

"Yes, Sir Badger," said the ensign, and poured salt

over his cereal. He made a remarkably quick breakfast and left.

Badger turned to me. "Spoke to me like a bloody butler, didn't he?"

"Yes, Badger," I answered.

"Twice," insisted Badger.

"He was a little nervous," I said.

"Nervous!" exclaimed Badger, his small red eyes flaming angrily. "What the devil's he got to be nervous about?"

Badger's main concern with the young officers was to see that their hair was cut regularly, to amplify the knowledge of regimental history taught at the Depot, and to teach them a short glossary of words whose use would help to set them apart from the rest of the Army. Only four of these words were very important. London was London, and not Town. A service dress jacket was not a tunic, since the tunics of the Brigade are scarlet. A servant was a servant, and not a batman, and why not? And, finally, the Brigade wore plain clothes when out of uniform. As Badger said, "Those fellows who live among the Wogs may wear mufti, but the Brigade has never served east of Suez."

As a man with a bad head for heights may wish to hurl himself into an abyss, so I longed with fearful fascination to say to Badger, "My mufti's at home, Sir John, so my batman's pressing my tunic so that I can go to Town for my furlough."

Within two or three days of my arrival at the Holding Battalion my tailor informed me that my uniform had progressed sufficiently far for me to be fitted. I informed the Adjutant, who deputed the Assistant Adjutant to accompany me so that the cut might be approved. The Assistant Adjutant told me of an occurrence which had much distressed the Bombardier Guards.

A young ensign had appeared before his Adjutant for approval. The Adjutant was dissatisfied with the young man, even to the point of addressing him formally.

"Mr So-and-so," said he, "your uniform is lamentable. You will change your tailor. Also your barber. You will have to get rid of those yellow shoes, and you will tell your servant to tone down the colour of your belt. Further, you had better grow a moustache."

"Certainly, sir," said the obliging youth, "would you like it fair or dark?"

When my uniforms arrived at last I learnt the purpose of the plus fours which we had been instructed to order, for all young officers donned these garments with boots and puttees for parades. I had expected that after the interminable drill to which we had been subjected at the Depot, and the considerable amount at Sandhurst, I could now try my hand on others. This was not yet to be. For after the form-up and the inspection at parades we young officers were handed over to a senior subaltern, and were whipped away out of sight behind the cookhouse or the latrines.

Almost at once we would be joined by one of the two Drill Sergeants, who would say, rhetorically, to the senior subaltern, "Permission to carry on, sir!"

When the senior subaltern had acquiesced the Drill Sergeant would drill us as an instructor chases recruits. As a sop to the conventions we should be called out in turns to practise a few words of command. These Drill Sergeants, who were, to confuse the ignorant, warrant-officers ranking immediately below the Regimental Sergeant-Major, were great men, well able to castigate junior officers.

True, they did not shout, "Wake yourself up, you idle, dozy, horrible man, you!"

But they could and did say frequently, "That won't do at all, Mr Winston, sir. You mustn't ever let the Adjutant see you do it that way, sir."

And we all knew that there was more subtle business between the Drill Sergeants and the Adjutant. The Adjutant would not discuss the officers with a Drill Sergeant, nor would a Drill Sergeant formally report on the officers, but information was given in an oblique conversation.

"Are the young officers ready to be passed off the square, Drill Sergeant?"

"Doing very well, sir, very well indeed. Lord Mayfair

is a little weak on his words of command, but he'll come to them with practice. Mr Winston doesn't seem quite to get the hang of Guard Mounting procedure, sir, and Mr Barclay hasn't been very well just lately, which has held him back a little, sir."

"Not very well?"

"No, sir. Not at all well, sir. His stomach seems very queasy, and he's liable to drop off to sleep, sir."

The Adjutant would store these little human documents in the archives of his memory, and in a day or two would say to the Drill Sergeant, apropos of nothing, "Have you the nominal roll for the next young corporals' drill cadre, Drill Sergeant?"

"Yes, sir!" would answer the Drill Sergeant, instantly suppressing a gleam in his eye.

"Is there room for two or three more?"

"Certainly, sir. The cadre could take another four, sir, if you wish it."

"I think I will add some of the young officers, Drill Sergeant, to give them more experience. I'll give you the names later."

"Very good, sir," would say the Drill Sergeant, knowing the names perfectly well.

And so for a while we marched and countermarched, saluted and yelled orders, until some of us were footsore and others strained their vocal chords. True, we had shed finally our side-hats, but, as with Job, if it was not boils it was bunions. And now our affliction was puttees. These articles must have contributed largely to the immobilization of our forces during the First German War. They continued to immobilize and harass the young officers at Portland Barracks. If put on sufficiently tightly to be secure they acted as tourniquets, and a numbness would spread up from the feet, as if we had drunk hemlock. If wound loosely, so as not to deny the flow of blood to the extremities, they would begin slowly to sag in folds as a prelude to complete collapse. A young officer whose puttees were in the primary stage of corruption could be detected by the fixed appearance of his eye; an expression one would expect to see on the face of a young lady at a social function who has been warned by a sixth sense that her undergarments will shortly tumble about her ankles.

Ambrose, whose legs were of a most peculiar shape, suffered greatly, and, as his puttees were always too loose, affected a constipated gait designed to relieve the articles of any shock which might lead to their undoing. He began to march as a mannequin learns to walk with a book balanced on her head. It had from the first been obvious to most of us that this method of circumventing the degraded tendencies of his puttees could only lead to Ambrose's own decline and fall. Thus when most of us had finished with the Square, and were practising in battle-dress for King's Guard, Ambrose could still be seen struggling with the writhing folds, like Laocoön in a draper's shop.

The function of the Holding Battalion was to maintain large numbers of officers and men in a state of preparedness to take their places on drafts to the service battalions. It is difficult to keep an edged tool bright and sharp without a whetstone. Our whetstone was Public Duties. The foremost among these guards and picquets was the traditional duty of the Brigade to guard the King.

When my own name appeared on the guard roster I was weighed down at once by a similar anxiety to that which most people experience before a football match or a boxing bout. I felt that it would be easy to make a mistake which would incur retribution from my superiors, and derision from the expert Cockney spectators. This fear was quickly dispelled by the Regimental Sergeant-Major, one of whose many duties it was to practise those warned for guard. I found that the great man was a Lance-Sergeant Smartly expanded to an infinite degree in vocal power, instructing ability, and physical bulk. Such confidence did he breathe upon nervous young Guardsmen, and equally nervous young officers, that their doubts were blown away, and most men became incapable of making a mistake in the ceremonial.

This same quality of instruction was to be found throughout the Brigade, and the fighting ability of Guardsmen, tough, and backed by tradition, was directly fostered by first-rate tuition in their various rôles.

I think the Sergeant-Major kept one of his more special eyes on those awaiting guard duty. One morning, after I had been benighted at the house of some friends owing to the failure of the transport system during some bad bombing, I came into the barracks early. I was hurrying across the square to reach my room for a bath and a clean-up when I saw the Sergeant-Major heave in sight. He bore down upon me with deceptive speed.

I returned his salute, and said, "Good morning, Sergeant-Major."

"Good morning, sir!" replied the Sergeant-Major. I made to slip away, but the restrained power of the voice held me. "Excuse me, sir," went on the Sergeant-Major, "what's the name of your servant, sir?"

I told him, puzzled.

"I must have a little talk with him, sir. He's not turning you out properly."

I accepted the rebuke, cleared my servant of complicity, and explained to the Sergeant-Major about the bombing.

"Bombs shouldn't stop a Guardsman cleaning his buttons, sir," the Sergeant-Major said, with just the right amount of jocularity. And then, to show that the incident was closed, "I believe you're a Canadian, sir."

I admitted this unorthodoxy.

"Very curious! Very curious!" muttered the Sergeant-Major. "There's another one in the Regiment." Then, as if thinking aloud about us outlandish problem-children of his, he added, "But he hasn't written a book yet."

I moved away, leaving the great man deep in thought. His whisper reached me half across the square.

"Take the back stairs, sir, or you may meet the Adjutant."

My first King's Guard went well. It could not do otherwise, with the bulk of the Sergeant-Major looming on the fringe of the Parade, and the small, spruce figure of the Adjutant shining beside him.

The tour of duty was forty-eight hours. The three officers

used the mess at St James's Palace, and the captain and ensign slept there. The subaltern slept with his detachment at Buckingham Palace.

There was a fine old-world air of privilege about the Mess at St James's. The food was good, and the stock of wine was still catholic. We invited mixed guests to lunch and men guests to dinner, and wound up the day at the cleared dining-table, circulating port by candlelight. This, I thought, was soldiering indeed.

On my fourth guard the circulation of the after-dinner port was interrupted earlier than usual by aerial uproar. The sounds were very local, and we could not feel that smug pity with which the temporarily immune looked upon more distant citizens who were receiving attention. My duty now lay at Buckingham Palace, where I was for the first time in charge of the detachment, and the Captain of the Guard told me to remove myself thither with all speed.

I hurried into my equipment, and made my way through St James's Park, which was lit by a thousand fairy lights which spluttered and sparkled on the grass. I remembered that some incendiaries were said to explode, and my exalted duty was robbed of a little glamour. The remainder of the glamour was blown away in the vicinity of Queen Victoria's memorial by the blast from a stick of bombs which straddled the Palace. I picked myself up and ran to the gates, anxious for human company. The gates were, I knew, locked at sundown, and the policeman with the key was not visible. The Sergeant of the Guard had already posted his sentries in the steel beehives. I made myself known, and ordered one to leave his post and to find the key. He doubled across the forecourt, and quite soon returned, opened the gate, and admitted me. It had come to me with clarity that the Palace had been bombed, that of all the targets in London it had the greatest propaganda value, that, out of the many million people in London, this moment was my responsibility.

I asked the sentry what had happened.

"Dunno, sir," said the sentry. "I reckon they dropped some bombs."

A crater in the forecourt and a dust-cloud over the ruins of the North Lodge were some confirmation.

I ordered the sentry into his beehive, and made him responsible for the key. As I doubled over to the Guardroom Lance-Sergeant Smartly came to my aid. His invisible presence told me that my first duty lay to the Palace, my second to the Guard, and that the rest could wait. The shelter under the Guardroom was very crowded, for, according to the orders laid down, the sergeant had put his off-duty men into it, and the police too had joined them. We sent the police away, and I saw one Guardsman, wedged on the stairs, thrusting at them with his rifle-butt as they went out. I thought this treatment a little cavalier, even though they were uninvited guests. However, after watching more carefully, I saw that he was protecting from damage the toe-caps of his boots, and, remembering the Depot, I had every sympathy.

The sergeant and I went up on the roof to visit the Bren gunner, whose duty it was to deny the tiles to hostile aircraft. From this viewpoint we looked anxiously for signs of fire, but nothing untoward was visible, save the drift of dust above the ruins of the North Lodge. We descended, and made the round of the sentries. These, so recently butchers, bakers, and candlestick-makers, were quite cool under their first ordeal by high-explosive.

On our return we went to look at the North Lodge. We saw a pair of boots protruding from under the rubble, and we were able to move enough blocks of stone to identify the legs of a dead constable. We found a fairly senior police officer, and suggested that he should extricate the body of his comrade, and check the rest of his men.

At Portland Barracks the Holding Battalion had very large companies, for at times the battalion must have approached the strength of a brigade. But it was difficult to learn much of one's platoon, since the nominal roll changed rapidly as drafts were found, and as new intakes replaced those gone. The companies had an operational rôle to dispute the amenities of Regent's Park and the Zoological Gardens with hostile parachutists at first light each morning, Sundays included. I did once suggest that the Zoo would be safe on Sundays, since it was unlikely that any of the aerial visitors would have a Members' ticket, but the suggestion was not favourably considered.

And so in turns the platoon commanders would join their platoons at the dead, still pre-dawn hour, and, peering in the darkness on the square, would check arms and ammunition. Then we would march out of barracks through the quiet streets and into the Park, where the section commanders took off their men to the various posts. The platoon headquarters was in a derelict bandstand, and, though at first we saw ourselves defending Monkey Hill to the last man, last round, as uneventful dawn followed uneventful dawn the astral musicians of the bandstand switched from martial music to a dirge.

At this time some one with psychological knowledge had circulated a directive that parachutists were demoralized on landing, and would surrender if one scowled at them. In fact, as I later learned, a parachutist is invulnerable during the first flush of his joy and surprise at successfully denying the laws of Nature and Sir Isaac Newton. But no enemy came, and our chill vigil was disturbed only by the melancholy howls of the rationed beasts.

We young officers used to attend our Company Commander's Orders each day, and occasionally Commanding Officer's Orders. The Other Ranks of the Army are, by virtue of the System, very helpless individuals. Under any conditions, many other ranks are not brilliant, but, with the opportunity removed from him to exercise any but the remotest control over his private affairs, even the most intelligent Other Rank finds himself in a quandary without help from above. It quickly became apparent that daily orders well and fairly conducted were the key to contentment, discipline, and morale. Most Army crimes can be traced back to a prime cause of the intrusion of home difficulties into Service life.

Men frequently require leave to return home in order to cut down the facilities which a wife allows a lodger, to compound somehow with the firm which has sold them furniture on hire-purchase, to remove a wife from uncongenial parents, or sometimes to attend a birth which is timed not to coincide with privilege leave, to speak before a magistrate on behalf of an erring son, and before a Don Juan on behalf of an erred daughter. The Army possesses a man body and soul on payment of a small weekly sum less stoppages, but if it is to obtain full value from him it must sometimes share him a little with the time which has gone before.

My company commander at Portland Barracks was admirably suited to this dispensation of justice in its widest application, for he was an elderly First German War soldier of wide experience and fatherly instinct. He not only saw to it that his men were given the opportunities they asked to redress home grievances, but was competent to advise on divorce, etiquette with the bailiffs, and remedial treatment for complications set up by a back-street abortion.

If these troubles are not dealt with efficiently and with sympathy a soldier becomes bad in his work, earns punishment, and often goes absent. Experience taught me that the officer of the Brigade, removed by upbringing from the home sphere of his men, yet fully conversant with it through generations of service to his dependants, was treated as a father-confessor to whom no intimate details were spared. Later on in the War I noticed that Other Ranks did not so readily lay their private worries before officers whose origin was more nearly their own. The gap was not wide enough. It was like blurting out personal secrets to the man next door.

Sometimes to mete out justice required quick and clear thought. One grey morning my company commander, after a late night bedewed with port, was confronted by a wily Guardsman named Golightly. The roar of the Company Sergeant-Major without made us all wince.

"Guardsman Golightly! Guardsm-a-an, 'shun! Quick march! Mark ti-i-ime! Halt!"

Then *sotto voce*, "Straighten your wrists! Get your heels together! See me afterwards!"

The company commander sighed and read the charge, at first with no more than routine interest, then with a rising inflexion which showed his perturbation.

"Guardsman Golightly, you are charged with (1) conveying spirits into barracks, (2) stating a falsehood to a Non-commissioned Officer in that you said you were Jesus Christ, which you were not.

"Sergeant Keenlyside!"

"Sir, on the tenth of the eleventh I was Company Sergeant in Waiting. I made the rounds at Tattoo. At 2217 hours I saw a light proceeding from the end lavatory of the company latrines. I knocked on the door and said, 'Who's there?' A voice replied, 'Jesus Christ.' I ordered the occupant to open the door, and found Guardsman Golightly within. He had with him a bottle of rum, and he smelt of spirits. I reported him in the usual manner. Sir!"

This, I thought, would test a Solomon. But the company commander dealt with Guardsman Golightly on the first charge and dismissed the second. As he said afterwards, "Who am I, a miserable port-drinking sinner, to say that Guardsman Golightly is not the Messiah?"

It had become the custom of some of us to frequent a pleasant little club which overlooked Park Lane, and to weather the nightly bomb shower in its well-lit bar. Not so many places of entertainment stayed open after dark in those days, and not so many people frequented those which did. But where life went on as usual the atmosphere was stimulating, and of a gaiety unknown in safer days.

But on one significant night it seemed that all London had stayed at home. At about nine o'clock in the evening I walked the mile and a half to the club without seeing a living soul, unless alley cats glow with the divine spark. The club, too, was empty save for its elderly proprietress.

I stood by the fire drinking my drink. It was unwise to stand near the bar, for the heavy crystal chandelier above it danced and tinkled to the tom-tom of the guns in Hyde Park, and to the thump of the imported interpolations.

A tall, slim, fair girl came into the club carrying a suitcase. From her remarks to the proprietress I gathered that she was just returned from the country, that her taximan had refused to navigate farther through the perilous streets which led to

Kensington, and that she needed stimulant before trying to charter another vehicle.

The proprietress must have felt that queer night a pressure of the inevitable, for she introduced us. Many of London's conventions had already been shattered by blast, and I at any rate could not struggle against predestination. We drank a little together, and later dined. We talked continually, although of what I think neither of us knew. At length I found a bold taximan and sent Tessa home, to return to barracks myself, a shaken man.

Tessa and I met daily, and twice a day if I could get free, during the next few weeks. It came as a shock when the Adjutant sent for me and told me that I was to be posted immediately to a battalion of the Ironside Guards stationed in Lincolnshire, and likely soon to go overseas.

Tessa and I spent the night before my departure in walking the streets of the West End during London's heaviest raid. For myself, I did not much notice the bombs. I was already numbed into insensibility by the bombshell which had so damaged me internally. We said a farewell amid the smoking rubble and writhing, flaming gas-mains, a setting which would have satisfied even a Russian dramatist.

CHAPTER V

SERVICE BATTALION

In the early afternoon Ambrose Winston and I alighted from our train at a North Lincolnshire coastal town. A watery gleam of May sunshine touched the precinct of the station with a revealing finger. We saw the scaly piles of fish-crates which fathered the pervading smell, and we saw the shabby houses which lined the shabby streets.

"I don't think we'll find much fun in this town," said Ambrose, with conscious understatement.

Outside the station we felt more at home, for the battalion had sent a truck to meet us.

During the ride we learned quite a lot from our driver. We learned that the town which we had just left was not much cop, and that, even if it had been, battalion headquarters was fifteen miles away, and the companies were billeted among inaccessible villages round about it. The battalion, and the Guards Brigade to which it belonged, was training hard, though whatever for he could not think. He told us, too, that the leave roster was up to date, and that therefore seven days' privilege leave came along every three months, and midway between was a forty-eight-hour pass. The pass, however, was of little use to him, as he lived in the south, and could not afford the fare for so short a visit home.

Viewed from the open canopy at the rear of the truck, the flat, despondent countryside retreated damply. The fumes of the exhaust, however, were sucked inside by the vacuum of our going, and Ambrose, who had drunk several glasses of Drambuie on the train, grew pale and began to hiccough. The Guardsman relapsed into silent melancholy.

The battalion headquarters occupied an ancestral home. It was one of thousands of such houses, of which the young masters were at the war, and the old ones immured in a distant wing, like ghosts dreaming of dead days. There was a different look in the eyes of the men in this battalion. The glance was harder and more aware. The Adjutant, too, had another manner, which did not seem to say "It's nice to see your face," but rather "Are you going to be any use to us?"

Ambrose and I were posted to separate companies. I followed my new company commander out into the yard, where a PU waited. Barry Martin cast an eye over it and the driver, for he inspected everything within view, at all times. I sat in the back with the Company Sergeant-Major, who told me that Mr Willoughby, of 12 Platoon, had been posted away; that I would, no doubt, take over from him; that the platoon sergeant was fairly capable; that there was a pair of wire-cutters missing from the platoon stores; that the Company Quartermaster-Sergeant had a spare pair not on charge to him; that he would use his influence to have these appear in the platoon stores; and that I was fortunate to be serving under Major Martin, who was an Ironside of Ironsides.

When the PU came to a stop I was conditioned by the dreary journey and depressing countryside to expect a dose of castor oil and early bed. However, I found that the Mess was in half of a large, cheerful farmhouse. The other company officers were in the anteroom, where there was a blazing fire, and I was glad to see that all of them were drinking what appeared to be whisky. Barry Martin introduced me to them, then told me to help myself at the side-table. It was whisky.

My fellow platoon commanders were younger than I; John Mayhew, Peter Petter, and Maurice Willoughby. All of them seemed eager enough to hear what went on in London, but after a while the talk came back to the battalion. In the months which followed I too found that the life of the unit came to fill my mind. There were no distractions in our isolated station, and the battalion seemed to have its own living entity to which all of us were subservient. In time I found that I came to look on newcomers as the Adjutant had looked on

Ambrose and me. One did not desire primarily a good drinking companion, but rather a good workman. Fortunately, the two qualities frequently go together.

It is vital in a Service unit that personal relationships are easy. This is important at all levels, from the Officers' Mess down to the section. A piece of grit not apparent in training may immobilize a large piece of war machinery when it is running at full pressure.

Barry Martin's Company Orders were almost grim in their efficiency. There was no Prussianism about them, but rather an insistence that no detail of company life was too insignificant for formal notice. The occasion for neither blame nor praise was lost by default.

On my first morning at Orders the Company Sergeant-Major asked leave to speak on behalf of a Guardsman who had overstayed his leave. He stated that the man had been upset by his wife's relationship with a foreman at her factory.

"Did you know of this, Mr Willoughby?" asked Barry.

Maurice looked uncomfortable, and admitted that he had been ignorant. When Orders were done Barry kept him behind for a moment. He joined me for the hand-over of 12 Platoon, and said, "Got a rocket about that absentee. It's a bit hard taking the rap for the foreman."

However, when we had checked the stores, and found the full complement of wire-cutters, Maurice went through the platoon roll-book with me. Although he may have missed the one incident in the private affairs of a Guardsman, he certainly gave me an amount of information about the men on the roll which would have surprised those discussed.

Barry Martin's standards were difficult to attain. After I had commanded my platoon for two days he told me that Guardsman Moore's boots were short of studs. Showing a proper concern, I asked to which section he belonged, only to receive a cold rebuke at this ignorance. Barry's mind could not plumb my lowest depravity, for I did not yet know Guardsman Moore by sight. I kept the platoon sergeant with me throughout the next day's training, and did not let him go until I could put a name, not only to the faces of the men, but even to their posteriors as they practised field-craft.

At the Depot I had often wondered why Lance-Sergeant Smartly had varied from day to day the articles to be laid out on the boxes at the foot of our beds. This was, of course, a running kit inspection. Serving under Barry Martin, I speedily learnt that I was held responsible for my men's deficiencies, and in self-defence I copied the excellent Lance-Sergeant's method. In a platoon it is of course essential that any particular article of kit be shown simultaneously by all, otherwise one mug, enamel, would do duty for forty odd men. Few, if any, private soldiers realize the fourfold significance of shortage of kit. Firstly, it renders the owner less efficient, since he is not fully equipped. Secondly, he tries to borrow, and so becomes a nuisance to his comrades. Thirdly, he resorts to stealing, and the loser in turn replaces his loss in the same way, *ad infinitum*. Thus distrust of a comrade is born. And fourthly, when, in a kind of inverse Hunt the Slipper, the man not in possession is found out, some one in a factory has to waste man-hours and material to turn out a replacement.

In training, too, Barry recognized nothing as satisfactory save perfection. The fine old hallowed maxims of the British fighting-man did not command with him the reverence to which many thought them entitled by virtue of their age. One could not say to Barry:

"I haven't practised it, but all will be well on the day." Or:

"I didn't make a recce, but I expect we'll find the way all right." Or:

"Well, it was an old map." Or:

"No, I haven't actually shot with it myself, but the platoon sergeant knows all about it."

At Sandhurst no stress had been laid on the importance of man-management, and I once had to suffer Barry's icy politeness for a week after an occasion when I fell below his standard.

I had marched my platoon twelve miles to some ranges on a dismal mud-flat by the dismal coast. We lay in a bog to shoot, plagued by an east wind. It was June, but hail and sleet fell alternately throughout the early afternoon, and we became chilled to the bone, and our trigger-fingers remained crooked as if we were a party of genteel tea-drinkers.

We marched twelve miles home again, too miserable to sing. I dismissed the platoon, told the platoon sergeant that I would return to inspect feet after they and I had had some food, and went over to the Mess. Barry came in as I was gulping a whisky. He asked me for details of our day, and I gave him a picturesque account of our discomforts, which did not much impress him.

Then suddenly, "Have you seen your men fed?"

"No," I answered. "The Company Quartermaster-Sergeant told me he had a hot meal ready for them, and would see they were all right."

"Go over at once and see that there are no complaints."

Barry said no more, and I got out quickly lest his fury should break the bonds of restraint.

Of course, he was right. The men were browned off, tired, cold, hungry, and grumbling. That was the very moment when it was so vital for their officer, who they knew was just as miserable, to remain among them until hot food and drink, dry clothes, and a rest had restored their spirits. They would say to themselves, "Stuck it proper, 'e did. It was a fair treat to see 'im wangle that extra 'elping of 'ash for us. Must've been 'ungry 'imself, too, poor devil."

Out of these tiny bricks of goodwill the strong edifice of morale is built.

A unit which has for a period been doing static training is in danger of growing roots. Roots are an impediment in war-time. Accordingly the battalion was jolted out of its routine by a two-day march of sixty miles to Sherwood Forest. There was nothing unusual about this march, which was the sort of practice done by all units, though thirty miles a day on hard roads carrying equipment is quite far enough for anyone not out on an endurance test.

It was, however, impressive to see how the battalion moved like a machine running within its capacity, and ready to respond instantly to the controls. The distances set between companies and platoons never varied. The halts came at exactly ten minutes to the even hour, and the men fell out, loosed equipment, raised their feet if possible above head-level, and lit cigarettes. Water-bottles remained unbroached without an order. This is a necessary rule, for the soldier in the ranks is improvident, secure in the faith that if he runs out of water, or anything else, some one, somehow, will help him.

At the first night's halt, which Barry's company spent in a rick-yard, I was surprised how strongly the men finished, for Guardsmen are heavy fellows, drawn from a class whose feet traditionally pain them. When the platoon had pricked its blisters, fed, and cleaned its weapons, and when Barry had been over to us, as if casually, but really to inspect us, I went off to see John Mayhew and Peter Petter. I found John entertaining his platoon with funny stories, and Peter accompanying his men on a mouth-organ, while they sang *My Brother Silvest.* Presently the three of us strolled over to Ambrose Winston's company. Ambrose was sitting on his pack, surrounded by his platoon. He, like them, was eating stew with a spoon from his mess-tin.

Evidently we had interrupted a general discussion. A beetle-browed Guardsman was asking, "Well, excuse me, sir, how would you roast a sucking-pig, now?"

Ambrose considered the problem, unhurried, while one or two of his audience ran their tongues over their lips. Pensively he made a heel-mark in the ground, ladled a lump of gristle into it from his mess-tin, and smoothed the place over with his boot.

"I should stuff it with a veal forcemeat," he said, coming to a decision, "and sew it up. It should, of course, be trussed with the legs together, underneath. To get the crisp effect I should brush it with oil, and cover it with greaseproof paper before putting it in a baking-tin. You must baste it well, and towards the end you should remove the paper to let the carcass brown. It's also very good stuffed with chestnuts."

The platoon sergeant let out his breath.

"I'll tell Q all about it, sir," he promised, looking into his mess-tin. "'E don't somehow seem to have got the hang of it."

Ambrose noticed his visitors, and we went with him to where his kit and his blankets lay. We winced when he took his boots and socks off. Ambrose, however, seemed to think little of his bloody wounds, and stuck lint and plaster on them, which he carried ready prepared in a little tin. I was surprised that he had got so far, and never dreamed but that he would have to ride in his platoon truck next day. But he did not ride, and I saw him again with his men on the following evening, eating with them before he went to slap more plaster on his feet.

It is a pity that the officer class is often misrepresented. The good officer is both protector to his men and father-confessor. In active fighting units he does not retain his command if he is idle, inefficient, or out of tune with his subordinates. It is only the officer uncertain of himself who dare not mix intimately with Other Ranks. The heredity of the traditional leader class teaches that men are led by serving them.

The battalion returned from Sherwood Forest to find excitement awaiting in Lincolnshire. Together with the Bombardier Guards battalion in our Guards Brigade, we were given seven days to move to a port of embarkation. Where we were to go, and what we were to do, was not divulged. There was, of course, speculation, and this was intensified because at that time there were few parts in the world where Allied troops might land without bringing down trouble upon their heads.

Ambrose and I were sent for by the Adjutant, who told us that we might be left behind, since there were in the battalion some supernumerary officers senior to us, and more experienced. We spent two or three days checking our men's kit and documents, both of us feeling like a Cinderella preparing her sisters for the Ball. We had little heart to join in the discussions and guessing games, until on the fourth day word came that we would move with our platoons.

The two battalions travelled by special trains to Glasgow, and moved into a hutted camp on the outskirts of the city. Rumours of embarkation blew hot and cold. The urgent days made weeks, and the weeks made months, but still we stayed in camp. Expecting as we were to go to war, we enjoyed ourselves with determination while the opportunity remained. The Other Ranks, however, were sensible enough to avoid the unconventional forms of alcohol for which Glasgow is famous. This was just as well, for the colloquialism 'old So-and-so was blind last night' may be optically true next morning.

The officers found that some of the citizens had unorthodox views on politics, the monarchy, and the King's uniform. John Mayhew entered into a discussion with one such stranger, and emphasized his points by tapping him on the waistcoat with the ferrule of his ashplant. The stranger grasped the end of the ashplant, and so enabled John to withdraw the sword it concealed, with which he continued to tap.

At last the orderly room clerks stated that our projected operation was off, and that we should move to Dumfries for the winter. This news was officially confirmed by the authorities, who are usually a day or two behind the clerks.

At Dumfries Barry Martin became second-in-command of the battalion. In the Ironside Guards promotion goes almost always by seniority. This has the advantage that there is no room for intrigue and for jockeying for position. On the other hand, if the system is too rigidly adhered to some soldiers undoubtedly feel frustrated if they have outstanding ability which must await its turn for recognition. This feeling is not necessarily engendered by a wish for higher rank, more pay, or more authority. But most men wish to fulfil the highest rôle of which they are capable, so that they may give rein to their capacity.

A breath of fresh air came to flutter the cobwebs of Army training. Some of the good Regular soldiers had reached ranks where their opinions carried weight. They had realized that drill, discipline, and aptitude on a rifle range were not in themselves sufficient. Those qualities, they said, were only a foundation, but were now the more important because of the superstructure which they must bear, and which must be firmly imbedded in them. For the soldier was to be taught to be a mixture of poacher and gangster, and yet to remain a soldier.

These visionary leaders may have drawn a parallel between the Allied armies and those prehistoric monsters, slow-moving and slow of thought, which had been unable in time to adjust their habits to changing world climate, geology, and flora, and had died the death. They saw clearly that a ponderous and flat-footed stance, a traditional left lead and right cross, would never defeat this all-in fighter from Germany. Perhaps commando training had inspired their views. At all events, that type of training was now to be given to all soldiers so far as it was applicable.

The Bombardier battalion and ourselves were each instructed to send an officer and eight non-commissioned officers up to the Scottish Highlands to go through a form of commando training which had the sinister name of Hardening Course. It was known that I walked up mountains for pleasure, and, possibly because of this eccentricity, I was ordered to go with the Ironside squad.

We alighted one afternoon at a remote station. The little platform was crowded with men from many units, who milled about under a heavy drizzle, sorting out themselves and their kit. I saw the Bombardier squad already formed up, standing like a rock amid the confusion. The Bombardier officer approached, and said at once, "There's no transport, it's raining, and we've got to march seven miles."

Then he eyed the scene with distaste, and added, "I think our squads had better amalgamate, don't you?" He used the tone of a white man remarking to another white man in a Hottentot village, "We'd better share a hut."

I agreed.

"When were you commissioned?" asked he.

I told him, and he replied comfortably, "You're a few days senior to me, then. I'll leave it all to you."

Our march was all uphill, and as our greatcoats became sodden their skirts clung to our shins. However, we dared not ease our pace, for it was clear that the other squads were in a competitive mood. The Guardsmen marched with the long, slow stride of the Roman legionary, and devoured distance with deceptive speed. From our rear, squad after squad challenged us with hasty stride, and, like a bicyclist chasing a lorry, touched for a moment our tail only to fall away again. One squad passed us with much shouting and éclat, but on the unrelenting upward slope they faltered and broke down, while our juggernaut tramped past them. My new colleague, Richard Peveril, with his ashplant, brought up the rear. Patently he looked upon the whole thing as a joke in bad taste, but, none the less, he seemed to find no difficulty, and maintained an air of the son of the house on a country stroll.

When we had seen our men settled in their wooden hut we went to the Officers' Mess, which was in a pleasant Georgian-style shooting-box. The atmosphere in the anteroom was heavy with gloom, as students foretold woe for all on the course. We learned that a commando troop were to act as instructors, and that they would teach the technique of mountain walking, outdoor cookery, and bivouacking. The students were to be divided into three groups in order that the syllabus might be staggered. Most of our informants felt that the students would be staggered too.

Richard and I were drinking an after-dinner whisky, in a mood of gentle sadness, when some of the officer instructors came into the anteroom to inspect their victims. My depression lifted when I recognized two of them as acquaintances of my Welsh climbing days. One of them, Percy Black, had few whole bones in his body, being a keen Rugby player as well as a climber. The other man was "Piton" Price. He had earned his nickname by his dexterity in hammering pitons into rock while ascending climbs, where lesser men dare not loose a single hand-hold.

Next day, to break us in, we students were taken off for a trek of about twenty miles across broken country. It was interesting to see how quickly the Guardsmen adapted themselves to this new experience, so different from any training which they had had before. They soon learned that a relaxed body, a detached mind, and a steady rhythm of movement gave the secret of something very near to perpetual motion. They speedily gave up their attempt to keep step with one another through the bogs and down the screes. They saw, too, that, where obstacles and inequalities of ground caused the leaders of our single file momentarily to check, the main body of the squad had also to stop or bump into the leaders. Thus rhythm was lost, and our string contracted and expanded like a thread of elastic. We solved this difficulty by dividing into two sections, which maintained a rough gap of some twenty-five yards, and within the sections each man stayed at some ten paces from his predecessor. Thus the minor checks were absorbed in our length, and the man in front was usually clear of an obstruction before his successor was baulked. Also, they learned that the inequalities of a mountain can be used as the treads of a stair, and that a long slope may be treated as a flight of steps on which there is no need to upset the flow of effort by slithering. Within a short time the Guardsmen had exchanged the discipline of the route-march for the discipline of the mountain expedition.

They had at first viewed the excursion with profound disfavour, but they now began to see that this unusual mode of progression had its technique as clearly laid down as any lesson in a military training pamphlet. Once this fact was grasped, there was from the point of view of Richard and me little more difficulty, for a Guardsman likes to go by the book, and here he had his book, though its lore was unwritten.

At last we reached the crest of a high ridge, and far below we saw our house and hutments. The Chief Instructor pointed to the buildings and told us to make for home individually. At once there was a wild rush down the hillside, the commando men tumbling into a clear lead. I told the senior sergeant of our squad, who was an Ironside, Sergeant North, to keep the men together, and then fled down the mountain, through the pell-mell students, in chase of the commandos.

A few students came into the camp fairly close behind the instructors, and then, at a ponderous double, followed Sergeant North and his Guardsmen, well ahead of the pack.

I had a drink that night with the Chief Instructor. He said, "Didn't you write that book about mountain farming?"

I admitted this.

"We're short of instructors," said he, "and the Guardsmen

seem able to look after themselves. You'd better give us a hand. We'll go on a recce to-morrow morning for a bivouac area on Ben Nevis."

Then he added, "I'm afraid you'll miss the assault course, but it can't be helped."

I expressed gratification, tempered by a suitable disappointment over the assault course. From the window I could see the ropes and swings and catwalks and pits prepared for this exhibition of sadism, and shuddered at the narrowness of my escape.

The next morning we found a good bivouac area in a thin pine wood at the foot of Ben Nevis, and, satisfied with our exertions, went on to find lunch in Fort William. That night I marched from camp the fourteen miles to our wood with the first of the three groups into which the course had been divided. We carried with us two blankets apiece, toilet kit, mess-tins packed with pemmican and oatmeal, groundsheets, gas-capes, and weapons. I slipped into my pack my sleeping-bag and an extra groundsheet, for the construction of a bivouac demands two groundsheets whose owners willy-nilly must sleep together. This contiguity is vaguely repugnant if the partner is not of one's own choosing.

The commandos taught the students to pair off on arrival, so that one could erect the mutual bivouac while the other made a fire and cooked the meal. Each pair were taught to block one end of the bivouac with boughs and sods, to cut springy branches, heather, or bracken for a mattress, and to lay one gas-cape over the mattress. The second man's gas-cape hung like a curtain over the entrance. Furthermore, we learned that warmth was preserved by banking earth, turf, or leaf-mould up the side as a seal against inclement vapours. The cook was shown how to make his fire in a very small, shallow trench edged with stones so that a mess-tin could span the embers. If the trench were scooped to follow the direction of the wind we found that the draught could be controlled by placing a flat stone across the windward opening.

We ate our pemmican and oatmeal stew, enlivened by the wily ones with a meat cube, drank a beverage made from a compressed block of tea, sugar, and powdered milk, and then for the most part crawled into our sleeping-quarters.

It had begun to snow, and I was glad to help Percy Black consume a bottle of whisky which, as he rightly said, would only have meant added weight to carry up Ben Nevis on the morrow, unless emptied. Sounds of snores and flatulence echoed through the wood, drowned now and then by cries of blasphemy as the more rudely constructed shelters tumbled in upon their occupants.

Percy and I speculated on the driving-force of war which moved in such a mysterious way to perform its blunders and wonders. We pondered why a diverse and unwilling party of rich men, poor men, beggarmen, and possibly thieves should need to spend a comfortless night in a snowbound Highland wood in order to defeat an enemy common to all of them, and who was probably toping in well-fed content before the roaring fire of his Continental cantonments.

But then, thought we, it was unlikely that we had the monopoly of masochism. Quite possibly some ardent band of Hitler's disciples was pursuing a parallel activity amid the hills of Bavaria. The gods who were looking down upon our chequer-board must have been chuckling in their omniscience as they calculated the moves ahead which would bring the opposing pieces face to face.

We arose early next day to our ascetic breakfast, eaten upon a clean tablecloth of snow. The Chief Instructor joined us for the walk up the powdered slopes of Ben Nevis. One or two of the students developed vertigo, though the way was not precipitous, and one or two broke down through minor strains or lack of the will to go on. But, by and large, the party kept well to its unaccustomed path, and we struck at last the ruined observatory which clung to the summit. The snow was hard frozen, the wind keen, and the mist thick about us. Here was no place to linger, and quickly we thrust down through the blankets of cloud until we reached a level where the pale sun flashed slanting on the ice-crystals. Hushed voices raised themselves again. Tales of little adventures had by the route were made and capped, and capped once more.

The glow of achievement quickly lights the fire of the spirit. Our hungry, tired, browned-off party, unused to the hills, now rated itself among the great expeditions of history, and had sloughed its despondency. It seemed to me that our untried armies, even then attempting to keep sharp the edges of their swords on the grindstone of barrack routine, would have been better stimulated among the mountains. War is a challenge, and the soldier, like the boxer, must fight frequently with the real enemy rather than with the sparring-partners of schemes and TEWT's if he is to remain a serious contender for its laurels. Short of a foe in battle, there is no sterner teacher than a mountain.

We reached the road in the early afternoon. The cripples were pushed into a truck, and the rest of us marched fourteen miles home again.

I came out on the following day with the next group. The Chief Instructor apologized to me before we started out.

"I'm afraid you'll miss one of our most interesting tests to-day," he said. "We do six miles in the hour in equipment."

It was Piton Price who brought the whisky this time, and again we sat late into the night until the Philosophers' stone had rolled almost within reach. But the solid understanding of Time and the purpose of the Universe and the abode of the Godhead fades always to a nebulous half-knowledge in the grey of morning, and we were little wiser as we trudged once more upward through the deepening snowdrifts of Ben Nevis.

A third time I made the now-familiar trip, and this time the squad of Guardsmen was among the group. They brought with them a spirit of competition, and attacked Ben Nevis as if its summit was a military objective. First on the top, they looked a savage band of ruffians, difficult to imagine on a barrack square. Yet if the Adjutant had been able to see them I think that he would have detected the underlying qualities of discipline and courage.

I was out of touch with events at the camp, and during the long march back from the foot of the mountain Richard Peveril told me the news.

He said that the whisky had run short, and that he would

really have been unable to carry on had he not been able to visit the instructors' room of an evening. The food, I learned, had gone from bad to worse, but hopes had been raised when students were taken into the snow-filled woods to see a demonstration of field cooking. It was felt that the spectators would be invited to taste the confections. The cooking was done skilfully over a small, smokeless fire made from half a dozen twigs, and in the bitter cold even hunger was stayed by the numbness which spread inward from the extremities of the beholders. But Richard claimed that he retained throughout a vestige of appetite, which only faded as he saw that the main dishes were, firstly, a blackbird, tiny when plucked naked, which was roasted on a spit, and, secondly, a pemmican stew thickened with disreputable inside parts of the blackbird. The bird was, indeed, offered to the students to taste, but one and all, while remarking on the delicious appearance and savoury odour of the titbits, declared a virtuous disinclination to eat between meals. The pemmican stew *à l'oiseau* was greedily dispatched by a Sergeant Instructor.

The final episode of the course was to be a forced march of seventy miles across the hills. We were driven out in hooded trucks, and were dropped at last in a snow-bound pass. The Chief Instructor led the whole course down a minor ice-glazed road. Richard and I consulted our maps, and decided that we had been set down in Glencoe, and were now heading for Loch Etive. After eight miles we had a halt near a farm, then marched on for a similar distance until the gleam of water showed like dull silver through the dusk.

The Chief Instructor called the squads to him, reminded us that we carried maps, compasses, blankets, and iron rations, told us that we were at the head of Loch Etive, and instructed us to make our own way back to camp, in squads, across country.

Darkness had now come. All round us squads began to prepare for the night. The teaching of the course was put into efficient practice, and fires sprang up quickly, while bivouacs took shape beside them. Richard passed a quiet word to

Sergeant North, and in ones and twos the Guardsmen melted away from the other students to form up in silence on the track. Away we went again, and retraced the eight uphill miles to the farm by which we had made the afternoon halt.

At the tramp of our boots a man came out, bearing a lantern, and, when we asked for shelter, he led us to an empty building, not unlike a village hall, which was next to the farmhouse. Presently he produced a few palliasses, a pile of rough coverings, baskets of buttered scones, and an urn of tea. A Guardsman always travels secure in the knowledge that tea and cakes will appear in his path, and none showed surprise at this hospitality. Feminine sounds had been heard in the farmhouse, and when the meal was done the senior members of the squad most punctiliously carried back the debris of our meal, and remained away until we sent for them to go to bed.

We had noticed on our maps that a steep gully, its foot opposite our farm, nicked the high ridge which screened us from the Glencoe road. We determined to take this way in the morning, and thus save ourselves the long detour which the road made. Our route lay across Glencoe, over the hills to Kinlochleven, and on again over the Ben Nevis block to Spean Bridge.

We started before daylight. The gully was fortunately so steep-sided and sharply defined that, once within its groove, there was no getting out. Soon all sound died save rasping breath and scraping boot-nails. Sometimes we traversed up one side or other of the ravine, sometimes we clambered up the bed of the stream which had gouged it out. Here and there the ice would not bear weight, being but thinly frozen over the swift water, and we all became very wet, until our trousers froze stiff about our legs. The glimmer of day came dully through a low and leaden sky, and showed us close by the head of our gully. We looked back whence we had come, and Sergeant North voiced the general feeling when he said, "Thank God I came up in the dark!"

Ahead of us, and far below, lay Glencoe. We followed the course of the river Coupall, which tumbled away northeasterly, until within an hour or two we scrambled on to the road about midway along the pass. Our route now lay due north to the high valley of the Leven, although the map showed that we must detour to the right to avoid the high ground of Aonach Eagach.

The mist was creeping low, and heavy snowflakes slid out of the white mystery above us. The wind tumbled them, undignified, into mounting drifts. We sat a moment for a smoke, and I told the Guardsmen that in such weather two hundred and fifty years before the dwellers of the Glen had been put to the sword or driven out of their cosy bothies to certain death from exposure.

Sergeant North remarked that the victims were fortunate in starting warm, and I realized that we were all becoming nearly frozen. We rose, and began to climb northward up the snow slopes. Visibility closed in to a few yards, and we could do none other than march by compass. The snow was deep, and not firm frozen, and the heavy men, weighted with heavy packs, sank to their knees at every step. It must have been about midday when the trend of the going levelled out, and gradually changed to a downhill slope.

Richard encouraged our weary warriors by stating that the Leven must be close in front, and that we would follow it down to Kinlochleven for a hot drink before we struck north again.

But hardly had he spoken than we came below the mist, and stopped aghast. A couple of miles below us, and stretching far away on the right hand, lay a great sheet of water. Richard and I hastily thumbed our maps once more, but, try as we would, we could will no loch to appear on the crumpled sheets anywhere within a score of miles of where we purported to be. The Guardsmen gulped, but said nothing, and submitted to follow our lead again downhill towards the water.

Surreptitiously Richard and I compared compasses. Then on the map, and in the mind's eye, we retraced our steps to Loch Etive. True, for most of the way we had come blind, either in darkness or in mist, but the feel of the ground had always tallied with the contours of the map. As ever in such instances, the human radar rebelled against the false message of the instrument.

"The compasses are out!" declared Richard.

"The maps are wrong!" said I.

However, as we neared the water we saw that artifice had had some hand in its birth. There was concrete at the western end, and a leat ran downward parallel to a leaping river.

Simultaneously we saw the answer to the puzzle. Some reservoir had come into being more newly than to be shown on our outdated maps. All else fitted, and the river was undoubtedly the Leven. Vindicated, we made short work of the few miles to Kinlochleven. Thus out of despair came forth the Guardsmen's tea once more.

The Ben Nevis block now lay between us and camp. We wished to be in on the morrow, and must therefore travel farther before nightfall. Ten miles up in the hills, on our direct route, the map showed a dot, probably a shepherd's bothy. We decided to try to reach it.

The squad began well after their rest. We followed a steep track which eased in gradient after a few miles. But on the featureless moor the track, if it were still there, was lost beneath the snow. Dusk closed in upon us on the heels of the mist, and the intermittent snow-flurries grew into a swirling, full-scale blizzard. The Guardsmen, too, were flagging. They had done wonders on their unaccustomed trek, but it was obvious that they could go little farther. Neither map nor compass could help us now, and we dared not think of a night in the open.

Of a sudden we smelt peat smoke. We followed blindly upwind, scenting like a pack of hounds, and within a few minutes ran full tilt into the wall of the bothy.

A fine old man, gnarled as a heather-root, played host to us, helped by his wife. They dried our socks, fed us on scones and tea, and presently led us through the snowstorm to an outbuilding, where there was a store of bracken for bedding the cattle who lay in their stalls beside us. When the men had repaired their feet we fell asleep on the bracken, lulled by the rhythmic chewing of the cows, and comforted by their warmth.

We were a sorry sight at daybreak. Hardly a man was moving freely, for, besides chafed feet, many had taken falls in our journey, and had stiffened up. Our boots and clothes were still wet, the fire was out, and a dark mist lay against the little window. I heard Sergeant North assert authority with Sergeants' Mess clarity.

"If none of you's not fit, you'd better be, on account of you won't get home alive else."

We limbered up a little as we lit the fire, fetched water, shaved, ate our oatmeal ration, and drank tea. Sergeant North asked permission to leave some of our rations for the use of the old couple, and the woman received an offering of oatmeal, pemmican, and dried apple rings. What she did with the pemmican I have never been able to guess. Richard thought she might nail a slab of it above the lintel of the cowhouse to protect the beasts from an overlooking.

As we started off the low-hung sun grew redly through the thinning mist. In a few minutes the vapour was gone, and for the first time we ceased to grope for our way. Spean Bridge lay some fifteen miles ahead, and in the clear visibility the signposts of the hills were easy to read. Ben Nevis and Aonach Beag stood white and solid for more than four thousand feet on our left front, and a ridge of high ground stretched across our direct way. We detoured east of the ridge, and struck a track which led down to Spean Bridge.

The Guardsmen were light-hearted, pleased to know that they would shortly have done exactly what the Chief Instructor had told them to do. The gaiety was infectious, and I stalked a blackcock with my .38 revolver, and saw him fly away with the disdainful air of a bird who regards any firearm save a twelve-bore shotgun as the instrument of a hooligan.

None of us was versed in Scots licensing law, but we had a feeling that if we reached the Spean Bridge Hotel before two o'clock we should be rewarded.

We did, and were.

While we were within some of our instructors appeared.

When they saw us they stared as though we were ghosts. We learned for the first time that there had been great concern about us, and that the authorities had been thinking up a reply to expected questions in the House of Commons. None had seen us leave Loch Etive, and none had heard of us *en route*. The rest of the course had floundered on the Glencoe road on the first morning, and the commando troop had decided against going cross-country in the rough weather conditions, and had returned by road in a prodigious forced march.

At Spean Bridge we were seven miles from camp. The instructors were pleased with us, and announced that we should walk no more, but should be fetched by truck.

"Truck be damned!" we all said, and instead formed up in threes and set off.

At camp they turned out the guard for us, and, more to the point, made a rum issue. The Guardsmen were given the next day free, and Percy Black took Richard and me deer-stalking. On the way back to the Mess in the dusk I told Percy how much I had enjoyed the irregular soldiering which we had just done. He agreed that he too enjoyed commando life, and said that several officers from the Brigade had been seconded to the commandos. Nothing more was said at the time, but two months later Percy sent me a letter.

CHAPTER VI

PRIVATE ARMY

Percy Black's letter came two months after the commando course. It was headed, with burlesque flavour, "1st Airborne Cavalry Squadron," and on the face of it sounded an ideal unit in which Percy might break more bones. He was very guarded in what he said, stating simply that he had left the commandos to join this new unit, itself part of a new formation which was commanded by Major-General "Boy" Browning, a Grenadier. He added that several Guardsmen had already arrived, and that he thought he could find a place for me.

I went to see the Adjutant, who showed goodwill, as did the Commanding Officer. Perhaps I had on my side the wish of the Regiment to have a finger in a new pie. The battalion was practising assault landings on the rough, bleak coasts of the Western Isles when my interview bore fruit. Regimental Headquarters had agreed to my attachment, and within forty-eight hours I had handed over my platoon and said good-bye.

I knew little of what I was going to, for although there was vague general knowledge of an infant Airborne Force, newly raised, there was secrecy about its size and purpose. Before leaving Scotland I telephoned Percy Black to ask more, and to say that I would report next day. He would give me no details on the telephone, but told me to take ten days' leave.

I spent most of my leave in the Lake District, scrambling about the hills of Wastdale, but went on to London for the last day or two, needing to see Tessa once more. For so intelligent a woman, Tessa had a curious mental quietude, a lack of turbulence in her personality, which was restful to experience. We moved in London shoulder to shoulder with a thousand other couples of whom the men were in uniform, who like a flock of starlings would rise in a body from one bar to alight, still chattering, in another. And yet we felt a detachment from this lively and well-lit round, as if it were but an irrelevant backcloth against which we danced our *pas de deux*. When there is much unspoken between two people they float on the crowded stream as in a glass bubble, seeing round a little, hearing a little, noting nothing save each other's unfinished thoughts.

When the time came to report to the 1st Airborne Cavalry Squadron at Newbury, in Berkshire, I met on the train a subaltern rejoining the unit after leave. He was not forthcoming when I questioned him, stating finally that he was to be posted back to his old battalion. He said that the Airborne Force had dictatorial powers, and that if they wished to be rid of anyone they had only to say "unsuitable for the Airborne rôle."

My train acquaintance directed me to the country house on the outskirts of the town where lay my new unit. The atmosphere was slipshod. There were no neat transport lines, no well-signposted stores and offices, only a few men to be seen, and these aimless and in varying dress and headgear. My guide led me to an empty anteroom in the house, pointed to a cupboard, said, "The drink's in there!"

And went away.

As I stood miserably Percy Black came in. I greeted him with the eagerness of a drowning man clutching a strong swimmer.

"Hallo!" he said. "Sorry I got you into this. I'm leaving myself in a few days."

I felt the dark waters close over my head, and must have gulped. Percy got an inkling of my feelings, and, as I came up for breath, metaphorically grasped my hair.

"You may like it here," he comforted. "The unit's going to be a small one, and at the moment it's about at quarter strength, with six officers and sixty men, or so. There's not much to do yet because most of the personnel are away on courses. It's a major's command. You'd better come and see him."

My new Commanding Officer, Major Rory O'Brien, was in his office. He was about forty years old, big-built, with a smooth pink face and silver hair. One could imagine him as a martial bishop of the Middle Ages, a roistering cleric with whom bed, board, and battle took precedence over the beatitudes. From him I at last learned something of the company into which I had come.

Rory told me that Winston Churchill had decreed that there would be Airborne soldiers. Accordingly an Airborne Division was now being formed. It would consist of two Parachute Brigades, one glider or Air Landing Brigade, and divisional troops, gunners, signallers, and the like, equipped to travel by glider. We ourselves were then attached to the Air Landing Brigade, and the Squadron would in time be fitted out with jeeps, so that it could act as divisional cavalry.

I then received a little lecture on the Airborne rôle. Rory said that the Airborne soldier must not consider himself any more intrepid than other fighting arms, and that the real point of difference was that he would travel comfortably to battle in a plane or a glider, rather than in a jolting lorry. However, he made the reservation that the method of delivery was expensive in petrol and material, and that once landed the passengers must justify the cost. He pointed out that there would be no real armoured or artillery support, and that therefore the Airborne soldier must be prepared to fight on his own for a period with the weapons which he was able to carry with him. Rory then gave me clearly to understand that I was a probationer, and dismissed me.

He sent for me again next day. He said, with a relish of a collector of rare specimens, that he had obtained two vacancies for a course at GHQ Battle Schools, and proposed to send another officer and myself to learn the new technique, so that we might return to instruct the Squadron. He added that we might leave at once, spend a night in London, and report in County Durham next day.

This concession was typical of Rory, for he did not believe

that anyone should be a martyr to discipline. The Army attitude at this time to the liberty of the subject was that, since the soldier was paid so much a day, he should be on call for all twenty-four hours of it. Many in authority found it easier to keep their subordinates on hand against contingencies rather than to plan out what contingencies might arise. This common practice was not all the fault of junior commanders, for the Army system of command is such that a sudden decision at a high level produces a chain-reaction with the speed of nuclear fission.

Thus, lest the Brigadier decide without warning to visit a company on training, the battalion commander holds his second-in-command at readiness; the second-in-command keeps a car and driver standing by; the PMC tells the Mess Sergeant to have all the waiters to hand in clean jackets; the Regimental Sergeant-Major practises the Barrack Guard in turn-out, and tells the Provost Sergeant to see that all the prisoners are properly shaved; the duty company is put at readiness to clean up the camp; and the company out at training is held in arrested motion poised at the start of the most spectacular bit of their programme.

Whoever it was who mentioned to some one that the Brigadier might be round rubs his hands at the end of the day, and says, "Well, he didn't come because he's gone on leave. But if he had turned up we were all ready for him."

My companion on the course was Horsey Bridgewater, a big, ruddy-faced young man, with the controlled large movements of a cavalry charger. He was to meet his wife in London, and as he talked of her, secure and happy in marriage, I envied him, and wished that I too could be sure of a lasting and successful union.

Tessa and I spent together another of those evenings in which there was a dreamlike quality, so that we were afraid to give voice to the unspoken words within us lest we wake up to a reality of difficulties, dangers, and the shadow of parting. We said good-bye again that night as always before, regretful at having left unsaid the things we now had no time to say.

Horsey and I caught the train to Durham next morning, and sat silent and morose until I espied in the corridor Tiger Badcock, the ex-Ironside ranker who was at Sandhurst with me.

"Hallo!" said Tiger. "You going on this bloody course?"

I told him that we were going to learn a new technique in tactics and training, and introduced him to Horsey, who studied with wonder the luxuriance and span of Tiger's still increasing moustache.

"Don't think you are going to a series of lectures," advised Tiger. "Haven't you heard about these new courses?"

Now that we were reminded of it, Horsey and I did remember gossip among the soldiers, and guarded comment in the Press about these new courses designed to make men impervious to fatigue and callous of bloodshed. We must have showed dismay, for the sadistic Tiger sat down with us and told us a series of horrible anecdotes about students on previous courses who had died or become mentally deranged.

When we arrived at the Battle School, isolated as it was from the haunts of men, Horsey and I found ourselves in the same platoon, together with Tiger Badcock, for whose company we now felt distaste.

That evening we were given a lecture by the Chief Instructor. At the back of the room stood a bevy of young men who had the superior air of torturers at a questioning, and who were obviously our instructors. If Horsey radiated the vitality of a man who habitually put a pinch of health salts into his morning tea, then these men provoked their livers with a tinful. They stood, arms akimbo, on the balls of their feet, and chatted to one another with the confidence of Oxford Groupers who are spiritually clean as well. Horsey said that they reminded him of Carruthers. It was some time before I realized that Carruthers was a composite being compounded of all the virtues. Horsey told me that Carruthers's motto was *Mens sana in corpore sano*, and that he had graduated from being head of his school into the Colonial Service, where he had ruled great territories by putting the black men on their honour.

The Chief Instructor's talk was more of a warning than

a lecture. When he had said that modern war was one of speed and movement, where familiarity with weapons was essential, even in the most unconventional positions, and where individual prowess could once more find scope, he told us that we would from the outset be harried to breaking-point. Finally he told us that we would always travel at the double, and shouted, "Move!"

Our sluggish brains told us that the exhortation was over, and we stampeded from the hall like a herd of startled bison. In the cold night air Horsey and I marked time at the double long enough to accustom our eyes to the dark, and so to avoid the many students who had in their enthusiasm prostrated themselves. I suggested to Horsey that Carruthers might approve of us washing down the news we had heard with a stiff drink. Horsey agreed, with the reservation that, although Carruthers was a man's man, he never allowed drink to get the better of him.

We met our own platoon instructor in the bar. He was a pleasant man, convinced of the value of the new battle drill. However, he gave us a new thought by stating that it was aimed to make the course sterner than the real thing, so that we would find action a relaxation. On this we went to bed. There was a Canadian next to me, lying on one elbow to study a photograph. After a moment he passed the picture across and said, "That's my wife with our kid. Guess he's quite a big feller, now. It's gone two years since I've seen him."

I sympathized with him, and at once a smile lit his face.

"My name's McDonald," he said effusively. "Guess we'll get to know each other here."

I said that I was by birth a Canadian, and at this McDonald began to talk without reservation. He was, like many of his countrymen who had gone overseas early in the War, not very happy. It seemed to these pioneers that the quick blaze of their first enthusiasm had consumed itself, and that, with their fires dimmed by waiting and by disappointment, there was nothing to warm their spirit against the coldness of absence from their homes. He endorsed what I had often felt, and which was later true of many American soldiers, that these exiles did not wish to remind themselves of some of the softness of life by seeking the company of the teen-age girls and the grass-widows of our garrison towns and industrial cities. More often than not they would have preferred a respectable tea-party in some family home, and to have helped mother with the washing-up. But the British do not readily invite people into their houses, least of all wild men from beyond the ocean whom they associate with grizzly bears. So that to escape from the bleak military life of their camps few roads were open.

At last Tiger Badcock put a hand on the light switch.

"All said your prayers?" he inquired. "You'd better have a kip. May be the last you'll get."

We were not initiated gently into the new training. On the first morning we began at once a spell of the hardest work which most of us had ever done, and the tempo was maintained until the last day, nearly a month later.

Within the platoons into which we were arbitrarily divided, each of us filled a new rôle daily, either student platoon or section commander, Number One or Number Two Bren gunner, mortarman, anti-tank rifleman, or grenadier. Quite often the piece of ground on which we were to be indoctrinated in the new tactical handling of weapons would be a couple of miles away. With a full load of equipment, arms, and ammunition, harried by our instructors, we would double to the area. We began to suspect that all routes were chosen to include briar-hedge and river obstacles, for we rarely began our work dry or unblooded.

Sometimes, on arrival at our destination, the instructor would allow us to sink to the ground for a few minutes, with the command, "Smoke!"

Few of us were ever able, for our matches would be sodden, and we without breath.

At that time Battle Schools were in their infancy, and were not approved of by some senior soldiers. But orthodoxy is not static in war or anything else. The correct tactics at Waterloo would have been incorrect a hundred years later at the battle of the Somme, and these in turn were outdated a quarter of a century later. The great conquerors of history succeeded not so much by the discovery of new weapons as by adapting existing weapons to new tactics. The German armies had evolved the handling of the armoured fighting vehicle from the point where it had been left in 1918, and had changed it from a steam-roller to an almost invulnerable charger. This had led to the war of movement, of which the Allies, still conditioned by the memory of the fixed lines of 1918, were struggling to find the method.

A war of movement, where troops must be represented as a series of dots, rather than drawn in a long, unbroken line, meant that many situations arose where massive fire-support was not possible, and where sub-units, units, and even formations must fight a battle with their own resources.

It was to teach the unit self-reliance that the Battle Schools were formed.

On our course we learned above all to use our full fire-power instantly, accurately, and from any position. We were taught to move in to the attack round a flank whenever possible, using the tactics of fire and movement, so that while part of the force was advancing another part harassed the enemy with fire. More important, we were taught to shoot to kill, not to indulge a taste for pyrotechnics, for the enemy must not live to fight another day.

The term Battle Drill was correct. The tactics we learnt were a drill, infinitely adaptable and expandable. They could be applied in any situation and on any scale, even where a corps made a flanking movement covered by the massed artillery of an army.

We were taught, too, versatile drills for clearing houses, villages, and woods; for fortifying houses; for laying booby-traps; for patrolling by day or by night. Throughout we were inoculated against the bemusing din of battle by explosions and by fire directed very close to us. Of course, people sometimes got hurt. I saw Horsey sit down suddenly one day, with a surprised look. When I went to him I found that a bullet had drilled through his shoulder.

"If you were Carruthers," he said, "you'd suck the poison from the wound."

I saw him that evening in hospital. His wife was on her way to visit him, he had been promised sick leave, and he reckoned that it had been the most successful course he had attended.

So, I think, did we all, tired and scared as we were. Even Tiger Badcock ceased to criticize. He remarked one day to my Canadian bed-neighbour, McDonald, "This is all good stuff, but I guess private soldiers wouldn't stand for it."

"Why should they?" said McDonald. "The private's paid to be a private, not a war-whooping Apache."

On the last day I telephoned Rory. He was sympathetic about the fifty per cent. casualties suffered by the representatives of his unit, but was glad to hear that we were all enthusiastic about the course—the more so since it was over.

"We leave here to-morrow, Friday——" I began.

"Report midday Monday," said Rory.

Back with Rory O'Brien's Squadron, events followed one another rapidly. The Airborne Division, grown from infancy to manhood, concentrated in or about Bulford Camp, on Salisbury Plain. The men were issued with red berets and the shoulder flash of Bellerophon astride winged Pegasus. Equipment of all kinds, much of it special, or adapted to our peculiar uses flowed in. Parachute aircraft, also glider-tug combinations, became increasingly available after a tug-of-war with Bomber Command. Our training progressed, and as units became practised in their own rôles they were blended into the bigger purposes of brigades, and the brigades at last formed a coherent division.

The Airborne men were volunteers. Some of the newcomers were wild men, some were bad men. Most of the wild men were broken to harness and retained, but the bad men were sent back to the Commanding Officers who had detailed them to volunteer.

Rory was most critical. It was sometimes difficult to see on what grounds some of his objections were based, unless Gaelic second sight revealed to him horrors hidden to the Sassenach. But this clairvoyance he reserved mostly for officers and key men in the Squadron, for Rory was a firm believer in decentralization, and allowed his subordinates within wide limits to pick their own men and pursue their own methods. From first to last the Squadron posted away sixty per cent. of the volunteers who came to it.

There were four Troops in the Squadron, each commanded by a Captain. I commanded 'A' Troop, Horsey, 'B,' Jack Johnson, 'C,' and Francis Winterbottom, 'D.' The Troop split into a headquarters and three sections, each under a subaltern. It was likely, therefore, that one of the Squadron's rôles would be to provide mobile, heavily armed officer patrols, an individual and exciting job. Rory, who had been in a destroyer as a very young midshipman during the First German War, did all he could to encourage this individuality, and allowed Troops to go away by themselves to train.

As Troop commanders, we four were in the position of men gazing on the pieces of a jig-saw puzzle and wondering how to begin, so that the picture might be completed before events interrupted. We had our subalterns, non-commissioned officers, and troopers; we had a variety of equipment which embarrassed us as a novice golfer might be by an over-full bag of clubs; and we had our vehicles, which few of our men could either drive or maintain.

The vehicles were the key to our rôle, and were also the most liable of our stores to deterioration. Under Rory's directions, we tackled vehicle training first. As for 'A' Troop, we went away for a fortnight to a remote high crown of downland, screened from sightseers by a fringe of woods. We moved our vehicles there by an act of faith in the deserted hours which followed dawn. For the first few days we ran four circuses—for jeeps, motor-cycle combinations, heavy motor-cycles, and lightweights.

At the start of the day the four circuses of vehicles and cycles would be separated, each chasing its own tail. Then, the combinations, still gyrating, would creep like a spinning discus across the down. The machine strove constantly to turn towards the sidecar, and, as the rider's arms wearied, did so, spoiling the arranged orbit of the circle, and presently spoiling every one else's orbit, too.

In addition, the other groups of vehicles were not without reproach, for every now and then some gallant member of the team, either giddy or bored, or perhaps because he was an individualist, would fly off at a tangent as a foreign body leaves a spinning turntable, and, bucketing across the downs, horrified at being alone in outer space, would erupt like a comet into the ken of the next ring.

However, as so often happens, order grew suddenly out of chaos, as a stirred-up pond clarifies when the mud settles. We returned to Bulford as a reasonably competent body of mechanics and drivers, in need only of the polish which usage would give.

During the two weeks which we had spent by ourselves in bivouacs we had learned a good deal about one another. The knowledge was useful when, almost at once, the Troop went off once more to shake down into its sections, and to practise dismounted tactics. This time we drove down to the New Forest, and set up our bivouac in the pleasant alleys of its ancient trees.

Troop headquarters consisted of twelve of us, with two jeeps and four motor-cycles. The most important man in my jeep was Corporal Baxter, the signaller, although just then we had not progressed to wireless training. The second jeep carried a three-inch mortar team. Among the four motor-cyclists rode the Troop Sergeant, Sergeant Mackintosh, a small, brisk young man, with that masterful nose which is often a more accurate guide to character than the most jutting jaw.

The three sections were of ten men each, their commanders subalterns, with a lance-sergeant and lance-corporal apiece. The subalterns turned out to be a capable trio. Dougal Pearson was a dark, hard-bitten Scot, thick of speech. Ian McMillan was another Scot, long, lean, and fair. George Field was English. All three were very young indeed.

During this stay in the New Forest we practised the battle drill which I had learned in my course, until all of us had the field-craft of shikaris, although in those surroundings we could not fire weapons.

Rory visited us one night, with a senior training officer from London. I think the stranger was shocked by our gipsy camp, for he stood silent for a while by the shielded fire, sniffing the roasting game. Presently he demanded to know where our sentry was.

"Here, sor!" came the rich Irish voice of Trooper McEntee, punctuated by the snick of a rifle-bolt, from out the shadow of a bush.

Our visitor seemed upset that our guards did not march up and down in heavy boots, waiting to challenge loudly the noises of darkness, but that instead they slunk soft-footed from shadow to shadow to meet the creatures of the night on equal terms. He felt, I am sure, that we should be content to advertise our presence to the unfriendly, so that we might be murdered in our beds in the proper manner.

The Troop's next journey was to North Derbyshire, to fire our weapons under field conditions. We selected from the map a rough and deserted-looking area of the Pennines, within forty miles of the Airborne Depot at Chesterfield, so that we could use this establishment to draw pay and rations, and obtain medical help should our weapons get the better of us.

However, we were, as it turned out, to operate from a comfortable base. We made the long run north, and arrived at nightfall at the head of a dale which melted into the slopes of Kinderscout. We had perforce to halt, for the road ended.

I went into an inn to ask whether we might for the first night sleep in a barn or an outhouse. The landlord did better for us. He owned a second inn in the hamlet, which was closed for the duration of the War, save for the bar. Here our new friend installed us in the ground-floor rooms, and throughout our stay showed us all the utmost hospitality. In North Derbyshire we found everywhere similar kindness.

For a fortnight we roamed the hills firing our weapons under varying conditions, until even the instructors at the Battle School would have been satisfied. They would have been particularly pleased with us on an occasion when we beleaguered a party of unauthorized sportsmen, themselves heavily armed, who, unknown to us, were forced for an hour to take cover under a clapper bridge, crouching waist-deep in water.

Personalities made themselves felt. The Irish Trooper McEntee turned out to have power over beasts. I once saw the head of a grass-snake pop inquiringly out of his battle-dress blouse. The same receptacle cradled many a rabbit, which he was able to pluck casually from the grass to its demise at the lip of his Squadron stew-pot.

Back at Bulford, I had found a Bombardier Guardsman who had relinquished corporal's stripes to volunteer for Airborne work, and, after a little intrigue, had managed to get him for my servant. Longman was a very big, calm man, and a born soldier. He was soon to become a section Lance-Sergeant, and in his place I had in view a Welshman, named, without originality, Jones, who was the best scrounger in the Troop.

Corporal Baxter, the signaller, was known as Gentleman Jim, for he was both good-looking and educated. When, later on, we came to do our wireless training I became used to hearing Corporal Baxter say, in refined tones, "The beastly thing won't work, sir. I think it's received a jolt."

These trips and others enabled the Squadron to become a versatile and skilled little unit. Superimposed on our own internal training was the Airborne training, arranged at a higher level. Most of the Squadron seemed to enjoy these aerial manœuvres, but Horsey and I discovered a distrust of them, feeling that to usurp the functions of the angels was *lèse-Dieu*. In the early days of the Hotspur glider our presumption only escaped retribution by repeated miracles. The Hotspur was a plywood craft, glued together by some of the easy-terms furniture manufacturers. It carried a pilot and nine men, and was towed by such elderly biplanes as were available. Since the Hotspur had a high wing loading, and the tug aircraft a low cruising speed, the glider yawed and wallowed uncertainly in the wake of the tug, travelling as it was at about stalling speed.

The Hotspur perplexed us, too, because although it could deliver our men to an objective, prostrate with air-sickness, it could carry nothing more beyond our personal equipment. It seemed then as if we would never go to war as Airborne mechanized soldiers. However, during the autumn of 1942 the mighty wings of the Horsa glider began to be seen with increasing frequency over Salisbury Plain. These great craft, towed by four-engined bomber planes, could carry a loaded jeep and trailer, and its crew, and three or four motor-cycles with their riders. They were comfortable gliders, and well-designed to land in the difficult zones likely on operations. Horsey and I felt a little happier.

Suddenly big events stirred us all. The Allied armada sailed to North Africa and Rommel was caught between the First and Eighth British Armies like a nut in the jaws of a nut-cracker. We did not then know how long the hard Boche would take to crack. But our chief interest lay in the activities of the 1st Parachute Brigade. The seaborne forces had landed along the North African seaboard on the 8th of November, 1942. The following day elements of the 1st Brigade left Bulford by air, arrived in Africa on the 11th, and were parachuted into action on the 12th. This swift sequence made us sit up. The speed and mobility of the Airborne arm had been convincingly demonstrated to the sceptics, and it was brought home to all of us that we too might well be blooded with as little warning.

Rory increased the tempo of our training, and all of us felt that the climax was at hand. We felt, too, the need to put right our personal affairs. Prodded by events, I found that I no longer wanted to live my private life in a past which was buried in a Welsh mountain. I told Tessa of this, and she agreed, without much excitement, to marry me. She came down to stay at a farmhouse on the edge of the Plain, and Rory gave me forty-eight hours' leave in which to get married.

Tessa, who has a genius for the unexpected, developed laryngitis on the day of her arrival. When we went together to the Registrar's office she was almost speechless, and had a high temperature. She brightened a little as the clerk took down particulars of my parents.

"Occupation of father?" asked the clerk.

"Gentleman," I replied, believing that to be the correct technical term.

"No! No!" exclaimed the clerk, impatient of undemocratic affectations. "What did he do?"

My father had died aged twenty-two, and had not determined his occupation, so I answered, "Nothing."

"Unemployed," muttered the clerk, writing busily.

Three months later our Orderly Room Sergeant told us that we were very soon to embark for Africa. In due course this news was officially confirmed.

Security of speech was very good indeed in the Airborne Division, and none of us, I think, even hinted of the future to our wives or families. Just the same, the Squadron concocted a reason for a last Mess party, to which most of the married men brought their wives. We set out to drink dry our cellar, lest the stock should fall into alien hands, and did so. Carruthers became rather a prig towards morning, and Dickie Oakes, the Quartermaster, who was the only teetotaller in the Mess, trod on a bottle, tumbled, and broke his wrist.

The date of entrainment for the port of sailing was made known to us. 'A' Troop went through its familiar routine of packing its possessions into the vehicles, and it was difficult for us to realize that, when we off-loaded, we would not be in Derbyshire or the New Forest.

On the last evening I cycled over to see Tessa. We spent our time together as so often before—a stroll, a glass of beer at the little inn, supper, a game of backgammon—but I watched the slow climb of the moon and listened for each chime of the clock. Tessa made arrangements with me for a tennis party the next week. Yet Tessa knew well enough that it was the parting, and kept her sure knowledge unvoiced, so that we said good-bye as if only for a day.

CHAPTER VII

AFRICA

At sunrise on our first morning in Africa we found ourselves on a stony knoll, our kit heaped about us in confusion. Round and about us as far as the eye could see were American soldiers, white and black, all wearing different hats, or the same sort of hat differently. We formed an island of insularity in a cosmopolitan sea.

At dusk the previous night our troopship had slid quietly to the quay at Oran, with us, her passengers, lining the rails like sightseers on a pleasure cruise. And, indeed, we wondered what business of war had brought us on our cruise, for a fortnight before the Afrika Korps had laid down its arms on the low, bare headland of Cap Bon, and had marched itself in a soldierly manner under junior officers into captivity.

The Quartermaster's men presently arrived with tents, which we erected as best we could, for the iron-hard ground rejected pegs as armour-plate scorns a bayonet, and the Squadron lines took shape. The environs of each tent were garnished with pathways edged by coloured stones, as the men tried, with the age-old pathos of the exile, to make themselves a home. But some senior officer had the misfortune to stumble in the dark over some one's edging, and the removal of the stones was ordered. The men would have preferred to lose a week's pay.

The light relief on this bare hillock was found at the latrines. These were perched unscreened on the low summit, and commanded a fine view which was enjoyed in a most democratic way by American colonels cheek by jowl with darky truck-drivers. All wore funny hats and smoked cigars while at their morning devotions. Rory O'Brien, seated on his deal throne, put one of his men who was passing by on a charge for failure to salute, and thus won instant respect from our allies.

Our vehicles were expected to arrive on another ship at the little port of Azeu, and I was sent with the Transport Officer to unload them. The Transport Officer was of remote Gallic extraction, and during our few days at Azeu he made numerous friends. Thus we lodged ourselves upon a pleasant French family who had a house close to the beach, where we shared an enormous feather mattress in an open courtyard with an elderly ex-Légionnaire. In return the old man guarded our clothes daily while we swam. At last our vehicles were on African soil, and I greeted with affection my own reliable jeep which had for nearly a year borne me to and fro in the out-of-the-way parts of England.

The Squadron was now mobile again, and, with the Air Landing Brigade, moved from the stony hillock to settle down on two airfields near Mascara, a hundred miles away. These had been condemned by the French as heavily infected with malaria, but none of our people fell sick.

There is no doubt that we were all very fit, and that our own germs were in good shape to counter-attack invaders, but our immunity to malaria and other tropical diseases was largely by reason of the new attitude which the British Army had adopted towards hot climates. Gone were the sun-helmets and spine-pads, and gone too was the mental attitude which flinched from sunlight. Instead we worked and played bare-legged and bare-backed, and the colour of our skin changed from white through salmon pink to mahogany. We kept our bowels open in fly-proof latrines, swallowed anti-malaria pills if watched by the Medical Officer, and covered our arms and legs after sundown against bites.

Very quickly we learned that we had not been brought to Africa by mistake, and that there was a Plan. The Plan was to invade Sicily with seaborne and Airborne troops. The Airborne force was to be made up of the veteran 1st Parachute Brigade, and the untried 1st Air Landing Brigade. But we, the 1st Airborne Cavalry Squadron, had no place in this expedition, and were instead to help the other glider troops prepare themselves, as a dresser titivates the star for a stage appearance. Dougal Pearson, Ian McMillan, and George Field were bitterly disappointed at this unheroic rôle, and even the more mature Horsey slunk silently about muttering to Carruthers. As for Rory O'Brien, he nearly choked with frustrated pugnacity, and devised for us a special rôle which he submitted to the highest quarter. He suggested that our squadron should alight on the mountainous spine of Italy and thence raid the coastal road and rail communications until such time as the mainland was invaded and the ground forces could relieve us.

The plan might have worked, at that. Anyway, I remembered it, and soon afterwards found the idea useful.

The time grew near to give the Sicilians their surprise. The Airborne fleet was to set off from air-strips around Kairouan and Sousse, an area upward of a thousand miles from Mascara, and orders came for the Division to concentrate at their jumping-off point. We, as the Divisional Cavalry, were given the job of shepherding all the transport on the long journey, while most of the personnel travelled the hot and dusty route by rail. For the convoy, the monotonous pace set of thirty miles per two hours was wearisome, but we, as whippers-in, had some latitude. We ran ahead to pick areas for the night's halt, we had opportunity to buy eggs and fruit, to shop a little in Arab towns, and to drink coffee with the vendors.

On the third night of our journey we stopped near Beni Mansour, where a staging camp still functioned. It was a moonlit night, and Horsey and I went for a stroll before bed. To the south of us rose a great range of hills, mystic in the dead light. The giants were unexpected after the hundreds of miles of shimmering flatness which we had travelled. Horsey and I had, of course, been talking of our wives, and at that receptive hour of the night our spirits reached a little way towards England, to return afraid of the void of distance.

For comfort we turned our eyes to the hills, and refreshed ourselves with sight of their calm beauty. I said to Horsey that I was determined to climb them before I left Africa, and received from him a suitable reply.

Three days and five hundred miles later we reached our new homes in an olive-grove a few miles from Sousse, and the hills were far away.

Events now moved quickly. Rory O'Brien made a shower-bath out of a petrol-tin hung from a branch; the Divisional ammunition dump blew up, rained mortar bombs on our lines, and wounded the second-in-command, who was replaced by Horsey (it is an ill explosion which blasts nobody any good); the Mayor of Temlett put in a formal protest, accompanied by Madame, about restrictive practices at the brothel, claiming that it was a gross reflection on the young ladies to limit the length of the evening queue; and we four troop commanders betook ourselves and our men to four air-strips, there to service the gliders awaiting the trip to Sicily.

The spirit of the air-strips was dust. Their sun-baked surfaces were an inch deep in red dust. We needed no sirocco to envelop us in fine grit, for every spinning propeller blew clouds upon us. We messed with the American Air Force pilots, crews, and ground staff, who were to fly our comrades to battle.

After a few days our palates revolted from their highly flavoured and plentiful rations, and longed for bully and biscuits. As far as my own air-strip was concerned, our tight little Troop grew yet closer knit, as if it were satisfied with and sure of its own structure, and mistrustful of transatlantic discipline.

With Rory's connivance, most of the Squadron's officers made a surreptitious arrangement to fly as passengers in the tug aircraft, for we were then inexperienced and eager to sniff the odour of battle. I suspected, too, and took good care not to be certain, that most of the Troop was booked for a joy-ride. But there was to be no hitch-hiking, for a little before the hour of departure an absolute embargo was put upon stowaways.

There was drama in the air that evening of the 9th of July, 1943. The Dakotas were lined, tight-packed in echelon, at the downwind end of the air-strip, and close behind each tug sat its glider, the nylon tow-rope coiled unsnarled between them. About each glider door stood knots of Airborne soldiers smoking and chatting with elaborate unconcern. It was strange for us to look upon these men whom we knew so well, with whom we had trained for so long, and to imagine them as they would be during the next few hours. For they were to go on a wild ride that stormy night, and to have a rude landing.

The casual groups melted into their gliders, the ply-wood doors shut, and the field was as eerily empty of fighting-men as the beach on which had stood the Trojan horse. In quick succession the Dakota engines coughed into wakefulness and the great dust-clouds bellied away and upward as if from a factory of Mars. The marshalling officer moved out into the fairway, and with expressive arms beckoned out the leading aircraft. The machine moved, slowly at first, diagonally on to the runway, straightened, and took up the slack on the tow-rope, until its glider followed it as a leashed hound its master, then with full roar the pair sped ever swifter over the hard clay. The glider took to its wings, unsteady for a moment, then the tug too found its native air, and both of them skimmed low and purposeful into the red eye of the sun. Plane after plane followed, close as a skein of geese, and suddenly was silence.

Three days later a war correspondent's dispatch came to us by way of Divisional Intelligence. It said:

> Date line in Sicily with Airborne Force 11/7—under great difficulties men of first glider-borne force to be used in action fought magnificently in Sicily during night before Allied invasion by sea. Over 100 gliders were brought 400 miles in wind almost reaching gale force. Landings were made in bad visibility under heavy anti-aircraft fire. Although it was now not possible for force to fight together units of about 15 threw countryside into night long alarm. Principal objective bridge outside Syracuse was taken initially by fourteen men who with together about seventy more fought way through in daylight held it for fourteen hours against increasing Italian opposition.

I was with this body of men as a spectator and full story—which I too exhausted write presently—is one of the most magnificent episodes of this war. The force surrendered mid-afternoon when only some 30 soldiers unwounded or unkilled and ammunition exhausted.

We had then been under concentrated fire 4-inch mortar, heavy machine-guns some hours. There was only one Bren gun in our party, the rest of the men being armed with Stens, rifles. 15 hours fight they waged with these with almost no cover, and left considerable numbers of enemy dead, whilst within one hour of capture we all managed to escape when Eighth Army Reconnaissance Unit began shooting guards. Another unit 5 officers 9 men with whom we linked up this morning had captured a 6-gun coastal battery in a fierce charge shortly after leaving their glider. Throughout night before invasion I could hear grim little actions going on in darkness as units fought towards rendezvous. I learn that blockhouses were captured, barracks shot up, patrols machine-gunned and wiped out, and that over most area S.E. of tip island whereon seaborne forces destined land was thrown into panic by these deadly attacks. There can be no question that comparatively light resistance met by Eighth Army and Navy forces in early stages due glider-borne troops' activities—more to-morrow—end.

One of the most pleasant features of the companionship of Airborne soldiers was the absence of line-shooting. Indeed, the deprecation of their exploits took the form of understatement. The commander of the Air Landing Brigade himself supplied the bathos on that wild Sicilian night. The Brigadier's glider, in common with many others, was released much too far from the coast. The pilot struggled to make land, only to see a high cliff loom up through the night. He made a stall turn, and simultaneously a searchlight blazed out from the cliff-top and the glider was splintered by tracer bullets. They plunged into the rough sea, and clawed their way out of the fuselage to cling a moment to a wing which was slowly sinking beneath them.

The Brigadier quickly took stock of the situation, and turned to his waterlogged brigade major.

"All is not well, Bill!" he announced. He then swam ashore and took charge of the battle.

After our comrades were sped to war our four Troops returned from their air-strips to Rory O'Brien's olive-grove. The days which followed were an anticlimax. We explored the coast for many miles round, moving by Troops, and often bivouacking away for a night or two where we found the bathing good.

I discovered that the 2nd Battalion Ironside Guards was resting near by, fresh from its glories in Tunisia. Few of the officers and men with whom I had served were remaining, but Peter Petter was irrepressibly present, and I dined with him once or twice in the Mess. The 1st Guards Brigade had fought often beside the 1st Parachute Brigade in the early and demoralizing days of the British First Army's activities, and I heard no words but praise for the dash and tenacity of the lightly equipped Airborne men.

Battle had taken a very heavy toll of the Battalion, and not many officers were left whom I knew. I did not see the ungainly figure of Ambrose Winston, and Peter told me that he was recovering from wounds. He had won a conspicuously good Military Cross on an empty stomach. It is not the shape of a man which determines his power of leadership, but the breed.

Rory began to talk again about his plan to paralyse Italy by landing the Squadron in the Apennines, and, with a flash of inspiration, I suggested that I should take 'A' Troop up into the mountains which I had seen near Beni Mansour, there to practise them in climbing technique. Somehow Rory got permission, and to Horsey's surprise I set off one morning, a day ahead of the Troop, to spy out the land.

We concealed ourselves on the first night in a patch of scrub. The party was made up of only myself, Corporal Gentleman Jim Baxter, and my servant Jones, and the Arabs were at that time attacking small groups of travellers. We reached Beni Mansour on the afternoon of the second day, and I went to talk to the Commandant of the almost disused staging camp. He knew little of the mountains, save that they were the Djurjura Alps, an offshoot of the Atlas Mountains, and that the French had built a strategic road through them. He said that a track to the southward led up to the strategic road, joining it at a height of five thousand feet near a mountain refuge, named Tikjda.

We made up our minds to try the track. We forded two rivers and travelled for ten miles straight towards the hills without them seeming closer. Then we ran into woods of conifers, and came on a group of charcoal-burners.

"Yes, m'sieu!" they said. "That is the road to Tikjda. Very bad place. Much snow in winter and many great monkeys."

This description might have applied to any European Alpine resort. The road which had been pointed out wound away at a gradient of one in five. It was an earth shelf six feet wide carved out of a steep hill-side. In bottom gear we climbed for fifteen miles. The wood of the charcoal-burners was lost in the depths below, but some way above us on the track commenced a thick belt of cedars and pines. On the fresh, cool breeze we could already smell the heavy scent of cedar, and I was reminded of summer days in the Laurentians of Quebec.

Away to our right, unveiling themselves as we slowly climbed, a fantastic jumble of rock peaks began to appear. Some were sharp like little Matterhorns, some were sheer like the Aiguilles of the Dolomites, some were to be reached by long, broken, knife-edged ridges, like the Coolins of Skye, magnified ten times.

Then we climbed into the cedar woods. At once the atmosphere of the place took hold of us, for it was that of a Shangri-La of fact, not fiction. We were exhilarated by the cool air, by the smell of the trees, by the ice-cold water springs, and by our remoteness from war and telephones and Army forms.

We came to the Refuge at Tikjda, and found it not unlike an Alpine inn. The Refuge was built on a tree-crowned spur. To the east, perhaps twelve miles away, was the perfect peak of Lalla Kredidja, some 8000 feet, the highest summit in the Djurjura, very severe and remote, with a belt of trees drawn across the face half-way to the top. To the north, with its lower slopes starting at the Refuge, was Ras Timédouine, a peak only ten feet lower than the other. This was a magnificent rock mountain, whose slopes rose like a wall from immediately behind the Refuge. A fine rock ridge ran away east from the summit, its crest guarded at intervals by rock gendarmes, until it melted into a col near Lalla Kredidja. West of the Ras Timédouine by ten miles or so was the Dent du Lion, a fine ridge of jagged rocks with a summit which looked interesting even from that distance.

From the French people at the Refuge we learned that these peaks were mysterious, practically unclimbable, riddled with ice-filled glacial caves, provided with air cover by eagles, and held by ground forces of bare-rumped baboons.

We slept that night on a shelf levelled by spade on the slope of the steep cedar wood. The starlight was the brightest I have ever seen, and, though the night was moonless, I could see through the tree-tops the cone of Lalla Kredidja, aloof and mystical. From below, two thousand feet down in the valley, drifted up a tuneless fluting, which grew as one listened into an eerie melody. The Kabiles were at their hidden recital.

The Kabiles are a race of European descent, related to the Berbers. After many wars with the Arabs they have betaken themselves to the fastnesses of the Djurjura. In these hills many lesser summits rise from the floors of the valleys, and the Kabiles have built their red-roofed villages on each little peak. The close-clustered hamlets look like so many fezzes capping the lower summits. In winter the villages hibernate under many feet of snow, the cattle, goats, and sheep snug in their stables, with their forage stowed in the lofts above. But in the summer the herdsmen with their flutes lead their flocks high up among the big peaks, and rarely make the long, sheer descent to their homes. They sleep in rough shelters contrived under overhanging rocks, always near a spring of water. When errands to the villages become necessary it is the women who undertake the journey, and who toil barefoot up thousands of feet of dangerous rock, to carry back to their flautist husbands their requirements. The Kabile women are of great beauty, until they break up under too much work and too frequent accouchements. It seems to me that the Kabile men have found the perfect contemplative existence, and have discovered a Shangri-La signposted ' for men only.' The whole race are scrupulously clean and honest. Possibly this is why they fought with the coastal Arabs.

The next day dawned cool and cloudy—the only cloudy day of the trip. Corporal Baxter set off in the jeep to await the Troop at Beni Mansour, and guide them to our camp.

I set off in Army boots for the high col to the east. Five miles' climb up the track was a great cleft in the ridge of Ras Timédouine, from the floor of which I could see for the first time the country to the north of the mountain. The cleft is known as the Gouffre d'Akouker. Ravens, flying high, were still thousands of feet below me. The valley on which I looked was shrunk like a relief map. Its little peaks were crowned with Kabile villages, and beyond it lay range on range of high hills melting into a fantastic jumble of broken country towards Bougie and the sea.

West of the Gouffre was the rock ridge of Ras Timédouine. I began to scramble up it, and in twenty minutes had reached the lowest part of the crest. The ridge climbed steadily to the foot of a huge dome, a thousand feet high, of solid rock, behind which lay the summit. On the right the rocks fell in an unbroken sweep to the floor of the valley which I had seen from the Gouffre. The floor was a mile away, but a day's return journey. On the left was, first, a rock wall a thousand feet high, then precipitous slopes of scree and boulders tumbling far away into a haze of depth. The strategic road clung apprehensively to the slope.

The first of the gendarmes was climbed by a chimney. It is difficult to maintain dignified balance with Army boot-studs even on a pavement, and on the rock ridge they were murderous. They proved especially trying on the rock dome. From the top of the dome a splendid pavement of rock permitted one to walk upright as if on the rooftop of an astonishingly high house, until one reached the cairn, half a mile away.

Since the French were convinced that no one had yet

reached the top of Ras Timédouine, I knew that this cairn must have been raised by supernatural agency. I looked about me for traces of the Abominable Snowman, and, sure enough, just below the summit was a great hole fifty feet across and a couple of hundred deep. Its sides were so sheer that even the nearly vertical North African sun did not touch its bottom, where lay a hard-packed bank of snow and ice.

The view was quite magnificent. Westward the Dent du Lion looked remarkably fierce, while to the east Lalla Kredidja raised its steep final pyramid.

Suddenly cloud dropped on to the Dent du Lion, and began to flow across the gap towards me. I had no wish to be caught up there alone in the mist, and in Army boots, and hastened the return. I tried a short cut down the rock wall, but my boots nearly got the better of me, and I had to finish the descent in socks.

After supper in camp some French people came out from the Refuge to talk politics, but we were early interrupted by the sound of car engines and the *putt-putt* of motor-cycles, and soon the Troop swept into camp, the eyes of the men as if standing out on stalks. None had fallen by the way on the five-hundred-mile trip, much of it over very bad roads. When the vehicles had been serviced, camp made, and food eaten the Troop drifted over to the Refuge to drink wine, seated on a little terrace which jutted like a balcony over the darkening gulf below.

The days which followed in this remote place were some of the happiest which most of us had ever spent. This was not due entirely to the contrast between our present freedom and former routine, but was because the place distilled an elixir from cool air, iced water, fragrant scents, and the beauty of great distances seen from a height. Our minds knew an Olympian detachment, so that personal anxieties shrank. Throughout our stay the men behaved like children loosed on a beach, eager, laughing, and carefree.

We worked hard, however, though none of us thought of our activity as travail. We exchanged the discipline of a military unit for that of a mountain expedition, and at the same time fostered individuality by making rendezvous—often miles from camp—to which the men were left to find their way by map. These assembly-places were arranged on our mountain scrambles at points beyond which difficulty began.

Our first rendezvous was at the Gouffre d'Akouker, where even cockney tongues were stilled before the magnificence of the view, framed for our eyes by the rock walls of the Gulf. Our dress was unmilitary—shorts and boots only. Our haversacks we wore like rucksacks, and they contained gym shoes, food, water-bottle, the short toggle-rope of the parachutist, ammunition, and a shirt. Our Sten guns were tucked under the flap.

We moved on this first day in the way taught by the commandos on my hardening course in Scotland. Troop headquarters and the three sections kept a distance of fifty yards or so between them, and within each party the men followed one another with a gap of several paces. Thus we avoided constant stopping at places of difficulty.

We had changed into gym shoes when we came to the solid rock of the long ridge of Ras Timédouine, and the Troop scrambled along at a good speed, and with obvious enjoyment. When we were on the rock dome, suspended like flies on a melon, some one shouted "Bears!" and the more intrepid adventurers climbed down the swelling bulge, weapons ready, hopeful of a hearthrug. However, the bears turned out to be baboons.

Later I learned that the French women who came up into Djurjura were very nervous of these animals, who, they claimed, were amorous, and no respecters either of maidenhood or the wedding-ring. One sometimes saw these hairy Lotharios prowling about in the woods, lower down, and I must say they had an insolent look in their eyes.

We sunbathed on the summit of Ras Timédouine, before retracing our steps to a place where it was possible to clamber off the knife-edge of the east ridge. The men were tired when we returned to camp, and next morning found some of them very stiff. We made an easy day of it, and clambered quietly up to the foot of the rock-wall to find some ice-filled caves of which we had been told. We had understood that these were quite small, and that sufficient daylight filtered inside to show the way. In fact, however, we should have gone with torches and ropes. The caves proved immense, and had been queerly carved by water and ice. They were similar in structure to the Grottes de Bétharram, in the Pyrenees, and it is interesting to recall that the Pyrenees and the Atlas mountains are of the same family.

It was freezing inside the cave. Daylight was soon lost in the depths, and we felt our way gingerly within, trying to avoid a turn into one of the many side passages. Matches in that immensity gave no light at all, and when I found my foot poised over nothing I called a halt. A flare of burning paper dropped in the pit did not reveal the bottom. We turned and crept out into the sunshine. Unfortunately, no opportunity recurred to revisit the caves with more adequate equipment.

I had in mind three more major expeditions; to Lalla Kredidja, to the Dent du Lion, and a visit to a Kabile village.

We tried Lalla Kredidja next. We traversed some tremendous precipices as we slanted upward across the west face of the mountain, and, just below the final pyramid, halted a while in a thin wood which clung to a slope which one would have thought impossibly steep for tree-roots.

A fine long ridge descended southward from the peak, and five thousand feet lower down we saw a reservoir. After a frugal lunch we made for the water. The descent was steep, rough, and trying and there were many toes blistered through stubbing up against the toe-caps of shoes. We were a hot, weary party when we reached the reservoir two hours later, and no one was in a mood to listen to the "Défendu" and "Interdit" of the French guard. Our knowledge of the language deserted us. We caught the expostulating hands and shook them amicably, then dived into fifteen feet of crystal-clear water, cold as ice. When we left we could hear the guards all shouting at once into a telephone in a hut a furlong away. I expect they will tell their grandchildren about the curious strangers who appeared from the summit of Lalla

Kredidja, and as mysteriously vanished in the direction of Ras Timédouine.

When the time came to visit the Dent du Lion we saw from our maps that a track of sorts led part-way into the mountain group, and we determined to try out our vehicles. It was a frightening experience, for the track, a mere shelf winding along the contours of steep hillsides, had crumbled away in many parts. There was no returning once started, and, had a jeep been stuck, all the vehicles would yet be there. At last, very subdued, we came to a huge grass-floored amphitheatre, its tiered walls formed by the circular rim of the peak itself, which gave us the impression of standing in the crater of a dead volcano.

It was impressive to see how confidently the Troop now swarmed up the rock. Indeed, having gone up one way, they scrambled down for a thousand feet to try another, and finally Dougal Pearson, Ian McMillan, George Field, and Sergeant Mackintosh led their parties directly up the face as if competing against each other in a guides' race.

As our fortnight drew to an end we made plans to visit a Kabile village. This was likely to be difficult, as they had purposely been built in remote and inaccessible places.

I had made the acquaintance of a benign old patriarch, whom I named the Prophet, and of his son, a sturdy man of thirty, termed John the Baptist. I had first met the old man as he tended his herds on a high plateau, and had accepted eggs and goat's-milk from him. He had a fine face, a white beard, clean finger-nails, and an air of gentle simplicity. At this first encounter the old man had shown great interest in my revolver. I was alone, and did not like to give it into his hands for examination. Furthermore, it was loaded, and I was sure that an ancient of such obvious divinity would be unused to arms, and would do some one an injury.

However, the old ruffian was quick on the uptake, and sensed my hesitation. In a flash he had reached into some inner recess of his garments and a .32 automatic had appeared in his hand with a celerity which would have confounded Billy the Kid. He showed off the weapon like a child with a new toy. There was a loaded magazine in the butt, and the old chap demonstrated safety precautions by putting on the safety-catch, aiming at John the Baptist, and pulling hard on the trigger. Then he waved his hand, and the automatic vanished whence it had come. We became great friends, and one day he agreed to let his son take my party down to the village which lay a mile from the Gouffre d'Akouker. It was a vertical mile.

We traversed a great slanting slab of rock, we passed through a cave as big as St Paul's Cathedral, and we slid for thousands of feet down extremely steep scree. The men were more subdued than at any time before, but they were fit. John the Baptist fell farther and farther behind. At last we lost sight of him, and halted. But somewhere in that maze of rocks we had lost him. We never found him again that day.

The village was like Drake's Appledore gone mad. Each house was detached and was set at a different angle to its neighbours. Narrow paths ran at all levels, sometimes over the flat red roofs of houses. There were queer deep arches like tunnels, and one place was like a medieval keep. Everywhere was spotlessly clean, and the only smell was farmyard. A pleasant Kabile took us in charge, but for all his politeness he quickly led us out of the village to a spring a mile away. At once a kind of durbar commenced. Lads brought us green figs, tomatoes, eggs, and live cockerels. We gave in return cigarettes, Army biscuits, and empty tins. The men were a little distrait, and I knew they were brooding over the extremely long and extremely steep ascent which lay between them and the camp.

We set a rendezvous at the crest, far above us, and sent the men off homeward in parties under their Non-commissioned officers. For half an hour we watched them toiling upward by a variety of routes, then the subalterns and I set off in pursuit, caught and passed them, and arrived first at the rendezvous. Now and again a little showing-off by officers is good for discipline.

On our last night the French at the Refuge arranged to light a camp-fire, and to roll out a barrel of wine. We sat about the flames until late, singing and making inflammatory martial speeches, punctuated by the loosing of Very lights. The evening only ended when McEntee, to demonstrate that the wine was done, toppled among the embers of the fire.

When we returned to Rory's Squadron, still among the olive-groves near Sousse, the men of ' A ' Troop walked apart for a while, relating wonderful tales which would have made Munchausen envious. It took the Squadron Sergeant-Major several days to persuade them that they were as other mortals.

The report of the expedition was well received by the divisional commander, and as a result Rory gained permission to winter the Squadron in the Djurjura should we still be in Africa. Accordingly, Horsey and I contrived to be ordered to journey once more back to the hills to prospect for suitable quarters. But first Rory had another little plan for all of us.

We had now come under command of the 4th Parachute Brigade, and Rory felt that, although we were glider troops, we should learn to jump out of aeroplanes as readily as our new comrades. We went, therefore, to the Brigade dropping-zone near Kairouan to undergo such synthetic training as was available. This training, due to lack of time and appliances, was fortunately not of such ferocity as that to be experienced at the Parachute Training School in England.

Instead we had a few slides holding on to a pulley which sped down a long, slanting wire, and learned to hit the ground in a compact ball when we released our hold. We learned how to collapse a dragging parachute on landing, and finally we practised jumping rapidly out of a mock fuselage. This manœuvre was my undoing. My three subalterns leapt immediately after me, and, being unnaturally keen about the whole business, gave me no time to get clear, but landed on me one after the other from a height of ten feet. I did not at once locate the damage to my person, any particular injury being submerged in a welter of bruises, but I did experience difficulty in sitting down, and found that I had to sleep on my stomach that night.

Next day we took off in a Dakota soon after dawn, climbed to fifteen hundred feet, and circled the dropping-zone, ready for the operation known as 'slow pairs.' This is an ingenious procedure for prolonging the suspense, for after each pair has hurled itself into nothingness, the one victim on the heels of the other, the aircraft makes a wide, slow circuit of the dropping-zone while the remaining occupants slide up towards the door, and the next pair stand desperately in the opening.

When my turn came I was in a state of partial hypnosis, fascinated by the spectacle I had watched of a full aircraft depopulating itself in flight. I stood in the door, Dougal Pearson behind me, and waited for the violent shout of "Go!" from the instructor. After standing for several hours, I thought it must come now, and went through the mental process of stepping out. But no command came. I relaxed, exhausted. After another infinite lapse of time, I tensed myself again, determined not to be caught unprepared, but time was going slowly that morning, and gave me an object lesson in relativity. My intensity held itself to a white-hot point for a little, then inevitably cooled, aided by a cold sweat. At this moment came a yell of "Go!" and unwittingly I was gone.

There was a lightning impression of the shadow of the tail-plane passing above me, of a buffeting from the slip-stream, and of a jerk as my parachute was tugged forth, bellied out, and developed. Then came a sickening sensation as I swung from the horizontal to the vertical at the end of twenty-two feet of rigging-lines. Thereafter all was peace, silence, and great relief. To one side of me, and a little above, was Dougal Pearson, feet and knees correctly together, hands grasping the lift-webs, his voice raised in a Gaelic pæan of praise. For a while we seemed to hang without any motion, and the dropping-zone lay below us, its features as inanimate as those of a scale model.

Presently I looked down again, and it seemed to me that the scale was now larger, for greater detail was visible, including a manikin, whose thin shouts just reached me. I thought that this must be an instructor, and cared not at all. Then, suddenly, the landscape sprang to life. It leaped up hungrily towards me, and I was powerless to ward it off. The instructor's thin shout became a bellow, and I now cared a great deal.

"Feet together! Feet together!"

Next moment I landed, rolled half over, and my parachute collapsed gracefully beside me. A thud announced the arrival of Dougal. We got to our feet in a most exalted frame of mind, and, having bent the laws of nature to our purpose, we would have recked but little of a platoon or two of the enemy.

An hour later we were airborne again, and this time jumped in half-sticks, so that on the descent I had several companions. There was a little breeze now, and I was swinging to and fro at the end of my rigging-lines. I heaved at my lift-webs with some dim-remembered instruction for damping the oscillation. Then I realized that I must turn myself to face downwind, and did so. The ground was doing its sudden spring by this time, and I hit it drifting forward, but on a backward swing. I took a fairly hard bump on my back, but thought nothing of it till I sat in the truck to return to the olive-grove, when every jolt sent the sort of feeling through me which one gets from a knocked funny-bone.

After one or two attempts to sit down in the Mess tent I went to see the Medical Officer, who had, fortunately, always been a friend of mine.

"Ha," he said, wiggling the base of my spine about, "you can wag your tail now. No more jumping till it knits together."

Next day Rory, always unorthodox, landed on his head, and thereafter suffered from double vision. To counteract this he wore a black patch over one eye, and now looked more like a pirate than a martial bishop.

A few days later Horsey and I set out again for Tikjda to discover winter quarters. I had devised a sorbo-rubber cushion for myself, shaped like an enormous doughnut, which mitigated the wort of the bumps on the long jeep journey, but I was glad indeed to step out into the cedar woods below Ras Timédouine. Horsey, who had frankly disbelieved my description of this place, and who had told me a long tale about the dislike of Carruthers for tall stories, took back his words.

In my report to the General I had, like a good soldier, kept something in reserve. This was the astonishing fact that in the mountain Refuge lived a young Hungarian dancer who claimed to be fleeing from some persecution of the gendarmerie. This secret weapon devastated the last of Horsey's defences.

When our servants had made up our beds under the trees, and we were reclining by our fire awaiting the results of their cookery, night came down with its African suddenness, as if Allah had said "Enough!" and with a gentle hand had drawn the curtain over the window of the sky.

On the heels of the dusk came the Hungarian bearing a jar of wine, and she stayed beside our fire to sing and dance to us. But her entertainment was as unremarked as if she had been the slave of a potentate, for against its background our thoughts played to and fro just as the firelight flickered against the ceiling of branches above us. For Horsey and I lay looking out into the indigo abyss on whose edge our camp was poised, and with few words we talked, as soldiers always do, of our wives, and I of the child which Tessa had told me was to come, as much a personality to me as though it had already independent life.

The drawbridges of these castles of the air bridged the gap between us and home. For me the aspirations linger; for Horsey the tale is different.

The very next day we completed the work which we were allowed a fortnight to do. Down the track towards Bwira we investigated a large building where we understood French children were entertained by Roman Catholic priests each summer. There was a religious flavour about the place, but I well knew that this would speedily be exorcized by the Squadron when it arrived in time for the winter snows.

Horsey and I had a very slight struggle with our consciences, our work done so quickly, and, purely as a matter of form, discussed the question of an immediate return to Sousse. However, common sense prevailed, and we realized that a thorough reconnaissance of the whole area would be a useful contribution to the cause.

We went up to the grassy hollow above the Gouffre d'Akouker, and there found my old friend the Prophet and John the Baptist, his son. Young Kabile children were perched on rocks above the rim of the hollow, flutes a-shrilling, wary eyes guarding stray goats, sheep, and cattle. As Horsey and I sat beside the elders a little maid of eight or nine years old brought us green figs wrapped in a huge leaf, her every action a poem of grace, her bracelets and anklets tinkling, her earrings swaying with a provocation already part realized.

I introduced Horsey to my former acquaintances, and we took up our talk of religions at the place we had broken off a month before. We were already in agreement about the Oneness of God, and speedily came to a concordat on the many roads which lead to Allah—each adapted to the personality of the pilgrims who followed it, but each leading by its different route through the bewilderment of the maze to the same ultimate peace.

On other days we climbed at leisure the spiny ridge of Ras Timédouine; the delicate spire of Lalla Kredidja; that remote canine tooth, the Dent du Lion: and the sheer wall of La Main de Juif. Our servants busied themselves about the camp and on maintenance of the jeep when we were about, and for the rest of the time haggled with Kabiles for leather wallets, straw sandals, or gastronomic delicacies.

One day Horsey and I started at dawn, threaded our way southward through the peaks of the Djurjura, and at last descended from the cool air to the hot desert breath, so hot that one cast about for shade or for the sight of water, well knowing that neither was to be had on that limitless, shimmering gridiron. Towards evening the hills of the Ulad Nail rose ahead of us, and as the sun switched out we came to Bu Sada, a starting-point for desert caravans, and a mixture of the primitive and the civilized.

We found ourselves a room in an inn, and, when we had eaten, made our way through the black and narrow canyons of the streets to the house of Messouada, the Queen of the

Ulad Nail dancers. A child of about twelve years old, laden with jewellery, led us to a plain, whitewashed room where a few desert Arabs, more magnificent than the imagination of Hollywood could compass, sat on rugs while they drank thimblefuls of coffee from tiny cups placed on the low tables.

Presently entered Messouada, a girl-friend, and the child who had let us in. We exchanged the social *convenances*, and amid the saccharine of manners the acid of money passed, and after that we and the Arabs became guests. The sordid was behind us, the Elysian ahead.

At last in came three musicians, a flautist, a drummer, and a man with a tambourine, and disposed themselves on their haunches in a corner, where they struck sundry discords for a while, until out of the discordancy grew a tuneless melody whose theme entered into us until we swayed and breathed and talked to its eccentric rhythm.

Messouada and her friend sat awhile at our feet, until a tapping of their fingers in time to the beat of the musicians spread until their whole bodies swayed. The girls rose, as graceful as two flighting birds, and posed and poised themselves with nodding heads on toe and foot until the players sped the tempo of their tune and the two dancers whirled and twirled about the room, anonymous in clouds of flying drapery.

Impossibly the beat of the drum came quicker, and first Messouada then the other threw off their many garments, piece by piece, in time with the swelling music. As they did so the musicians swung about, backs to the room, and, as became good followers of the Prophet, stared into their corner.

There is some alchemy of the East which inhibits Western prurience, and to us the two whirling white bodies were as sexless as a pair of lovely ornaments. The dances of the Orient have about them, too, a power of hypnosis got through rhythm and infinite, patient repetition, so that when our hostesses broke into the gross and ugly stomach dance, cramping their muscles grotesquely, aversion grew to acceptance, and at last to soothing pleasure.

It was pale dawn when we and the Arabs said good-bye, exhausted, not so much by wakefulness, and not at all by emotion, as by the rhythm of sound and movement which had penetrated within us and made impact as a high note can shatter a wine-glass.

We returned next day to the cool, clear air of Tikjda, and scrambled more among the surrounding hills. When at last we came to leave for Sousse Horsey and I felt a reluctance which was almost prescience, and, to drain the dregs of this time which remained to us, we took the coast road eastward, through Bougie, Jijelli, Philippeville, Bône, and Tabarka. The sea was at our left hand to cool us in the heat, and our way ran through low hills, sometimes along *corniche* roads, and sometimes through forests of cork oak.

When at last we reached the Squadron all was bustle in the lines.

"Hell!" said Horsey. "It looks like an exercise starting."

We hurried over to report to Rory, who was in his office tent, and to tell him that we had found perfect winter quarters for the unit.

"You're just in time, you two," he said, when he caught sight of us. "We're invading Italy in thirty-six hours."

CHAPTER VIII

RORY INVADES ITALY

THE plan was this. A major Allied landing was to be made on the west coast of Italy. Simultaneously, as a diversion and as a foothold for future operations, the 1st Airborne Division was to secure Taranto on the east, and to push up the east coast. No aircraft were available for us, and a scratch naval force was concentrating at Bizerta to ferry us across the sea. This consisted of a British minelayer and five cruisers, the battleships *Howe* and *King George V*, a destroyer flotilla, and an American cruiser. There is within the functional bulk of a warship little space to spare, and the Airborne troops were to tuck themselves out of the way about the decks during the twenty-four-hour crossing. Obviously, little transport could be embarked, but the minelayer, the *Abdiel*, was expected to take jeeps and some anti-tank guns in her cavernous interior.

The Squadron was to be under the command of the 4th Parachute Brigade, and was with that formation to force a way northward from Taranto, while the 2nd Parachute Brigade consolidated a hold upon the port itself. These troops were all that could be embarked on the first lift, and it was hoped that the remainder of the Division would follow within a few days.

It seemed to us that the Airborne participation in the invasion of Italy was an afterthought to the main plan. We wondered how a force of warships unequipped for an assault landing hoped to put us ashore in a major port, and, once ashore, how our two brigades expected to take and hold Taranto, let alone push north—even with the help of Rory and his Squadron.

When I heard Rory's news I hurried to 'A' Troop lines, where Dougal Pearson was in charge, ably seconded by Sergeant Mackintosh, whose masterful nose was jutting with aggression. The men were stowing in the vehicles all the impedimenta of war, each item in the place we now all knew so well, ready to be found in light or in darkness.

There was no more to be done. We were all of us so used to immediate mobility that so far this was for us a routine. After the familiarity of preparation we had constantly to remind ourselves that when next we reached for a weapon it would be not in play but in earnest, and that all that had gone before was but a rehearsal for the curtain shortly to rise on our first performance.

I had noticed the absence of the fine, upright Bombardier Guardsman, Sergeant Longman, who had for a short time been my servant, and was upset to hear that he had been removed to hospital with some obscure tropical ailment.

There was something irregular about the enterprise on which we were to embark. It seemed to us that it was not a set-piece plan, doomed to mud and tragedy, but that the intense individuality of our little unit would find scope to express itself. We felt, therefore, that pre-battle exhilaration which is different from any excitement in life.

We spent a busy evening between the Mess tent and our own particular jobs, for, though all was ready, we feared vital omissions in our preparations, and had frequently to put down our half-finished drinks while we rushed out to check what had been done.

Horsey brought Carruthers in to dinner. We were assured that he was dressed in a dinner jacket, a rule which he never broke. Carruthers was given an empty chair next to Horsey, who talked to him so factually that as the evening wore on, and our duty of finishing the drink stocks neared completion, he took concrete shape to some of us. Throughout Carruthers was rather a prig, and we were glad when the sun set upon him.

We were to move to a port the following evening. Early in the afternoon Rory sent for me. In the tent Jack Johnson of 'C' Troop was already waiting.

With his black patch, Rory had about him the air of Nelson off Copenhagen, and as it turned out the parallel was close.

"There is a little difficulty about our vehicles," said Rory. "The hatches of the *Abdiel* are too narrow to take jeeps, and we are only to take a small proportion of our transport on the Divisional convoy which moves to Bizerta to-night. It is most uncertain how much can be embarked. I want you two to move off independently with your troops before the convoy forms up. You will dispose yourselves in an out-of-the-way place on the outskirts of Bizerta, and await my further orders."

Jack and I, knowing Rory, at once realized that we were being made party to a private adaptation of the Squadron's instructions, and that Rory was determined to ship as many of his vehicles as he could contrive.

A little before dusk we mustered our two Troops, and, in the conspicuous absence of Rory, said good-bye to Horsey, and drove through the trees on to the main road, already busy with dispatch riders and Staff jeeps. We did our best to look on proper business bent, and moved purposefully through the Divisional area at a pace which would cause no remark; then at last on the open road we sped north for Enfidaville, Tunis, and Bizerta.

Dawn had not yet come when we reached the fringes of the port. We pulled off the road and slid into a dip in the ground, put our lights out, and dismounted to brew tea. When we had drunk Jack and I set a guard, told the rest to snatch some sleep, and ourselves lurked by the roadside.

Presently, far off, the lights of the convoy showed in chain across the plain. As they neared us group after group swung off to right or to left, and the lights flicked out. We had not long to wait for Rory. Quite soon he dashed up in his jeep. I gathered that he had now got some official connivance, for he said, "Down to the quay, and see if you can find any space for your vehicles."

Jack and I doubled down into our hollow. We told our Troops to be ready for an immediate move, and ourselves leapt into my jeep with the celerity which the situation demanded if the Italian campaign were to achieve the success which we felt that only our assistance could bring. I pressed the starter, and nothing whatsoever happened. I leapt out again, baulked of my Rolandesque urgency, and probed in the machine's vitals without success. I dug out the starting-handle, swung the engine, heart in mouth, and Old Faithful sprang to life. Without further inquest we fumbled our way through the unknown streets until we came to the water-front, now lighting up with the sudden sun as the auditorium of a theatre leaps progressively out of the darkness.

Against a bollard leant an American sailor, a rating, who wore a little, funny, round white hat such as the mill-girls buy at Blackpool during Wakes Week.

"What's your ship?" we asked.

"U.S. Cruiser *Boise*," answered the sailor, shifting his gum in a democratic manner.

"Where for?" we asked.

"Taranto," said he.

"What chance of embarking a few vehicles and some troops?"

"How come?" he inquired.

We explained, patiently, "We are trying to find space for some jeeps, trailers, motor-cycles, and troops. Is there room on the *Boise*?"

"Guess so!" said he, relieving the bollard of his weight while he whistled over the dirty waters of the harbour. Many small vessels were bobbing off-shore in the choppy sea, and one of these, a Landing Craft, Motor, swung towards us. Our acquaintance made an arrangement in an unenthusiastic way, the LCM manœuvred to tie up, and Jack and I tore off back to our Troops.

We returned to the quay simultaneously with Rory, who had with him Squadron Headquarters. We learned that the other two Troops were waiting farther along the water-front, and hoped to be embarked with official approval. But Rory had rather a hunted look, and, after a hurried parley with the skipper of the LCM, he told us that the aircraft hangar of the *Boise* was, fortunately, empty, but that it would not contain all our transport. Jack and I, therefore, left behind all our motor-cycles save four, and told our Troop Sergeants to take charge of these and their riders, and to follow on with the second lift of the Division. Then Rory, with his Headquarters, and Jack and I, with apiece three subalterns, eighteen Other Ranks, five jeeps and trailers, and four motor-cycles, drove on to the LCM, and were ferried out to the *Boise*. As we cast off Rory gave a sigh of relief, and cast a last look up the quay, as must the fleeing chief of Ulva's Isle have searched the heather for pursuit.

As soon as I could I found a way to the hangar. I collected an American artificer, and together we removed the starter-motor of the Jeep. With foreboding we withdrew the armature, and saw that the winding was burnt out. Sadly I replaced the dead component, reflecting that it was indeed ill-luck to experience my first mechanical trouble at this moment.

Towards tea-time we got under way, and confusion was confounded by order as meals were arranged, and as the men, with British versatility, made the most of any shelter on the deck, and prepared beds on the iron plates, comforted by groundsheets and greatcoats. Almost at once the ship's loud-speaker system came to life. It said, importantly, "Crackle! Crackle!" then added, "The Italian Government has to-day signed an Armistice with the Allies. The Italians will in future be regarded as co-belligerents. Screech!"

Immediately Rory called his Order Group. The orders were simple, if elastic. We were told that the attitude of the Italian forces to the Armistice was unknown, and that we might expect from them every gradation of conduct from co-operation through indifference to armed hostility; that the German strength in the area was not great, but consisted of a Parachute formation who were hard fighters; that the German reaction might be sharp; and that we could expect that some of the reinforcements which they would undoubtedly hurry to contain the Salerno landing might well be diverted against our own skeleton attacking force.

The Squadron rôle was simple. There were, broadly speaking, three roads leading north from Taranto. The right-hand, or eastern, route bore across the heel of Italy, through the little round houses of Apulia. The centre road ran through Masafra and Mottola to Gioja del Colle. The left-hand, western road circled round through Matera and Altamura. Jack was to go right, I was to take the centre, and a squadron of the Special Air Service in jeeps the left. We were to keep in touch with each other by wireless, and with Squadron Headquarters. Our object was to discover Italian reaction, to brush aside Italian or German resistance within our scope, to converge if the opposition allowed on Gioja, whose airfield was needed to fly air support to Salerno. The 4th Parachute Brigade would follow us up as best they could but would have no transport.

In the controlled turmoil of a ship sailing on an operation there is little quiet. The Americans played the host—though the ship was dry of liquor—in a fashion which kept us in a glow of camaraderie, and they had, too, the hard look of fighting-men not always to be seen on the faces of Servicemen. But, though they offered us bunks, it was a wakeful night. The officers studied maps, and went over the plan again and again, for we were as yet tiros in the martial art despite the long years of training. The Other Ranks huddled together on the decks for warmth, until most of us went to sit with them through the night.

In the early afternoon of the next day came a smudge of smoke on the horizon to starboard. *Howe* and *King George V* moved protectively between the smoke and us, and presently word passed that we had witnessed the Italian fleet steaming to surrender. On the port side land appeared, and soon we picked out villages and houses as we steamed at speed under the sole of Italy.

In the late afternoon we came to the fringe of the minefield which covered the approaches to Taranto. The small fleet lay off while a destroyer edged through, to return after a while with an Italian pilot. At this the *Boise* and H.M.S. *Penelope* made straight into the harbour. For an invasion the scene was badly set, for we swung in broadside with the last of the daylight, *Penelope* next to us, against a quay deserted save for a few loungers who obligingly caught our mooring-lines.

A handful of Special Air Service men swarmed ashore to set up posts at the inland fringe of the port. The rest of us disembarked by ladder and waited, a little apprehensive of air attack, as our vehicles were unloaded. The remainder of the fleet were anchored some way out, preparing to discharge by lighter.

As we awaited the last of our vehicles I told Corporal Gentleman Jim Baxter to net his wireless in to Squadron, and his Number Two to net the forward-link set to our three sections. Presently he returned to say that the rear-link was not co-operative. Before I could suggest that he thump the set on the side—a sovereign remedy for sulkiness—the young commander of the 4th Parachute Brigade came up to hand over to me an SAS officer who spoke Italian. He said that an interpreter might be useful.

It was near midnight before we moved off the quay. Jack Johnson, of 'C' Troop, and I shouted a "Good-bye!" to each other, and after that the Troop moved slowly without lights through the bombed streets of the town. In a little while we were sharply challenged by the SAS post on our route. I had delayed my order group, hoping for some crumbs of information, but, since there were none, I told Dougal to lead with Number One Section, Troop Headquarters next, then Two and Three Sections. All motor-cycles were to travel in the rear in the interests of silence. I remembered the tremendous fire-power of our few men, and as a last injunction reminded the subalterns to open up with all they had if we struck opposition. The SAS dragged their improvised barrier to one side, and a moment later we were on our own.

The night was moonless, but bright starlight allowed us a glimmer of perception across the countryside, although our road was left darker than the Pit under its shadowing trees. Dougal's two jeeps crept ahead, and I drove mine myself, striving to keep a distance and at the same time to hold them in view. The scattered houses had thinned out, and we were in the open countryside, when Dougal's section halted. I heard the rest of the Troop behind me quietly dismount and lie down with a clink of weapons.

This is it! I thought. We are ambushed alone in the night.

I crept forward to listen to the excited whispers ahead, and as I strained eyes and ears heard the words "It's no whusky, you cluck! It's brandy!"

From the relapse into his mother dialect I understood that Dougal was labouring under intense emotion. As I reached him, he seized my arm and thumped a great stack of wooden cases piled in an angle of a fork-road.

"It's all brandy," he said, in cracked undertones, as might a pilgrim who had descried the Holy Grail. "Every bloody case of it. Shall I no' mount a guard?"

I reminded Dougal of our primary duty to prosecute war, but suggested that he should put a case or two on his trailer against medicinal need. The Troop moved slowly on. Quite soon the quiet was shattered by a single shot whose reverberation played against our tautened, inexperienced nerves, and would, we felt, advertise to all Italy our presence on the Massafra road. There were more whisperings ahead.

"It came from that house," said Dougal, when I went up to him.

Across the road was a high garden wall, broken by an arch in which was set an iron gate. Some one was muttering through the grill. I hissed for the SAS man, and told him to mutter back.

Presently he explained "The old man thought you were Germans!"

"Tell him he's a bloody liar," I said, "and if he doesn't go back to bed we'll come back and burn his house down with him inside."

"Shall I no' lob a grenade over to teach him his manners?" asked Dougal, in the stern tones of a young man brought up under Scottish discipline.

I dissuaded him, and at the same time told Ian McMillan to leap-frog to the lead, and Dougal to tack on at the rear of the Troop. It seemed unfair to let Dougal have all the fun.

Before we moved, however, there came from behind us a tremendous explosion, whose displacement whipped past our ears like a clap of wind. A flash played across the sky above

Taranto. We stood a little, wondering. But war is a narrow business, and we quickly saw that this was no concern of ours.

Ian set off at a great pace, but within half a mile stopped so suddenly that I nearly ran into him.

"There's something across the road," he said, when I had joined him. Together we wormed nearer. Sure enough, the obstacle was a mighty road-block of vast concrete cubes painted white with black stripes, and a twisting gap between them. We heard movement from their shadows.

I wondered if the block were held by Germans or Italians. The simplest way to find out was to ask, so I sent again for our interpreter. He lay down beside us, and called into the night. An instant chatter replied, its volubility disclosing identity.

"They're Italians," he answered, unnecessarily, "and they say they're friendly."

We called up some troopers to cover us, and walked up to the block, where we were warmly welcomed by a *capitano* in a Gilbertian uniform. We declined the proffered embrace, and, while our SAS friend interrogated him, called some troopers up to take away such weapons as we felt we could use, and to remove vital bits from the rest. It seemed unwise to allow these volatile individuals to sit armed behind a minor fortification.

The interpreter had by now finished his catechism, and informed me that there was a similar road-block a mile ahead, and that its defenders were friends of the Capitano's, and were also, and always had been, pro-British.

Ian led us speedily to the next block. As its whiteness gleamed suddenly ahead of him, the dark was lit by the flash of small-arms fire, and a storm of ill-directed tracer bullets zipped about us. The next moment I was startled by a similar phenomenon travelling in the opposite direction. It took me a moment to realize that the twenty-two trigger-happy stalwarts of 'A' Troop were justifying their destiny.

Presently both parties became bored, and during the lull the SAS linguist began to shout epithets into the night. Some sort of mutual understanding was reached, and we walked up to the source of the pyrotechnics. There were fully a hundred

Italians armed to the teeth, which flashed from all sides in conciliatory grins. We were most of us angry at the ill-mannered display, and Ian's nine men disarmed the boors somewhat roughly. I bethought me of the Capitano a mile behind us, and, telling the troop to wait, drove back.

The Capitano was standing on a concrete block giving a 'Sister Anne! Sister Anne!' commentary to his subordinates. My servant Jones helped him to reach the ground, and we put him in the back of my jeep. On our return to the Troop I had the interpreter explain that, as a co-belligerent, we would welcome the Capitano's local knowledge, and that, the better to see, he should sit on the bonnet. Thus equipped with our human Asdic, we moved on.

After a couple of miles the Capitano showed marked unrest, and I had just time to close up with Ian to tell him to go carefully when the road ahead was lit by a blaze of tracer and Very lights, and the staccato of light automatic weapons was punctuated by the thump of grenades.

'A' Troop followed its now well-tried routine of spilling out into the ditch. A moment later three or four vehicles came tearing towards us under full headlights. They slowed as our jeeps became visible, and we swarmed about them, to find that they were the SAS patrol from the westerly road, and that they had doubled back on our own central route. Their commander was Roy Farran, who had already a great reputation as a guerrilla.

"There's an ambush half a mile ahead," he said. "We shot our way through. We're going back now to report. We've got three German prisoners to turn in for interrogation."

All this sounded very comfortable, but our orders were to go on. I supposed that it was our duty to move into the aroused ambush. As I pondered one of the three prisoners decided to leave, and we all felt a little better after we had emptied our magazines. Farran said "Good-bye," and we were left alone with our problem.

Firstly, I told Gentleman Jim to get through to Rory on the wireless-set with which my jeep had been burdened for twelve months in readiness for this moment. The thing made a buzzing noise, and Corporal Baxter told me in pained accents that transmission was bad. I wrote a brief message on a signal pad telling Rory what to expect on the road, and stating, with a terseness which I hoped would tug at his heart-strings, that 'A' Troop was about to try conclusions with an ambush. This precious document I entrusted to a pair of our motor-cyclists whose capabilities seemed more reliable than the invention of the co-belligerent Marconi.

I did not at all know the form about real ambushes, but was fairly sure that it would not be playing the game to enter one in jeeps. Accordingly, I ordered Ian to remove himself and his section a little way from the defenders of the road-block, and to take in his charge all vehicles and drivers. The rest of us put on gym-shoes, changed our steel helmets for berets, and moved off in two parties through the fields on either side of the road. We had not gone far when a revolver duel developed over the way. I went over to see what was happening, and learned that our SAS friend, an individualist, had gone prowling on his own, and that he and George Field had demonstrated on each other the uncertainty of night marksmanship.

We soon reached the area of Roy Farran's ordeal by fire, but those who had been lurking were gone now that the trap was sprung. We deduced that they would make a similar play farther on, and pushed ahead more rapidly. In a few minutes we were much surprised to see a flicker of light on the road towards Taranto. Speedily it approached, growing in intensity until we saw several pairs of headlights bearing down upon us. We waved the convoy to a stop, and found that it was formed of half a dozen petrol tankers. On their tail was Ian with all our jeeps.

A rotund Italian in colonel's uniform descended from the passenger side of the cab of the leading truck and explained in head-waiter's English that he was removing petrol to Bari for safe-keeping from the Germans. Since the Germans were then occupying Bari, and were, indeed, probably only a few hundred yards up the road, we did not feel that we could accept the Colonel's reason. Consequently, we removed the weapons of the party, and left the convoy in the care of Ian.

The dark was wearing thin, and a glimmer of day showed to the east. Most of us were having the third sleepless night since Sousse, and felt that to be shot at while resting in a jeep was preferable to being ambushed on foot, so into our vehicles we climbed, and drove quietly off.

The dawn came quickly, and upon a hill ahead we saw in medieval situation our first goal, Massafra. We had little time to view it, for down the straight, tree-lined road came a burst of tracer. There was a deadly accuracy about it which foretold Germans. We swung our jeeps among the row of trees, which gave shelter in enfilade, and in no time at all Troop Headquarters were lying with George's section on the one side of the road, and Dougal's section were huddled against a dry-stone wall on the other.

"Kick the bloody wall down!" I yelled to Dougal. Incredibly, he did it, lying on his back, and he and his section vanished through the gap towards Massafra. The rest of us opened up a pulverizing fire, and I, realizing the inadequacy of a revolver at six hundred yards range, seized a Bren and sent the contents of a mazagine towards the point of origin of the tracer. I learned for the first time the comfort of hitting back, and since that moment have been convinced that morale is squandered unless the soldier has the tools for the job.

At times the tracer whipped so close that it clipped the stubble in which we lay, but, as it played to and fro as a garden hose waters vegetables, the troopers who were momentarily free of it replied with satisfying ferocity. Then, from a point down the road, Dougal's stalwarts opened up from a flank. The rest of us leapt for the jeeps, and did a kind of cavalry charge under cover of Dougal. Two minutes later we were in Massafra.

A swarm of olive gentlemen, some accompanied by ladies, burst upon us. Our SAS comrade translated that the Germans, —several of them inanimate—had withdrawn in trucks, and that the commander of the liberating forces was invited to join the Mayor in the square.

Corporal Baxter chipped in to say that Squadron was coming through on the disturbed ether. I put on earphones, tried to remember my RT procedure, and told Rory that Massafra was clear, and that Ian McMillan was sitting beside a lot of petrol. The machine then spat at me and went to sleep. Relieved, I drove into the square. A rather gross individual proffered a bunch of keys, which I returned. The ceremony over, wine and grapes were thrust upon us, and after some minutes I judged it wise to remove the young men from these and other adult temptations.

We laagered on the far side of the town. McEntee disappeared while the rest of us shaved, to return with his beret full of eggs. With these and the brandy, we were enjoying breakfast when the roar of a Continental bus-engine made us leap to our feet. Preceded by Rory in his jeep, a small party of 156 Parachute Battalion, accompanied by the battalion commander, drew up in a commandeered charabanc.

"Don't sit there!" said Rory. "Push on to Mottola. The rest of the Brigade is following up, and I've brought Ian along with the other section."

With hard-boiled eggs in the one hand and mugs of brandy in the other, we slid into our vehicles. My tail, damaged in Africa, was becoming pained by constant travel, and, indeed, most of us were tired and bad-tempered as we drove off, Dougal leading.

The nature of the country quickly changed, and after two or three miles we saw the road twisting uphill ahead of us through a broken, rocky landscape. We reached the winding stretch, and came to a place where the road swung in a wide left-hand bend. From the outer curve the ground rose sharply in a crescent-shaped ridge, while on the inside of the curve there rose, like a hub, a little conical knoll. Across the diameter of the bend we saw Mottola, sitting astride a pointed hill, its sprawling feet contained by a rampart part-way up the slope.

As we looked a gust of bullets swept through us; some flicked Dougal's clothing, others riddled the haversacks which were strapped on his jeep's bonnet. The weary Troop stopped sharply and leapt for the ditches. As I lay in shelter I thought of my poor jeep, exposed on the brow of a little rise, without whose willing wheels Corporal Baxter and I would be as unhappy as unhorsed cowboys.

I saw ahead a little hollow, just off the road, which promised shelter, and jumped for the driving-seat. Even as my foot pressed the starter-button my tired memory prompted me. I remembered the inquest in the hangar of the *Boise*, and the view of the burnt-out armature. Another part of my brain told me that I should in a second or two become a target, and that I should be hard put to it to regain my ditch, let alone fiddle about with a starting-handle.

Meanwhile my foot, unchecked, pressed the button. The motor worked. The engine started. The jeep and I fled to safety in the hollow.

The starter-motor did not work again in the days which followed, and had to be replaced when spares came up. I can only attribute this private miracle to the generation by fear of excess electricity in my foot.

I crawled to the rim of my saucer, and saw that part of the fire came from pill-boxes set on the ridge beyond the curve, and part from the knoll inside the bend. We were therefore caught in a cross-fire directed from above us. As this unpleasant fact became apparent there came a crash from the rampart of Mottola, and almost simultaneous explosions told that the road behind us was under shell-fire at point-blank range.

Most of the small-arms fire was directed on the Troop to my rear, and I was able to get forward a little without molestation, my Bren with me. With the visual help of my own tracer, I sprayed each pill-box in turn. There was a marked diminution in the volume of German fire.

It seemed to me that if we could take the knoll we could turn the tables on the men along the ridge, and, by remaining below the tip of the little hill, could also obtain shelter from the shell-fire. But when I looked about me the neat pattern of the Troop, so often practised in training, was sadly disrupted. Few men were visible, being busy at a polished display of field-craft and camouflage, and such as I could see were of mixed sections. From the volume of fire which came from the mostly unseen positions I knew that they were enjoying themselves.

At last my shouts brought response from Dougal and Ian. We held a strained conversation against the din, lost our tempers with each other, made friends again, and decided to take the little round hill by a left-flanking movement. The attack went like a set-piece demonstration at the Battle School. Dougal and Ian left their Bren gunners behind to fire on the hill-top; then, collecting what men were ready to hand, they moved rapidly up a ridge which melted into their objective. On the way they picked up George Field and his section. I crawled forward a little to keep the pill-boxes occupied.

Out of the corner of my eye I saw smoke drifting across the German positions on the hillock, and guessed that the subalterns, determined to do the thing in style, were putting down a screen with their two-inch mortar smoke bombs. Very soon there came the chatter of Sten guns on the knoll, and a moment later I saw red berets moving freely. The pill-boxes were still firing when a quiet voice behind me asked "What's going on?"

"How the hell should I know?" I replied, without turning.

"Well, it's your battle," the voice reminded me, and I looked round, to see the Brigadier kneeling behind a scrub-bush. A couple of minutes later Rory came up, and, as if they knew, the pill-boxes fell silent.

The Brigadier gave us our orders. We were to consolidate on top of the hillock and stay there until the 156 Parachute Battalion came up by various means to clear the pill-box ridge. Rory went off to collect our transport into a hollow below the knoll, and I trudged up to the victors on its crown.

George Field was lying down, overcome by an excess of excitement and exertion under a hot sun.

We disposed ourselves to receive the counter-attack which we thought inevitable, and, almost at once, came—as we thought—the usual German mortar prelude. The first bomb fell beside me, and, activated by nervous reaction and fright, I leapt in the air and landed on my suffering tail with a howl of pain which led Ian to rush to my succour with a Field Dressing.

We located the point of origin of the bombs, and sent some bursts of Bren fire towards it. On this a cautious head was thrust up, capped with a red beret. Through my field-glasses I recognised the healthy complexion of Horsey. We persuaded him that the hillock had undergone a change of occupation, and presently he joined us to receive congratulations on the only really accurate direction of two-inch mortar fire which we had ever seen.

The shelling switched to our transport in the hollow where Rory had partly concealed it. Almost at once a jeep trailer was hit, and gave a fine display as its explosive contents began to go off. To my horror, I recognized the trailer as mine, and I realized that the considerable amount of pipe-tobacco which I had accumulated was lost.

We became worried about our ammunition reserves, but Rory said that there was a truck-load back along the road. However, no one was very keen to drive it up under the noses of the Mottola artillerymen, until a little cockney of Squadron Headquarters announced that he would have a dab at it. He brought the vehicle like a racing-car up the exposed road and bumped it cross-country to the comparative shelter in the hollow.

"Well done!" said Rory. "We need that ammunition."

"Strewth!" exclaimed the cockney. "I didn't ought to've done it. I thought the old bus was full of blankets."

Some days later, he stoutly maintained that his Military Medal was won under false pretences.

The day wore on. The multiplicity of weapons possessed by the Troop no doubt gave a false picture of our strength, and may have deterred the mounting of a counter-attack. At any rate, none came, and I noticed several of the men nodding to sleep in their positions. It was mid-afternoon when we heard the slow stammer of Brens and Stens from the pill-box ridge, and we realized that 156 Parachute Battalion was at work. They did the job quickly. At once Rory prodded us all to our feet.

"On to Mottola!" he cried, as that other one-eyed veteran,

Marshal Ney, might have shouted, "First into the breach, *mes braves!*"

First into Mottola we were, and uncertain of our welcome. But again the Germans had pulled out, and we were subjected to a versatile Latin demonstration, which included an obese gentleman with a bunch of keys, dark-eyed beauties with bunches of grapes, and their mothers with bottles of wine. 'A' Troop had woken up enough to enjoy this hospitality, and seemed set to continue into the night, but Rory, that flail of God, was impatient again to hurl the Squadron against the powers of darkness. He broke in upon our celebrations, and, while acknowledging that we must all by now be somewhat tired, gave us a last task. Three miles along on the Gioja road was the village of San Basilio. The Brigadier wished to know if the Germans were prepared to make a stand there. Rory added to 'A' Troop two jeep-loads of Francis Winterbottom's Troop, who had come up from Taranto.

'A' Troop were by now fairly seasoned warriors, for a few hours' skirmishing with intent to kill transforms the abstraction of training into the practice of war. But, as the men were tired, unwisely I put Francis's men in the lead, followed by Troop Headquarters, then One, Two, and Three sections.

We were assembled on the outskirts of Mottola, in readiness to move off, when up the open unknown road ahead of us a vehicle approached fast. We stared a moment, puzzled, then with one accord concealed ourselves. The vehicle sensed trouble, hesitated, and came to an uncertain stop inside our ambush. We saw that it was a Mercédès with a Spandau on a swivel mounting next the driver, and two wide bench seats facing each other in the rear. There were half a dozen young Germans in it.

'A' Troop made its presence known. A fine blond officer moved a hand to the Spandau, and the air became very tense as the trigger-fingers of our troopers quivered. The blond German relaxed, and a moment later we had bundled all of them out. The officer had a neat .32 automatic belted round him, and I achieved an ambition by disarming him and strapping the weapon about my own waist. Amid the plaudits of the heterogeneous Airborne units behind us Ian's section marched the captives back to Rory, the troopers almost goose-stepping with pride as they made their offering of real live Germans.

We started down the road to San Basilio. We veterans watched aghast as Francis's novices advanced boldly down the centre of the tarmac at a round twenty-five miles an hour. I was trying to make up my mind whether to accelerate to warn them to use more cautious tactics when the job was done for me by an armoured car which poked its snout from out the houses of the village to loose off a stream of cannon-fire at the first jeep. The jeep shuddered to a stop, and jerked like a wounded animal as shot after shot struck into it. The crew leapt out, but two of them were caught by the machine-gun fire which was now streaming about us, and they died on their feet, held upright by their vehicle.

The rest of us were in an exposed place, and for a little it was not easy to raise a head. True to our tactics, the Troop was not, however, caught all on one side of the road, and I called to Dougal across the way to repeat his flanking efforts, since there was a little cover on his side. McEntee crawled forward with a Piat in order to deal with any advance from the armoured car or cars, and one by one, as they took stock of the situation, the rest of the Troop came to life. From some mid-way spot in the no-man's-land, a Fiat saloon car started up and sped towards us. The Spandaus riddled the body-work, and it stopped on the road verge. I heard a jeep behind me, and our SAS attaché slid to a standstill.

"Can I get our chaps back from the shot-up jeep?" he cried, "And pick up those Wops in the Fiat?"

He was gone before I could stop him. We could do little but forget concealment, and step up the rate of our fire to give him cover. He would have died but for Dougal, who had got forward to a position where he could pour a heavy flanking fire into the Germans. We later learned that he had put one full Bren magazine into a lorry-load of infantry, killing and wounding twenty-eight of the passengers, and that two lorries behind were roughly treated. If the Germans had proposed a counter-attack, they were dissuaded.

The SAS man came back to us with the two survivors of the lost jeep, and two Italian civilians from the Fiat. One of the Italians was wearing an open-necked white silk shirt, and across its front was written a straight line in bullet holes, each clean and round and but faintly edged with red. He was alive, smiled at us, and said, as we tried to give him some comfort, "Gently! Gently!"

We knew now that San Basilio was held. We bought the information about the little village with two lives, and the price, in war, was cheap. But there are many hamlets, villages, and towns in an embattled country, and so often the purse of manhood is drained before each has taken its fee. And spurious coinage is of no use in war, so that the coffers of strong breeding are drained.

Back in Mottola, Rory took me to the Brigadier, and I described to him the lie of the country towards San Basilio.

"You will reconnoitre again at first light," said the Brigadier, "and 156 Parachute Battalion will follow up."

We laagered in some fields outside the town. The men checked their vehicles, moving like sleep-walkers, and, as their tasks were done, fell asleep on the ground. Squadron Headquarters were mounting guard, and 'A' Troop had no responsibility until we woke two hours before dawn.

Nodding over a mug of brandy, I asked Rory, "What news from Jack Johnson and 'C' Troop?"

"There has been no news since he left Taranto," answered Rory. "It looks a little bad."

Before I fell asleep, I remembered something else.

"I heard a tremendous explosion last night."

"That was the *Abdiel* blowing up. No one quite knows what happened yet. A great many of the 6th Parachute Battalion were lost, also all the anti-tank guns, and the reserve ammunition."

The crest of the wave on which I had ridden for twenty-four hours was crumbling now. I had tasted the exhilaration of war, but after the stimulant came depression, and although there had been no sleep for three days and nights, the rest on this fourth was only fitful.

CHAPTER IX

CARRUTHERS MAKES A RESCUE

It was a stiff, cold, ill-fed, and miserable Troop which grumbled about its weapons and vehicles next morning. The night had been punctuated by bangs and alarums, and few of the twenty-two had slept soundly. Horsey joined Rory to see us off for San Basilio as grey streaked the east.

"Carruthers was always an early riser," he reminded me. "He used to say that a man's faculties were at their sharpest before dawn. He could never stomach a lie-abed."

I told Horsey how best to treat Carruthers, my sense of humour still asleep, and we drove off through the wakened, silent groups of 156 Parachute Battalion.

We branched off cross-country to the left, the light-weight motor-cycles following the jeeps quite willingly. We investigated a farm or two, where all were still asleep, and where the continued quiet calmed our nerves. At last we struck a track which ran in from the west, and, covering each other dismounted with weapons, entered the village to learn of Dougal's marksmanship the night before, and that the Germans had faded into the countryside.

I hurried back in my jeep by the main road to Mottola to apprise Rory of the position. Some way along the straight stretch of road was the stricken jeep of the previous evening's encounter, two of its crew leaning against it as if idly waiting, streaked with dried blood which matched the red of their berets.

'A' Troop breakfasted in San Basilio, and when an advance guard of 156 Parachute Battalion moved up with the rest of

Rory's Squadron we were given our orders to branch off up a by-road to investigate a long ridge of high ground which overlooked the way to Gioja. At a little distance from San Basilio the by-road ran through a cutting, the surface rising over a little hill. Beyond, the road ran down to the foot of the ridge five hundred yards away.

Our three sections had taken turn and turn about at leading, but by chance it was for Dougal to advance down the bare road through the cutting. I had a premonition of trouble, and disposed the rest of the Troop on foot to cover his movements. He had gone perhaps two hundred yards when a sudden screech of Spandau fire startled us, and we saw the white lines of tracer ending abruptly in Dougal's two jeeps. In a moment or two clouds of smoke rose from both vehicles, and, little by little, but with growing intensity, their spare ammunition began to splutter and explode. Dougal evidently had some No. 77 grenades to hand, for under a cloud of white vapour he hustled his men to cover in a ditch.

The rest of us sprayed the ridge with catholic bursts of fire, but the target was too big for us, and presently we concentrated all weapons on a white farm-house near the crest. This switch of aim had a marked effect, and we took it that the Germans were lying about the house and buildings. The German fire turned to the rest of us, and Dougal had a respite while the duel went on. But his position was obviously an impossible one. He and his men were lying in a shallow, wet ditch, with no cover in view, and their continued existence could only be a matter of time.

Rory came up with Dave Younger, of 'B' Troop, fresh from Taranto, who was towing behind his jeeps two archaic pieces of ordnance, looted, one would guess, from a museum. He said that the Brigadier was delighted at these acquisitions, which he felt lent tone to the campaign.

We deployed our artillery in a dip behind the cutting. Rory went to superintend the laying of the pieces, and I poked my head out of the cutting to direct the fire. There was a good deal of informal chit-chat before the rusty breeches were closed upon the ancient charges. Some intrepid man let the first piece off, and the shell sailed gently overhead to land a little to one side of Dougal.

"Up a thousand!" I yelled.

The next shot, assisted, no doubt, by an overdose of elevation due to the layer miscalculating the metric sight-graduations, sailed over the top of the farm on the ridge and was never again seen. "Down five hundred!" I called, feeling that a mean average might be more successful.

To every one's surprise, the next shell scored a direct hit on the white wall of the farm.

At this Ian came up.

"Can I take a jeep and try to get Dougal's section back?" he asked.

The same thing had been in my mind, and I felt that this was my day, and that I should be successful, and furthermore, in so close a little family as 'A' Troop, I thought that the unhappy youths of Dougal's section would expect me to get them out of trouble here, just as they had done when they were argumentative with the Military Police of Salisbury, Wilts.

With the terrifying, erratic barrage of our two pieces, the gay abandon of our many Bren gunners, and the careful sniping of three young men possessed of rifles with telescopic sights, there was little difficulty or danger in reaching the stricken section. I avoided the road, and took the jeep through the fields, zigzag, at speed, like a destroyer during an aircraft attack. The men were indeed unhappy. Two were wounded in feet and legs, one was burnt by the phosphorus of his own 77 smoke grenade, all were wet and browned off. I think they were glad to see me, but only in the fashion that a wayfarer greets an overdue omnibus on a cold and rainy day. We draped the wounded men over the bonnet, the rest clambered within the bodywork, and in a couple of minutes we were back in the cutting.

The situation was now stalemate. We could not with our few men advance out of our cutting under the spouts of the German Spandaus sited on the ridge. They, however, could not advance upon us over the open ground. The impasse was, however, resolved by four ear-splitting explosions as four mortar bombs landed among us in a salvo spread over as many seconds. At the same time sounds of strife reached us from San Basilio, to the rear, and we later learned that Squadron Headquarters was justifying its existence against a strong attack from the Gioja direction. Rory leapt into his jeep, told us to stay where we were at all costs, and tore down the open road to his headquarters. He was pursued by mortar bombs, but was untouched. Our SAS friend, however, who offered to remove our wounded, was no Rory, and a near miss filled him with fifty-six lumps of metal. He professed to be not seriously incommoded by the necessity of carrying with him this extra weight, but was none the less sent off to hospital at Taranto, together with Dougal's wounded and the first of the injured from Squadron Headquarters.

The situation deteriorated. The mortar-men were working from a hollow below the ridge ahead of us. Our musical-comedy guns became impossible to service, and the cutting in which the rest of us lay was a death-trap. We could not reply to our antagonists, since the guns, even if a crew could survive to work them, had too flat a trajectory to drop shells into the German hide-out; our two-inch mortars had not quite enough range; and our Troop three-inch mortar was embroiled at San Basilio.

Away to our right was a dry-stone wall, and beyond it a sort of common covered with tufted grass. 'A' Troop had always thought that the best concealment on these occasions was in an open space, and not behind trees and rocks whose prominence became aiming-marks for the unfriendly. Accordingly the Troop sprang to their feet, bundled into such vehicles as were left, and charged the stone wall. Our jeeps burst through it in fine style, bucketed over its foundation, and bounced over the tufted field beyond to a hollow where lay the dried puddle of a winter pond. Leaving the vehicles in this slight cover, the men took up positions in the open field, and, sure enough, the theory of concealment worked, for the troopers melted into the ground, and though the mortars searched and searched no one was hit.

We became bored after a while. I thought that we could hit into the mortar pit by pushing a Bren forward for a couple of hundred yards to fire in from a flank. Ian's section sergeant volunteered for the job, and with McEntee and a youth named Taylor, a studious, quiet young man of about nineteen years, he made his way forward while the rest of us distracted attention.

Unfortunately, Ian's sergeant succumbed to the hunted man's temptation to seek cover. He and his party advanced without harm, but, instead of taking up position in the open, they elected to go behind the only tree which grew for a radius of a quarter of a mile. The expert, professional Boche, who had no doubt watched our amateur antics with amusement, then fired one single mortar-bomb. It landed in the branches of the tree, exploded, and for a time the stammer of the Bren was silenced.

Presently Ian's sergeant crawled back, wounded.

"McEntee's dead," he said. "I passed out for a bit, and when I looked round Taylor wasn't there."

At this the ghostly chatter of a Bren burst out from near the tree, and for a long time the boy Taylor lay not far from his dead friend and restricted materially the movements of the German mortar-men. He was for his staunchness given an immediate Military Medal, and promoted King's Corporal.

We became very unhappy. The mortar shower rained steadily upon us. The Germans in the farm became more aggressive, and the Troop, now seventeen strong, was quite isolated in bare country.

Furious sounds of strife came from San Basilio as Rory's Headquarters wrestled with the Boche attack, and far to our left I heard the screech of Spandaus as 156 Battalion, using us as a pivot, began to fight forward in a wide circling movement to the ridge ahead of us. We had no idea of the German strength, save that they were very well off for vehicles, and the issue behind us and to our left was much in doubt.

For once the wireless was working. Curious bits of news came through to Gentleman Jim.

"The rest of the Brigade is having a battle at Castalaneta," he passed on to me. "The General joined them, and was killed a short while ago."

Then again: "I hear things are very sticky at Salerno, sir. We won't be so happy if the landing fails, will we?"

I became browned off. I thought that, with the help of the three-inch mortars and a few more men, we could push the Germans off the ridge ahead of us. I told Gentleman Jim to get through to Squadron with my suggestion. It was evidently Horsey to whom he spoke, for quite soon a runner crawled to me with a verbal reply via Gentleman Jim. The runner was smiling happily, and I saw that he was passing glad tidings to the rather apprehensive troopers who lay along his route. There was a noticeably cheerful atmosphere left behind him.

"Captain Bridgewater's compliments, sir," said the runner, beaming. "He says that a Mr Carruthers is coming to our help as quickly as possible."

It was as skilful a way as Horsey could contrive to let me know privately that the Squadron was committed to the hilt, and that we must fight our own battle.

The long day dragged its length, and the Troop, virtually sleepless for four nights, dozed between spasms of activity when they discouraged any presumption from the occupants of the ridge. The battle noises on our left waxed stronger as the men of 156 Battalion fought their way forward. I feared for them as I contrasted the stutter of their few slow-firing Brens with the vicious screech of the innumerable German Spandaus.

As for 'A' Troop, in our tired, half-dazed state, I do not think we quite knew when the fight was over, for we lay a long time before we realized that the countryside had grown silent. At last Rory drove up the empty road from San Basilio. He had fought off the attack on his headquarters, and had then gone off to stimulate 156 Battalion. Now he wanted us to rendezvous with the Squadron at San Basilio.

In the village street Rory lined up the young men of the Troop, so recently immature, and now aware initiates who had undergone the ordeal which confers manhood upon adolescence. He fixed the ranks with his one piratical eye, and said, "You have done well. Get some food, and then go to sleep. Unless there is an attack, you will have no duties to-night."

Rory was at once disobeyed, for the Troop lay down in its ranks on the hard road and passed foodless into slumber. None of them awoke when a German fighting patrol probed noisily at the Squadron lines in the darkness.

The next morning I took George Field and two Bren gunners as escort, and we drove out to the lone tree whose branches had detonated the bomb which had killed McEntee, and which sheltered him now that he was dead.

The Bren gunners posted themselves to watch the country-side, eerily quiet and menacing, while George and I dug a grave beneath the tree. We wrapped up McEntee in a blanket and lifted him awkwardly into his cold bed.

The sentries lay bare-headed at their posts, and I read snatches of the burial service.

"He that believeth in Me, though he were dead, yet shall he live."

"The Lord gave, and the Lord hath taken away; blessed be the name of the Lord."

"Man that is born of woman hath but a short time to live, and is full of misery. He cometh up, and is cut down like a flower."

I wondered whether the Eternal belief had not always been with mankind, for it would not have been so very different to have said, "Those whom the Gods love die young."

We filled in the grave, the Bren gunners scrambled to their feet, and we drove back to San Basilio leaving McEntee in the peaceful place. So many had died, and were yet to die, in that war, but this one unimportant death was our own concern, and the gap in our close-knit ranks was a wound which did not readily heal.

I passed that way weeks later. Some one had dug up McEntee to steal his boots.

In the following few days the pace eased a little. The rest of the First Airborne Division was ferried over from Bizerta, and with them came the remainder of the Squadron. But, even with this increase in strength, the situation was not very good. The Airborne force was by now a long way from its sea-base at Taranto, and was most inadequate in numbers to cover the ground over which it was spread. Its artillery and anti-tank weapons were negligible after the disaster to the *Abdiel.* And, with the battle at Salerno yet far from won, we wondered why the Germans did not launch a determined counter-attack upon us.

To conceal our sparse numbers, the Division kept up a constant aggression, and the Squadron patrolled by night and day over considerable distances. In its way this restless patrolling was as great a strain as a pitched battle repeated again and again. For even on a patrol where nothing happens the nerves remain taut against the prospect of sudden sound and fury. Each move is as enigmatic in its possible consequences as the gentle cast of a fisherman's fly, whose descent on to the quiet pool may provoke a frenzy in the water.

One day I was ordered to conduct a reconnaissance party from 156 Battalion, so that they might prospect a line of approach for a coming attack on Gioja. We went in jeeps by a covered route which I had found, at whose end was a farm with excellent cheese and a flat roof for observation. My seasoned companions of 'A' Troop made light of our daylight drive. They had developed an irritating piece of stereotyped cross-talk, which they intoned in the accents of a music-hall officer.

As we drove along Gentleman Jim went into the routine:

"Wheah are the enemay?"

"Theah!" came in chorus from his well-trained comrades.

"Oh!" said Gentleman Jim. "Carry on, men!"

They repeated their little act as we neared the farm. Off in the fields to one side I had just noticed a German patrol plodding along as unconscious of us as the rest of our party was of them.

"Wheah are the enemay?" demanded Gentleman Jim.

"Theah!" I said, pointing.

"Oh, my goodness, sir!" said Gentleman Jim.

The attackers from 156 Battalion penetrated to the centre of Gioja that night, but were thrust out again by sheer weight of numbers next morning. However, a couple of days later the town was ours. Here we had news of Jack Johnson and the vanished men of 'C' Troop. Jack had been killed in a skirmish somewhere among the round houses near Locorotondo within a few hours of saying good-bye on the quay at Taranto. His Troop were ambushed later on that first day, and, trapped in a sunken road near Gioja, had died almost to a man. A couple, badly wounded, were discovered in a hospital in the town, and they told us that the Germans had constantly visited them with presents and delicacies. The Germans have a dual national personality. The operator of the torture-chamber may snatch a few moments from his work to relax in a beer-garden to hum sentimental songs with a child on each knee, fondled by the hands which so recently wielded a whip.

We remained a few days in a large farm outside Gioja, where the only incident followed a cry in the night of "Fire! Fire!" The farm was built on an arched foundation, whose grottoes formed a store for fodder and a lair for beasts. Our ammunition was stacked in the catacombs, and was now surrounded by smouldering straw. We worked in respirators for some hours before the explosives were safe, but the fire, billowing smoke, remained active, unperturbed by the antics of the Gioja fire-brigade.

We slept above this furnace for two nights, warm as toast through the chill darkness, and then, receiving an order to move, handed over our cosy billet to the 21st Independent Parachute Company, who signed for the fire as part of the accommodation stores.

I never really knew how Rory contrived to receive orders to carry out the more interesting and flamboyant operations. At any rate, it was plain that he had again pulled out a plum with his intriguing thumb, for our move from Gioja was to occupy Bari. Bari is a coastal resort and considerable port.

'A' Troop, somewhat restored in strength and in vehicles, entered the city without resistance, and at first without much remark. Our jeeps took their place in the traffic, obeyed the police signals, and their occupants behaved with decorum. Short of an ill-mannered Wild West entry with guns blazing skyward, there was little we could do to infuse drama into the situation. Dougal in particular was as glum as a child robbed of a party.

We found our way to the fine promenade, and so conditioned had I become to the curious situation that I stopped my jeep outside the Imperial Hotel, a fine millionaires' hostelry, and booked myself a room. Further to secure my tenancy, I booked another for Rory. We then took over a school within a stone's throw, and Bari was occupied.

Quite soon Horsey appeared with an advance party from Squadron, and as we chatted on the pavement outside the school a seedy-looking man sidled up and said that there was a large prison camp on the other side of the town, and that there were large numbers of British within.

Horsey had been as disappointed as 'A' Troop had at the prosaic entry into Bari, and seized this opportunity for dramatics. We rounded up the nearest dozen of 'A' Troop, piled the whole lot and ourselves into two jeeps, and did our best to ride off in all directions, like Leacock's horseman. We did at last control ourselves enough to ask directions of polite carabinieri, and presently came near the confines of a vast wired camp which contained innumerable hutments. To our minds, excited by our errand of 'to the Rescue,' there seemed to be thousands of Italian troops standing to at posts without the wire, quite apart from a strong guard within. To supplement these gaolers was a regiment of Field Artillery.

"I'm not quite sure what Carruthers would advise if he were here," said Horsey.

"Demand the Commandant," I suggested.

"Probably," agreed Horsey.

This we did. We had the sense to keep moral control of the situation by refusing to enter the Commandant's office, and, after much excited chatter from his staff, he came out to our jeep by the gate. Horsey and I tried to think how a Hollywood hero would deal with the situation, and it came to us that he would have shot the Commandant, and tied knots in the barrels of the cannon. This was impracticable just then, we felt. Instead we asked for the nominal roll of prisoners.

Even though this thick folio was headed and annotated in Italian, a cursory glance down its columns made it clear that the prisoners were largely political, and that their races were legion—that is to say, Balkan. There were Albanians, Greeks, Jugoslavs, Croats, Bulgars, and stateless mongrels, but among the explosive and expletive-sounding names appeared no Smiths or Browns or Joneses or Macs.

However, Horsey and I were not readily to be baulked of a magnificent gesture. We put the Commandant in the middle of our troopers, and, leaving him as a hostage, went through the gate into the central wire compound. Segment-shaped pens radiated from the compound, and in each were segregated either nationalities or possibly political complexions. At a guess, there were a couple of thousand prisoners. The occupants of each section tried all to attain the front row against the wire in order to cheer us and bombard us with their hats. The noise was frightening, but at the same time inspiring. We felt that we should mount a rostrum, break out the Union Jack, cry "The British are here," and deliver an address on Freedom and Democracy.

Instead, we took a bunch of keys from the Italian Adjutant and flung open all the gates of the pens. Any stray Italian gaolers sprinted for the main entrance, and before we could move Horsey and I were embraced almost to death by the ill-flavoured crowd. This ceremony over, the factions gathered separately for a moment, there was a hush; then with a roar each mob flung itself upon the crowd nearest to it, and a mêlée began such as few men have been privileged to witness.

Horsey and I fought our way outside. The Commandant, hair *en brosse* and monocled in imitation of a Prussian, was the first man whom I had seen literally dancing in anguish. His subordinates had turned olive green, and were giving tongue in volume proportionate to their rank. Horsey and I looked appalled upon our handiwork, as might two scientists who had unwittingly unleashed some new force of the Universe.

But all passion must in the latter end spend itself, and slowly the tumult died. We re-entered upon the battlefield, and with difficulty gathered ringleaders together, to whom we at last made it clear that they must take their adherents back to their pens to await a formal liberation by a much larger force. To our surprise, the antagonists departed meekly, their venom for the present sated.

"I think Carruthers would go now," said Horsey, legging it for the gate.

As an afterthought, we bundled the Commandant into an overloaded jeep and took him back to the school, where Rory had arrived. The last I saw of him he was standing in front of Rory's desk making a futile attempt to be uncommunicative. Rory thumped the glass top of the desk so hard that he broke it, whereupon the Commandant began to talk. Later that day some Military Government people went out to the camp in order to earn their pay.

As English newspapers began to reach us we saw that for some days we had been the arrow on the maps of the campaign. This was a pleasant conceit, and we were not too pleased when elements of the 78th Division started to advance through us. However, the Air Landing Brigade, the Independent Parachute Company, and ourselves were joined to these newcomers with orders to maintain contact with the retiring Germans and to push on to a first objective at Foggia, to the north. Here lay a vast plain, which to all intents and purposes was one great airfield.

We used to drive out daily to the battle, returning at night for a bath and dinner at the Imperial Hotel. But presently the distance became too great to commute, and one night Rory did not return with the half-squadron he had with him. For he had left Horsey behind with his main Headquarters, and myself with 'A' Troop, since he did not trust the guardianship of Bari to the few thousand additional soldiers who had now arrived. When another night had passed Horsey and I took a jeep to search for him.

We drove most of the morning through the crawling transport of 78 Division. In the afternoon the traffic was lighter, and soon we had the road almost to ourselves. Now and again we met a stray group to whom we addressed our inquiries, but the fog of war was impenetrable to all save newspaper correspondents with their God's-eye view, and our questions remained unanswered.

It is eerie to drive along a silent road, to ford streams beside demolished bridges, to pass upturned, smoking vehicles, their dead still warm beside them, but no live soul to see. Horsey and I felt great discomfort.

"I think Carruthers would go back for a sun-downer," I said, in a low voice.

As I spoke there came a crash of artillery from a point about a mile ahead. Which way it was directed, and who had let it off, was not apparent. We drove a little closer, dismounted, and went forward on foot. We came to the rim of a large hollow, whose farther lip looked over the south end of the Foggia plain.

In the hollow we saw a squadron of Churchill tanks, a troop of 25-pounder field guns, some sappers, and the red berets of Rory and his merry men. There were present several officers senior to Rory, but it seemed to us that he had taken charge of the mixed force, was having great fun with the guns, and proposed shortly to launch the Churchills in a charge, spear-headed by his half-squadron's jeeps. He was able to spare a few moments for us, inquired kindly after our health, asked whether we had enjoyed the drive, and if the rest of the Squadron was doing garrison duties adequately at Bari.

We replied that we had been rather concerned about Rory's fate, but said little more because we had not the heart to spoil his enjoyment by discussion of things official.

Rory turned back to coerce the more senior officers to follow his plan of action, and Horsey and I foresaw that we should be press-ganged into a jeep charge across the mine-strewn plain against the emplaced enemy. But somehow it became known, no one understood how, as is usually the way in war, that the Germans had withdrawn, and that the hot heroics of a charge must be put aside for a cold-blooded follow-up through booby-traps and demolitions.

Rory sighed, and told us that we might as well return to Bari, and that he would possibly be back next day.

This was the last irregular, self-determined effort of the Squadron. The early elements of 78 Division were followed by New Zealanders, Canadians, and the ponderous supply services. Our original carefree tactics, inspired by the shade of Rupert of the Rhine, could find no room for expression among the beflagged Staff cars which carried with them the text-books of an advance. Perhaps it was as well, for we had had the greatest luck in our slap-happy attacks and our inexperienced patrols, and fortune is inconsistent. The wheel had spun wrong from the first for some of us, like Jack Johnson, but for the most the winning sequence had lasted longer than average.

The Squadron had one last run, outstripping competitors, into Foggia, and then, even as we wondered what the Italian winter would be like, came reports from the Orderly Room clerks of a move home to England. These rumours came near to confirmation as we retraced our wheel-tracks from the north, struggling against the tide of war flowing whence we had come, until once more we were housed not very far from Bari.

Our heavy baggage was still in Africa. It had been moved, we were told, to Bizerta, where it was lying rain-soaked on the open quay. Horsey was detailed to fly over to make arrangements for the impedimenta to be sent to us. Horsey and I had in common a profound mistrust of flying machines, from which, naturally enough, sprang a dislike and a fear of aerial transport. Early one morning Horsey went off to the airfield. I saw him leave the Mess, his cheerful face glum.

He was back, all smiles, by lunch-time.

"The thing wouldn't start," he said, confirming our theory that planes were more temperamental than, as well as being as noisy as, prima donnas. "I've got to go again to-morrow."

I have said before that death casts a long shadow. I had several times seen the silhouette of his finger laid across a face, and had had the feeling, too, that there was a subconscious, acquiescent acceptance in the other. Be that as it may, Horsey and I had grown to be very close friends, and perhaps it was not unusual for us to seek each other's company that evening, to dine at an hotel, and to sit afterwards late into the night. We talked, of course, of his wife, and of Tessa, who was so near to the time for her baby. What plans we made for peace I now forget, but for Horsey they were not fulfilled.

Next night Rory looked so worried, so unlike his usual self, that I asked him what the trouble was. He told me that Horsey's plane had left Italy, but had not made a landfall over Africa. Simultaneously we told one another that the crew would have taken to their dinghy, and were by now probably drinking brandy on one of His Majesty's warships.

But the days passed, and the vitality of Horsey was drowned in silence.

The men of the Squadron—for the boys had grown up of a sudden—enjoyed those last few weeks in Italy, while we awaited passage home. They liked the cooler but still sunny weather, and they found a taste for wines. They discovered, too, that the frank, free Latin love-making was a healthier and more jolly sport than inarticulate fumbling in the shameful darkness of an English bedroom.

We drove at last to Taranto, and there on the quay took leave of our vehicles, for which we had formed a personal affection. They had borne us faithfully and well in many strange places, but were now to pass into the service of others. We embarked on a Landing Craft Infantry, a welded, sardine-tin sort of ship, adequate only for the shortest trips. Somehow the whole Squadron crowded aboard her, though our numbers left little room to stand up, let alone lie down. We learned at once that the galley could do little to help us, and that we must set up our own field-cookers to leeward of any wind-break.

We set sail with some sister ships which bore the Air Landing Brigade, and for six days wallowed south-west across the Mediterranean until, cramped and hungry, we landed at Philippeville.

It was while camped here among the sand-dunes that a mutilated cable reached me. It had gone direct to Sousse, had followed to Italy, and was now back in Africa.

It said, so far as I could understand it, "Louise and Mother both well."

At times like this the man in the Services had not the advantages of his civilian brother. I wanted to know just how well was Tessa; whether she continued well; whether the child was a Miss or a misprint. I wished I could have been with Tessa; above all, I wished now that I could tell her I was returning.

We embarked after a day or two on one of the Canadian Pacific's drunken Duchesses, the very ship on which I had sailed back to Canada fifteen years before. The voyage was long, the speed of the convoy a crawl, as the swift thoughts of each of us flew ahead, only to circle back perforce to await our corporate company. But the sun lost strength to the wind, the air grew moist, and at last we lay fog-bound off the Mersey bar, unable to set impatient feet on the damp soil of our country. After this island welcome we slid into our berth on the Liverpool waterfront, and in the best Army tradition were whisked throughout the following night by special train. We arrived in Lincolnshire in the small, cold hours, and were forbidden to tell of our return.

CHAPTER X

STAFF COLLEGE

WHILE I was overseas Tessa had been staying in Hampshire with the wife of that cousin of mine whose name had helped me at my first interview with the Ironside Guards. When leave was given to our newly returned division I set off from Lincolnshire in the bitter pre-dawn cold of that bleak county, yet so warm from excitement that I doubt if frost-bite could have touched me.

I knew so much of Tessa, and so little. She had joined her life with mine as if casually, without knowing much of me, and that which she did know could not have been the better side. Yet our joining was not casual; our lack of care to probe each other's minds was perhaps because we knew that all time was ours to discover what we were.

Tessa's letters to Africa and Italy had been in their way unrevealing of her thoughts about the coming baby; they had not told much of her health, happiness, worries, or wishes for the future. There had been a quaint Victorianism about them: "I continue well" in reply to questions. And when I asked whether her condition progressed easily, or, as with some women, uncomfortably, I would get the answer, "We both continue well."

As the double-clicks of the carriage wheels reeled off the rail lengths southward they put a period to each tumbling thought and restrained it, as a part-opened gate restrains and sorts a pushing sheep-flock.

Tessa met me alone at the station. I saw her, very tall and fair, as the train drew in, with her look of Alice in Wonderland unimpaired by motherhood. As we met—she the scarce-fledged bride and I returned from the wars to a quick-left wife and unseen child—said Tessa, "Hello! Isn't it cold? I expect we'll have tea in the nursery—muffins, you know."

The baby was asleep on the lawn, muffled in her pram against the December chill. We approached as warily as a patrol to a booby-trap, but that sixth sense, soon lost with age, warned the still bundle. The child opened her eyes, calm and knowing, and I saw that Tessa had borne a miniature lady, who had, in her luxurious hair and eyelashes, and in her fine-formed features, none of the baby. Tessa shied away like a puzzled mare startled by the mysterious presence of its first-born, yet knowing that there must somewhere be a connexion.

"Oh, dear!" she said. "It's awake."

When I returned to Lincolnshire a problem was posed by the authorities. The Airborne arm had by now evolved from a stunt to a respectable formation. The Regular senior officers who had built the technique and tradition of this new arm had been the best, the most versatile, and the most far-seeing of their type. There were at the top many Guardsmen, and they had, by insistence on discipline, and by attention to detail, won acknowledgment from the rest of the Service that the Airborne soldier was indeed a soldier and not an intractable acrobat. The original Airborne Division was now supplemented by another, the Sixth Airborne, and the two formations were to be welded into the First British Airborne Corps, under the original commander of First Airborne, General "Boy" Browning.

For better or worse, the hush-hush private-army days were numbered, and it was foreseen that trained Staff officers would be needed to administer the expanded force. Airborne problems are peculiar to that type of warfare, and it was therefore advisable that the required Staff should be taken from men who already had experience of the new arm. A dozen vacancies were allotted to the new Corps for the next Staff College course, and I was told to volunteer for one of them.

It was, however, a rule that candidates must have two months' Staff experience, and unwillingly I was posted from the intimate companionship of Rory's Squadron to face the unknown perils of Divisional Headquarters. This move was most frightening, for my time in the Army had been confined to commanding a platoon in the Ironside Guards, and a troop in the Squadron. I had enjoyed regimental life with regimental comrades, and had picked up a working knowledge of the structure and organization of units, had learned to be responsible for Other Ranks, and to see to maintenance of weapons and vehicles. But outside this narrow orbit all else was to me as void as the cosmos. I knew that our Quartermaster provided food and stores for us, but had never considered how he in turn procured them, and in my mind dismissed the agencies of the RASC, RAOC, REME, RAMC, and the Divisional AQMG and substituted simply Santa Claus. I felt it indelicate, and in a regimental soldier improper, to probe into mysteries which might in the latter end explode my blind faith, and would give me a lot to worry about. I had felt, too, that it would have been insubordinate to express surprise at the order which grew out of chaos after the form up for a divisional move or the start line for an exercise.

This had been a comfortable philosophy, shared by many others, and had involved a minimum of mental exertion. I was horrified at being told to go behind the show-booth to see what made the puppets work.

At Divisional Headquarters I was a spare General Staff Officer, Grade 3. This grade is referred to informally as G3, and in my case I was a supernumerary clerk without any knowledge of the job. Although I had a distrust of these Headquarters people, shared none of their enthusiasms, and was much upset by the amount of work which they did, I made one or two friends, selecting those who had access to transport, and attaching myself to them as they ran their errands.

But, after a very short time, I became overcome with unhappiness. I missed Rory, and the rascally men of 'A' Troop. I would have petitioned to return to my unit, but that the details for the Staff College course reached me, and I learned that married officers might live out. This enticement was more than a newly wedded officer with a brand-new child could be expected to resist. But, just the same, the atmosphere of so superior a headquarters as that of a division was too rarefied, and on a sudden thought I waited upon the commander of the 4th Parachute Brigade and asked whether I might widen my experience by a tour of duty with him.

The Brigadier was the officer to whom I had tersely replied during 'A' Troop's siege of Mottola, and who was now my daughter's godfather. He consented to ask for me, and I moved some miles away, to the Brigade Headquarters Mess, where life was much more like that of a unit, and with the help of some beagling and shooting passed quite merrily.

Tessa, Louise, and I moved down to Camberley in the early spring of 1944. The renting of our furnished house was arranged at a high level by the Adjutant of the Staff College, and we shared the ample room with another student and his wife. The house was some two miles from Camberley, along a road easy for cycling, and was fortuitously placed within strolling distance of an inn.

It was with awe that I cycled to the Staff College to report myself. Nearly three years before I had felt a similar trepidation as I entered the same gates to continue up the drive to Sandhurst. I remembered the reverence with which I had been wont to hurry past the sacred College, eyes downcast, as Ambrose Winston and I had gone about our humble occasions in Camberley.

I now felt that I had entered too light-heartedly upon this course, and recalled the numerous stories which I had heard of students whose brains had snapped under the strain, so that they were driven to suicide or else remained for life shut up in an institution, where they identified themselves with ADOS, DAQMG, CREME, DMS, or RTO Bagshot.

But the first day or two revealed many things. The greatest surprise was to find few among the Directing Staff or students who were what the ordinary soldier would call 'Staff type.' Almost all the Directing Staff were taken from regimental officers, and they did a one-year tour of duty at the College before returning to active soldiering. The students, too, were a bemedalled lot of regimental officers, nearly all of whom had seen service in the Far East, Middle East, or during the brief and mainly inglorious excursions to Norway or France. It was, therefore, a comfort to find that I was to be in daily contact with ordinary intelligent men, and not with intellectual theorists.

To leaven the British ingredients were a few Americans and some Poles.

We learned that the course was divided for instructional purposes into three divisions, each of about seventy students, presided over by a General Staff Officer Grade One—that is, a G1, or lieutenant-colonel. The divisions were subdivided into syndicates of ten, each of which was under the direct instruction of its own Director, also a lieutenant-colonel. To co-ordinate the activities of every one was a Brigadier General Staff, under the Commandant, a major-general. In this Olympian atmosphere even the Adjutant was a lieutenant-colonel.

We were told that the syndicates were shuffled at the end of six weeks, and again at the end of twelve, so that during the eighteen weeks' course a student, though remaining always in the same division, would have a change of his syndicate director and fellow-students. I had had a fear that there would be an examination at the end of our time, in which we should be required to write out from memory the organization of the British Army, the War Establishment and G. 1098 stores of an armoured reconnaissance regiment, a movement order for a corps proceeding by night along a single axis, an operation order at army level for an assault on Berlin, and a critical survey of the use of armour by the Germans in their break-through to the Channel ports in 1940. But there was no examination. Instead, the progress of students was under constant review, and at the end of our time our Divisional G1, assisted by the three syndicate directors with whom each student would have had contact, submitted his judgment to the Brigadier GS and the Commandant, who added their own observations.

However, the mental exercises which I had wrongly feared in the lump at an examination were not denied us. For such things became daily routine.

The syndicate in which I began my studies was typical in composition. The Director, known as the DS, was a cavalryman who had been a brigade major in an armoured formation in the Middle East. Among the ten students were gunners, sappers, a New Zealander, a Polish Staff officer, and an American lieutenant-colonel. The Pole could say "Good morning, please," in English. The American was more fluent.

In the early part of the course we were much concerned to learn the correct abbreviations for all military terms, and also the organization and equipment of all formations and units. It was necessary to learn the abbreviations in order to conform to common usage without introducing a gay element of doubt into written messages, and also, I suppose, because they were shorter. It was quicker to write "Fd pk coy RE" than "Field Park Company Royal Engineers." And an intimate knowledge of the vehicles and loads of all units was essential if one was to plot the time past a point of a mixed column, so that it might avoid jamming the passage of an armoured division.

When this knowledge was partially digested we went on to discuss as exercises problems of movement, and of tactics. We were guided to a decision by ingenious methods. Each student was appointed to his own particular rôle, and if the walking-on parts were limited the syndicate would be divided into two identical sections of five, consisting, perhaps, in each case of a mock Brigadier, Brigade Major, Staff Captain A, Staff Captain Q, and Brigade RASC Officer, who was known by the delightful abbreviation of "Brasco." I noticed that the more senior one's rank the less was the work, for the brigadier had only to think out his plan in general terms and to leave the intricate details to his subordinates.

When at Sandhurst we had watched the blackboard outside the Company Office. At the Staff College we watched our pigeon-holes. These were necessarily capacious receptacles lining one of the passages, and after each day's work we approached them with sinking hearts to retrieve the thick wads of paper on which our problems were posed for the next morning. On the eve of exercises the folios would be particularly thick, and we would spend the evening marking up maps, trying to retain in our minds the mass of detail, and finally doing the work which went with the part allotted to each of us. Those who lived in at the College had some small advantage here, for if a real-life tank officer found himself commanding an infantry brigade there was always a foot soldier available whose brains he could pick. On the other hand, we married men living out had the use of our wives to mark up our maps. This help was a great time-saver, for the vital area of any scheme was diabolically chosen at the intersection of four maps which had to be folded and co-ordinated, with probably an offshoot of the ground turned over on the back of the map-board. To read and locate several dozen map-references, plot axes of advance, and mark in friendly and hostile dispositions took two or three hours. The brave little women, with their brows so fair all furrowed, performed this task while their hero husbands wrote their plans with fevered haste. Nerves male and female were strained to breaking-point, and matrimonial tolerance withered and died.

It is trying for an overworked soldier, his mind oblivious to all else save signal intercommunication, when he leans over his wife's shoulder to peer at the map-board, and demands, "Where have you put the Sigs?" and is answered meekly, "There's a packet on the mantelpiece, dear."

At the allotted time each syndicate would go to its room, where under the guidance of its DS a solution to the problem would be put forward, supported by detailed written orders and instructions. The DS at such times was more of a chairman or question-master than a tutor. It was his purpose to launch a discussion, work it up to fever-heat between rival opinions, then to withdraw from the battlefield until the combatants flagged, when, by a skilful word or two, he would renew the frenzy. In this way many possible and most impossible answers were put forward, so that our minds grew flexible until we could see all sides of a question, and not just the obvious.

When all passion was spent, and we had ceased to be even on shouting terms with each other, the DS would tell us the

School solution. At once our mutual differences were forgotten as we turned to yell derision.

At first we had expected that any answers which did not agree with the School solution would be judged wrong. But this was not so, for, unless some plan were demonstrably absurd, the DS would always accept an innovation as a perfectly possible alternative.

The man with the soundest ideas in my first syndicate was the Pole. Within a month he had progressed from "Good morning, please," to a good vocabulary in broken English. He was then able to explain to us how he had managed to complete his written work during his early days. He had been wont to translate the College paper into Polish with the aid of a dictionary. He would then compose his solution in his own language, and render it back into English. We natives had quite often to work after midnight, so one must assume that Poles never sleep.

As we became accustomed to the type and scope of the mental exercise demanded of us, the pressure of work was steadily increased. My first DS gave warning of this mounting tempo, and said that there might be times when we would feel overwhelmed. If so, he advised us metaphorically to let the flood sweep past, and to regain our breath on the bank. I took this advice one night, when I felt despair at completing my work before morning. But perhaps the flood was not adjudged to be at its high mark just yet, for I had scant sympathy next day.

On the whole, however, I think that it rested largely with the student whether or not he felt overworked. There is a type of mind which delights in detail, and in its own industry. This mind reveals itself physically in copious note-taking. There were students who scribbled furiously throughout discussions and lectures, so that they might have secret pleasure in the small hours transcribing their jottings into notebooks. This vice was pure fetishism, for readable and exact précis were daily issued on the current subjects. The DS did not encourage the meagre mind which loved detail for its own sake. Their object was to instil into us the detail to be used purely as a tool with which to express ourselves on a much larger canvas.

The only type of student which was really unpopular with the DS was that which had no ideas at all beyond the formal, and which if uncertain stayed dumb. Several of the more wily quickly noticed that these clerkly people, whose abbreviations were always correct, but whose answers were uninventive, were unpopular with their mentors. It became the thing, therefore, to disagree with the School solution, and, indeed, with the more obvious types of solution put forward by the students, and instead to advance opinions which, if far-fetched, were workable. It is said that the machines designed by Mr Heath Robinson were all operative. This virtuosity was positively encouraged by the DS, who took it that we had seen the more proper answer, had taken it as read, and had put forward our less orthodox ideas in order to broaden the discussion. This assumption was not always correct, for frequently a quicker-witted student would hold forth impromptu to disguise lack of study the night before.

It was expedient to have certain work in typescript before submission to the DS. Most of the note-takers hammered this out on their own machines, but others used a typist in Camberley who had official sanction to deal with even Top Secret subjects. This Scottish lady, a Miss McTurk, had done work for so many courses that her opinion was highly valued. One young gentleman, who had other plans than work for a certain week-end, called on Miss McTurk one Saturday to ask her to compose for him and type out an essay on Napoleon and the Hundred Days. This the lady kindly did, and the tired student found it waiting for him in his pigeon-hole on Monday. With the essay was a note saying:

"I have done your 'Hundred Days' for you, but I noticed that all the other students asked for 'General Wellington in the Peninsular War,' so I have enclosed another paper on this."

As soon as we were able to write military language, and had mastered the standard layout for various written orders and instructions, the scope of our activities was enlarged. Our exercises were now mostly done out of doors, and each syndicate or sub-syndicate would have a vehicle placed at its disposal to plot its tactics in the field. On these excursions the note-takers would tramp for miles across the countryside. The less painstaking would lunch at a convenient hotel, make a plan off the map, verify their decisions by a quick look at the ground from the seat of a PU, and thus achieve a correct, or at least an alternative, answer.

When reproached by the more earnest, these Rabelaisian types pointed out that in war a detailed and open examination of the ground would be impossible, and that those who wandered boldly about the fields of Hampshire with map-cases and satchels of books were cheats.

Midway through the course, a week-end's leave was granted. Tessa and I, with the infant Louise, took relays of taxis to evade the twenty-miles hire limit, and went to a well-known and light-hearted hotel near Maidenhead. We had made up our minds to enjoy this break, and did so on the Friday night of our arrival, and at the weekly dance on the Saturday. It is possible that we were a little conspicuous, and, as Tessa has never contrived to look married, we may have given rise to a little chatter. At all events, on the Sunday morning we thought it wise to have a drink before lunch, and since Louise was not feeling co-operative we decided to wheel her pram outside the open window of the bar. As we settled the pram under the sill an astonished voice floated out from the hush within: "Good God! Look! They must be!"

I found myself less in a whirl during the latter half of the course, and though the spate of work flowed faster and faster, yet there was more time to look about one. By some chance there was on this course a clique of politically minded students, intellectual note-takers of the Left Wing. Tessa and I had inclined towards Socialism all our lives, but from study of these people we saw that the ideal and the practice of this policy were wide apart, and we felt more comfortable when we had put our own vague Socialism into cold storage. We decided that a few more generations must add to the accumulating wisdom of man before he could handle with safety this dangerous 'ism.'

The protagonists of the creed were obsessed. Their work at the College was coloured always by their politics, and dogma was introduced in a most ingenious way into purely military matters. Neither did these adherents of Marx inspire confidence in the gospel which they preached. They were, many of them, inverted snobs, who saw good only in the private soldier who had got himself into trouble, and none in the generals whose efforts were directed towards preserving these students' right to free speech. They decried, too, the traditional fighting blood of the yeomen and the aristocrats whose flow had through the centuries bought Britain's greatness, and which was again being poured forth to preserve her independence. Instead, they pandered to the misfits whose shallow roots were not embedded in the country's long history of courage and leadership.

One student, at least, who had been in civil life a solicitor, would demand leave of absence to defend conscientious objectors. This is not to pour contempt on a man who feels that he must not take life, but rather to say that a soldier, of all people, should not professionally defend him. But inconsistency was the quality of these people.

There was among this gallery a perfectly normal student whose manners were good and whose war service had been brave and exemplary. I caught him off guard one night towards closing time at a Camberley hotel, and asked him point-blank why he had attached himself to this menagerie.

"Well," he said thoughtfully, "I've always wanted to go into politics after the War. I thought it all out some time ago. I decided that the Liberals were finished, and that there was so much established brain-power in the Tory Party that it would take a long time to make one's mark, so—I became Socialist."

As the course moved towards its end the perpetual uncertainty of Service life made itself felt again. It must indeed be difficult for the civil worker to understand how a Serviceman is entirely a creature without volition, and how wife, home, children, hobbies, and personal inclinations must be kept always secondary to the purpose of war. The Serviceman does not whine at being the slave of the lamp of Mars but finds in his abnegation of individual rights a little quiet glory. Just the same, he remains human, and we, our secure spell drawing to a close, wondered where in the wide world we would be sent when these peaceful days were done. Speculation was the more difficult since failures were not made known until the last day, and since the successful would by no means all be placed at once.

My production of a couple of books in pre-War days, an achievement frequently suspect in robust Army circles, stood me in some stead at last, for on the penultimate day I found in my pigeon-hole an envelope in which were directions to report as GSO2 Public Relations to SHAEF. Lest these things be readily forgotten, SHAEF was Supreme Headquarters Allied Expeditionary Force. I still had some combatant inclinations, but after three years as a regimental officer I was quite prepared to move for a while to London, where obviously I could see my wife and child. Thus ever the human element crops up to confound the machine of war.

Tessa and I took a quick week-end leave, our child left with sympathizers; then I went to take over my desk in London. At the door of a large building I showed the chit on which my appointment was written, and was led at once to my office. This was a spacious room, well furnished, supplied with several telephones, two fine leather-topped bureaux, and, at one of these, a fine golden-topped lady secretary.

I was expected, for the girl rang up some superior person to say that the new G2 had come, and then in answer to my questions began to tell me what my work would be.

Ha! I thought, as the glorious prospect unfolded, this will make Rory sit up when he hears about it!

For it seemed that most of my labour would be over the luncheon table, and that I was to entertain in a manner befitting Supreme Headquarters. I learned, too, that a soft-sprung motor-car awaited my whim in the square without, and that close to London rested a chromium-plated aeroplane to whisk me withersoever I listed. On my desk lay a box of Camel cigarettes and a box of chewing-gum. I was going to ask the lady secretary to lunch with me, so that she could tell me more, when a brigadier came in. He was nice, but firm.

"There's been a bit of a muddle," he said. "The Airborne people have demanded the use of all their own candidates from your course. You'd better go and see the postings people at the War Office."

With sorrow I took leave of the secretary, and of the desk-diary in which my luncheon engagements were to have been noted, and tramped round to confirm this news.

It was indeed true, and next day I reported to Headquarters First British Airborne Corps as GSO2 Operations.

CHAPTER XI

THE SEVENTEENTH PLAN

HEADQUARTERS First British Airborne Corps was sited in and about a large mansion near Rickmansworth. The house had been built by some fairly recent Captain of Industry as a symbol of success, and gave one the feeling that in its private days the Old Masters had been ordered for the walls on a yardage basis.

I reported first to my G1, and then went to see the Camp Commandant, who controlled billets and servants. The Commandant was a Bombardier Guards captain named Patrick Bush, thin and saturnine, like Don Quixote. He offered to farm me out on some unsuspecting local person, but said he could have a tent pitched for me on the lawn if I wished to be nearer my work. I chose the tent, since it would entitle me to Field Allowance, and since I intended anyway to return most nights to London, where Tessa had taken a furnished house in Chelsea. Bush was most impressed at this Spartan choice.

It took some days to gain a working knowledge of the Headquarters. It seemed as if most of the Staff were brigadiers, and that those who ran errands for them were lieutenant-colonels. As a new-fledged major, I was less than the dust.

The Airborne Corps was made up of the First and Sixth Airborne Divisions, the Special Air Service Brigade, and the Polish Parachute Brigade. It was itself a part of the First Allied Airborne Army, which disposed of three American Airborne Divisions in addition. Used to the humble politics of a small unit, the grandeur of this company was overwhelming, and the thought of the responsibilities to come frightening.

However, for a time no one took much notice of me. During

working hours I lurked with two other G2's and a number of G3's in a large chamber called the Operations Room. I had expected to be given the chance to use the correct Staff College abbreviations and to try my hand at moving real live columns of transport up and down the country. But there was little to write and not much to do. After a while I realized that all the work of a large Headquarters is done at and above G1 level, and below Warrant Officer Class II level. The middle classes, to which I now found I belonged, were scorned by the senior clerks as incompetents, and tolerated by the higher-ranking officers as errand boys. For our main purpose was to take messages on the telephone, and to move daily the flags on the war-map, which were in any event almost static during the early weeks of the Normandy campaign. Unfortunately, the operations room required always the presence of one G2 by day and by night, as the holy place of a temple demands a certain grade of votary. However, one of our number was a conscientious and ambitious young man, and was never happier than when in the Sanctuary.

The Headquarters was in a state of flux. Firstly, the establishment of a headquarters newly formed to command two divisions of a type never before known in war was experimental. Secondly, our Corps's superior formation, the First Allied Airborne Army, was as tentative in composition as we ourselves, and, being commanded by an American, we had necessarily to learn how each other's minds worked. Thirdly, between D-Day on June 6 and mid-September no less than sixteen different operations were planned in support of the Allied Armies, first within their bridgehead, and more especially later when they broke out and began to stream across occupied Europe But an Airborne operation takes some time to mount, for intricate co-ordination is necessary with the Royal Air Force who both fly and escort the troops, and later resupply them by air. And the rapid change of events on land made nonsense of our plotting before it was ever put into practice.

Two Royal Air Force Groups, Numbers 38 and 46, had now been formed to carry and resupply the Airborne Forces, so that all planning was done on a combined basis. It was a far cry from the early days when we were taken to war by scratch assortments of aircraft grudgingly loaned for the occasion.

For some time it was not clear what physical part our Headquarters would play during an operation. It had by many been thought that the essential departments would follow up with the seaborne tail of the fighting-men, and would arrive without exertion or excitement to occupy prepared billets in a cleared area not too near the battle. To our horror, however, we learned that General Browning fully intended to fly over by glider with the first lift, and to take charge of affairs by landing in the centre of the battlefield. He proposed to take with him a small tactical headquarters, in which would be most of the denizens of the Operations Room.

This news was depressing, for at this late stage of the war nearly all clerical men were Category—that is, unfit. Furthermore, few men about the Headquarters had seen much active service, and those who had were patently out of practice. I heard also that the G1 would probably remain behind to direct resupply, and that, of the two G2's who would go in his place, I would probably be responsible for the immediate defence of our gallant band of typewriters. It was proposed that our glider pilots would form a wider perimeter round us. This prospective responsibility was disturbing, for here was none of the *esprit* of a unit, and none of the time or facilities for training. There was also a certain interdepartmental jealousy, so that if one had occasion to speak crossly to a man the head of his department would ring up to castigate the officiousness of the G branch. Almost all the heads were brigadiers.

I went down to the Camp Commandant's office one day to have a good grumble with the Bombardier, Patrick Bush. Patrick was always in the midst of some crisis, but stayed unflurried with the calmness of a divinely inspired martyr at an *auto-da-fé*. He cleared his office and shouted for tea. As we drank I mentioned my fears for the safety of tactical headquarters.

"There were some new arrivals this morning," drawled

Patrick, in the voice of a man who is bravely carrying yet another burden. "Perhaps some of them can fire a rifle."

He pushed over a nominal roll, and I saw at once the name "Guardsman Longman, Bombardier Guards."

One has to be wary in dealings with either Adjutants or Camp Commandants, for they have found that the hand of every man is against them, and have developed a protective armour of negation. Nearly all visitors to their offices come only to present a petition which usually involves more work. It is best, therefore, to state a case with Oriental circumlocution. On this occasion Patrick himself made the opening.

"It's a pity Longman isn't a warrant-officer," he said. "My Company Sergeant-Major's leaving soon, and I'd like to replace him with another Guardsman."

Patrick's Company Sergeant-Major was a Bombardier. I offered to try to procure an Ironside warrant-officer for him. Patrick looked at me cannily, waiting to hear the *quid pro quo*. I told him that Longman was an old friend, and that I was tired of sharing a servant. At this Patrick sent for the new arrival, and in a few minutes the enormous ex-Sergeant Longman came into the office.

He recognized me with an impassive flicker. Longman told me that he had been taken ill during the time when Horsey and I had been away on the solitary trip to Tikjda, and had been invalided home as unfit to fly. As a result, he had lost his rank. With regret I offered to see him reinstated, but Longman declined, saying that he was quite happy as a Guardsman. What he meant was that he had all the opportunity to swing the lead, and none of the responsibility of stripes.

It does not pay a soldier to become sick or wounded in the service of his country, for he loses both rank and the pay it carries. It is better financially to stay in healthy and safe areas—or, best of all, to remain a civilian.

I felt happier comforted by the massive presence of Longman, though he reminded me so much of the unregenerate days with Rory's Squadron that the Operations

Room with its telephones became intolerable. However, others were also a little concerned about the combatant readiness of the Corps's tactical headquarters, and I wrote for the BGS a memorandum on training, all in the best Staff College style, with abbreviations. The plan was agreed to, and three battle courses, each of a fortnight, were arranged. The heads of departments, however, nearly sabotaged the scheme when they learned that we proposed to work, not on the near-by golf-links, but on the Derbyshire end of the Pennines, for they wanted their men on call.

Regimental Headquarters, Ironside Guards, always kind to their extra-regimentally employed, had been helpful about Patrick Bush's new right-hand man, and sent an iron-grey warrant officer, solid as a slab of granite, named Company Sergeant-Major Obelisk. The Company Sergeant-Major, though obviously fearing no man, came in to see me before facing the unknown hazards of life under a Bombardier. We went along together to see Patrick Bush, and the two of them made friends at once, true to the Guardsmen's freemasonry.

In Derbyshire little had changed since the visits of 'A' Troop nearly two years before. Again the little inn was put at our disposal, and we began work at once.

Corps Headquarters had been so concerned with bigger issues that it had perhaps overlooked the fact that many of its personnel, though bright at clerking, were rusty from disuse as soldiers. Many times great projects have faltered and died through failure of the lowly human element.

We started with simple battle-drill at section level. The students were intelligent, and speedily found an interest in minor tactics, and in the art of out-manœuvring an enemy while minimizing their own risk. At the end of the first week they were proficient on a platoon basis. We then ventured further, and spent our days travelling fully laden at high speed about the slopes of Kinderscout, where, contrary to all laws, we practised field firing until the gullies and crags echoed. It was easy to forget that so many of the men were Category, and at first it was a little hard on the halt and the lame, but in the hills, breathing the invigorating air, the cripples themselves forgot their ailments and confounded the Medical Boards by ending the course as agile as young goats.

At intervals during the three courses we had cryptic messages from Corps to be ready to return at short notice, but the final summons never came, and the scheme was completed in full.

On our return events on the Continent were compelling, and plans at Corps Headquarters were discarded almost as soon as begun. The Sixth Airborne, who had dropped in a high wind the night before the morning of D-Day to seize the crossings of the river Orne, and thereafter to hold the left flank of the bridgehead, were now streaming vengefully northward to settle a score three months long. At home the First Airborne was straining for action, spurred by the news of the Sixth Division's notable exploits.

The armour came to the fore. The river Seine was crossed, Paris freed, and the Belgian frontier reached and passed, until, on September 3, the fifth anniversary of the declaration of war on Germany, the tanks of the Guards Armoured Division clattered into Brussels. A week later the Irish Guards, by an unorthodox tank charge which must have shocked the correct Germans, captured a bridge over the Escaut canal, and our forward troops were poised on the border of Holland. To achieve this lightning advance, and to continue, it was hoped, through Holland into Germany itself, 30 Corps, under General Horrocks, had been streamlined for a self-contained thrust into the blue. The Corps comprised the Guards Armoured Division and the 43rd and 50th Divisions.

There were now three hurdles left before the winning-post, the rivers Maas, Waal, and Lower Rhine. With these behind, and the strong defences about them destroyed, the Siegfried Line was turned and the route into Germany lay through attackers' country.

Here lay the premises for a bold decision. It was not, perhaps, necessary to force these river-crossings one by one according to the laborious text-book. Montgomery made a different plan—a perfectly sound plan, but one, just the same, which had somewhere in it an unexpected touch of the gambler. He decided to lay down a carpet of red berets to ease the passage of the tracks and wheels of 30 Corps. In the plan's final form the thickness of the Airborne carpet was fortunately much increased, so that two of the three objectives were handed to the American 82nd and 101st Airborne Divisions, while the British First Airborne was detailed to the farthest goal of all, the Lower Rhine at Arnhem. The whole of this very considerable force was put under command of General "Boy" Browning, the first commander of our own original Airborne Division, and now the commander of our own Airborne Corps.

This, then, was the seventeenth plan since June 6th, D-Day. Most of us necessarily knew the plan in outline, as we had known the earlier discarded projects, and as departments were affected they knew at any rate some detail. Yet no one seemed to go about his business like a man weighted with the secrets of destiny, and the security of his knowledge was guarded in common talk as if unconsciously. This effortless care may well have been the result of years of training to guard against the loose word, for surprise is the deadliest weapon in the light armoury of the Airborne soldier, and, from the first struggling beginnings at Bulford, security had been a watchword.

In early September 1944, almost to a day twelve months after Rory O'Brien's invasion of Italy, I was sent down to Harwell airfield to prepare for take-off.

From the nature of their purpose, airfields are bleak, windswept places, for shelter to the man is obstruction to the flying-machine. Harwell conformed to the general rule, and the transit camp outside the perimeter was a tented field comfortless to living creatures.

There are many factors to be reconciled before an Airborne operation may be mounted with confidence. Few are under control of the men most concerned, for they include such matters as the availability of aircraft for transport, escort, and resupply, and the descent at the right time and place into the always uncompleted jigsaw of the ground plan. The factor of the weather is under no one's control. Because of these imponderables an Airborne operation may be long delayed, the nerves of the participants not being improved by the procrastination.

In this present case the specially formed 38 and 46 Groups of the Royal Air Force were ours to use, but, as to the ground plan, so fluid was the situation that not even the men on the spot could dare to forecast their future. Although we humbler men fretting about the airfields of Britain did not know it, we were awaiting the day when 30 Corps was at the borders of Holland, the Guards Armoured Division crouched at its head like a compressed steel spring, so that as our force dropped from the sky to seize the crossings of the Maas, Waal, and Lower Rhine, they might at one stroke carve their way through sixty miles of German-held country to relieve us and exploit our gains. Beyond Arnhem, aided by surprise, the way lay clear into the industrial Ruhr and North Germany. All of us knew that if we gained full success the next Christmas might indeed usher in a season of peace—and even some goodwill.

Mid-September drew close, and we were briefed party by party in a Nissen hut. Thereafter the hut was left open to enable all who wished to study the air-photos and models of the ground on which we were to land and fight. But after the briefing none could leave the barbed-wire confines of the camp, except in escorted parties on to the airfield to load the Horsa gliders with our jeeps, trailers, and motor-cycles, and the other impedimenta of a Corps Headquarters going to war as never before.

Loading ramps were placed opposite the wide side-doors of the Horsas. Up these we drove our laden jeeps, manhandled them round the acute corner into the fuselage, pulled up the trailers and the motor-cycles, and chained the lot to strong points in the floor. It is essential to balance the load most carefully in a glider, for the craft is uncontrollable if it is nose or tail-heavy, and so there is a chart for every variety of load, so that its components may be lashed to the appropriately numbered strong point.

Once the loads were in each glider party practised ditching drill in case of a watery descent into the English Channel, for, though we did not expect risk of attack so near home, tow-ropes might well snap if the air were bumpy or the piloting unskilful. The drill was simple. We seized a red-hafted axe from its clips beside the main door, and went through the motions of smashing a plywood panel in the roof. Next each glider, according to its load, worked out the distribution of passengers to seats, and adjusted the safety-belts to fit the variety of shapes and sizes. In the case of each craft it was essential to detail at least a couple of men to ride in the tail of the craft, for once the jeeps and trailers were in, the centre of the fuselage was blocked except to contortionists.

These rear passengers, whose position would render them air-sick, had a most important job. Obviously, unloading facilities would not be awaiting us in Holland, and it was necessary to drive our vehicles out of the back of the glider. To achieve this, the tail of the Mark I Horsa was detachable. To remove it the men at the rear had cutters to snip the control-wires, and spanners to loose the eight bolts which held the massive tail. The sequence of action was to cut the wires, then, one man to each side of the tail, to undo completely three of the four bolts on either side, leaving the fourth held by one thread. Then simultaneously the pair would give a last turn to their remaining bolts, whereupon the tail would drop off. If, however, one man was behindhand in this final unloosening one side of the tail would drop, and the other would remain held to the fuselage by a twisted and distorted bolt which no coercion would affect.

Assuming the tail correctly off, and dragged clear of the opening, there were two light metal troughs to be laid from the hole in the fuselage to the ground, and down these gangways we proposed to run the wheels of our vehicles.

There was a school of thought which, from the stimulating surroundings of the Mess bar, favoured a commencement of this unscrewing during the final glide to land. Most of us were unenthusiastic about this innovation, and preferred to linger a little longer in our vulnerable glider on the ground, rather than to have some excited soldier get to work with his wire-cutters while we were aloft.

This more general drill settled, each party was now concerned with itself only. Of the Harwell flight, General Browning was to take off first, followed by the BGS in Number Two, myself in Number Three, and thirty-odd other tug-glider combinations on our tails. We in Number Three—and I do not think we were unique—took pains to cultivate the goodwill of our two glider pilots, a very young subaltern and a sergeant. I do not know what return we expected from this, but there must have been some illogical idea that we would be landed more safely if they liked us. It did not occur to us that they would, in any event, be unlikely to crash the glider with themselves in it out of spite. We really need not have worried, for our two conductors were typical of the quality of the Glider Pilot Regiment—pleasant, capable, and unflurried.

There were eleven of us to travel in Number Three, including the two pilots. We detailed the G3 Intelligence and his sergeant to be sick in the tail seats, for we felt that by reason of their corps they would have the sense not to monkey with the fastenings until we had reached earth again. The two glider pilots had their own little perspex cabin in the nose, and the remaining seven of us sat facing one another on benches along either side behind the cabin and in front of the jeep. In the event of a heavy landing, we were apprehensive that the jeep would free itself and run over us, and I, in addition to this road-hazard, had in front of me the gear of the front tricycle wheel, which in adverse circumstances had been known to come through the floor and geld the nearest passenger.

On landing there was nothing that we people at the forward end could do to help with the tail, so we practised a speedy exit through the main door and the taking up of a defensive perimeter about the craft.

Throughout these manœuvres the stalwart and imperturbable Longman had ever been beside me to offer cups of tea. During our glider drills I noticed him in the seat beside me carefully adjusting the safety-belt to his big frame, and as we hustled out to lie prone about the craft he was again near by, a Bren in one hand, a Sten in the other. This sort of ghostly manifestation of a man who could only be with us in spirit got on my nerves. In the end I said, "Longman! you know you're not allowed to fly. I want you to take my kit back when we've left——"

"I've kept a place in the trailer for your camp-bed and the small tent, sir," answered Longman, in a patient and soothing voice. "You'll be more comfortable if you have them with you. I understand that there is a good weight-margin allowed for in the loading tables."

"But look here!" I protested. "What about your ear-drums?"

"That will be all right, sir," said Longman, as a family butler to the young master. "We've been briefed to fly in at only 2500 feet, sir."

That the day was at hand was patent when a Field Cashier appeared to distribute to us waterproof escape packets of assorted currencies. A total of £10 was considered enough for this exploit. I noticed that our French francs were issued by the Bank of France. I had in my wallet a thousand-franc note with which I had been left in Africa on the day when Bank of France notes became invalid, and were superseded by Algerian currency. After much argument I persuaded the cashier to change this into English pounds, and felt thereafter that the expedition was to be under favourable auspices.

In the afternoon of that day, the 16th of September, the rest of our little tactical headquarters came down to Harwell, and it became known that the morrow was the day.

Five hundred miles away, poised on the Dutch-Belgian border, 30 Corps was massed to crash for sixty miles across Holland to join us at Grave, Nijmegen, and Arnhem. As their hardened spear-tip, the Guards Armoured Division was crowded nose to tail ready to burst out of the hard-won bridge-head beyond the Escaut Canal. In the rear, squadrons of rocket-firing Typhoons crouched in close support.

At home men of the American 82nd and 101st Airborne Divisions, the Polish Parachute Brigade, and our own First Airborne were making their last preparations on the airfields of eastern England, and their own pilots and the pilots of the fighter escort were being briefed.

This great operation, planned to be carried out in daylight, could not equip itself with enough tug and parachute aircraft to take the whole force in one lift. We were to fly in low over hostile ground studded with the flak positions which guarded the bomber route into Germany. Therefore slow planes, and planes without self-sealing petrol tanks, were unsuitable. The airfield ground-staffs stood by to service and patch up the returning machines from the first wave, so that the rest of the force could be dropped next day by surviving aircraft.

The air Armada was to concentrate above the bulging Norfolk coast, then to fly in a long column with both high and low fighter cover across the width of the English Channel towards the Dutch islands. We should pass over flooded Walcheren, and near another island named misfortunately Overflak. We memorized the position of the larger towns lest we should make a premature descent, and then each of us studied the photographs of our own glider's particular landing-zone. A couple of miles to the east of ours lay the sinister dark line of the Reichwald Forest, which was within the German border. We should turn above the Reichwald, cut loose from our tug, and descend as if from Germany into a field of clear triangular shape, bounded by two converging roads. A mile or so to the north was the black blob of a moderate-sized wood in which we were to rendezvous with our companions.

There was no more to be done. Mindful of my cashed thousand-franc note, I went across that evening to the Royal Air Force mess, intent upon a drink and the purchase of a stock of tobacco. For I remembered my unhappiness in Italy when an ill-meant shell destroyed the trailer which held my store. The Mess was very gay, with an exhilaration which cannot be absorbed from a bottle, and the comradeship and *esprit* generated on the eve of a great adventure would have uplifted the veriest coward.

I asked the PMC about some tobacco. He offered to get me some, and returned with an ounce or two. I explained, with some diffidence, that I had hoped to buy a pound or more. As he demurred a little, thinking rightly that this was an inroad on his stock, a pilot's voice spoke up.

"Go on!" it said. "Give it him. Remember he's got to stay over there."

This appreciation of the soldier's lot was not always forthcoming in inter-Services relationships.

Sunday, the 17th, dawned fair. At eleven o'clock we moved over to the airfield, and the force split into groups, each about their own glider. Some one had chalked on the door of Number Three "Top Secret! To be opened personally by G2 Ops."

A sacrilegious hand had scored out "G2 Ops" and substituted "Saint Peter."

British humour can be very trying. I eyed Longman, but his face had closed down like a visor.

Some Medical Officer somewhere had once given me a little round tin in which were five capsules. These were said to be an antidote to fear, but to impair the faculties not at all. I looked at the tin, wondering, for any questions I had ever asked about the capsules were always brushed aside with a furtive air as if they were not jujubes but ju-ju. Presently, when I was chatting to the General's pilot, I bethought me of trying one on some one else, and proffered the tin hospitably. But the pilot, who seemed to have heard of these confections, shied sharply away, and stated firmly that with his important cargo he would not risk sudden paralysis. As a make-weight, he added that he understood the taker of such pills, while possibly impervious to nerves, must not for forty-eight hours partake of women or alcohol.

In the end I gave a pill to Longman and swallowed another myself. Thus fortified, we emplaned.

The door slid to. In the tube-like fuselage we forward passengers strapped ourselves in and sat looking at our opposites like strangers on the Underground. Longman produced a Penguin book and began to read. In the perspex nose of the Horsa the two glider pilots played about with all their little levers, and looked so happy that I, who always feel that aircraft fly literally in the face of Providence, tried hard to think of some sobering remark to make. No inspiration came, but instead a roar from down the tarmac mounted above the idling four engines of our own Stirling tug, and we knew that Number One was away with the General. Immediately Number Two took up the running, and in the wake of its noise our tug gave deafening pursuit. Strapped impotently, pulled remorselessly by a force we could not see, we sped across the airfield, the Horsa rattling and creaking. Of a sudden the earthy sounds died, and instead was the swishing of air past our sides.

I undid my safety-belt and glanced at Longman. He was utterly immersed in his book, following the lines with his great forefinger.

CHAPTER XII

HOLLAND

A LITTLE after midday we were above Norfolk, where we circled awhile to await the converging streams of air-traffic. The morning was one of sunshine and shadow, and the outlines of the white cumulus clouds drifted black across the fields below. We were not too high to see people on the roads and in the gardens, perhaps strolling home from church, or idly attending the pleasure of their Sunday joint. It was a day of peace and death.

To the north, in Lincolnshire, Tessa and the baby Louise were staying with friends, and I was glad they were not alone in the house in Chelsea. Tessa would wonder why my letters had stopped coming this last week or two, and when lack of word continued would construe uncertainty into worry as rumour took the place of news.

Presently our great flying column turned purposefully across the sea. At about this time Major Boy Wilson with his 21st Independent Parachute Company was drifting down into the quiet country west of Arnhem to lay out markers for the main drop of First Airborne. Word had reached 30 Corps that the operation was begun, and the pent-up power within the Escaut bridgehead had burst its restraint, and, behind a curtain laid by the Corps artillery, was fighting forward through difficult country and against stern resistance to enter Holland during the middle of the afternoon.

I stood up, and through the pilot's cabin saw diminutive white horses flickering on the sea below. Gliding down towards them was a Horsa, its tow-rope broken. I never saw it hit the sea, and watched instead the swarms of fighter planes returning in relays to rearm to strafe again the German flak positions along our route, and the route of those to follow. Unseen above us at 20,000 feet was the high fighter cover, and visible on either side were the tug-glider combinations of our group, rising and falling lazily in juxtaposition.

In the fuselage most of the passengers were asleep, or at least comatose, lulled by the swelling and dying, swelling and dying of the wind which rushed along our sides.

One of the pilots spoke over his shoulder and pointed ahead, where a hazy smudge grew momentarily into sharper focus till we saw clearly the Dutch coast. We were dead on course, and the islands lay like enlargements of the maps which we had all so closely studied. Once over the mainland, much flooded, we saw here and there pillars of black smoke which told of the attention of our fighters to the German flak posts. More than once we caught a glimpse of wheeling planes, buzzing about some hostile spot like angry bees. Their work had been well done, for only a thin sprinkling of bursts studded the air about our ponderous, slow-moving column. The pilots became more tense as we neared the end of our journey, and peered intently at the ground to pick up visually their exact position from memorized land-marks. When a glider cuts loose down it must go to a fair landing-place, for there is no engine to help the pilot should he change his mind about his destination.

For a few minutes I was lost, and then way ahead showed the long, straight, dark line which was the fringe of the Reichwald Forest and Germany. I lost sight of the forest as we turned for the run-in. The pilots were completely absorbed, ready to release the tow-rope as the tug brought them into position to reach their landing-zone. Of a sudden the craft jerked. The rush of wind along our sides eased to a whisper, as when a car free-wheels. The nose went sharply down, and I had a glimpse of our unmistakable triangular field, clear so far as I could see of obstructions. The subaltern pilot turned and grinned, gave the thumbs-up, said, "Safety-belt!" And became oblivious to everything save his controls.

I sat down, shouted to the others, and we began to strap

ourselves in. Longman remained asleep till I nudged him.

"We're there!" I said.

"Very good, sir!" he answered, and, before seeing to his belt, retrieved his book from the floor, dog-eared his page, and put the volume in a pocket of his Airborne smock.

The acute angle of the floor levelled. There was a clatter as we touched ground and bounced a little, then, as we settled finally, a continuous creaking and straining of wood and metal while we ran across the field, decelerating from about seventy miles an hour. We seemed to run a long way, our nerves strained as they were to anticipate a crash, before flaps and brakes took sudden effect to stop us with a jolt. Now was the moment for us to discover the real quality of our landing-ground, unpredictable from maps and photographs. And while we struggled a moment with the strained door, the outside world invisible, we wondered whether bullets would whip through our plywood screen or await us without.

The door opened with a wrench, and we sprang out to take up the prearranged positions about our craft. Farther away was sporadic small-arms fire which told of the American 82nd Airborne, who had landed a little ahead of us to secure ground for the resupply drops, and to fight their way to the great road and rail bridges across the river Waal at Nijmegen. Our immediate neighbourhood was quiet, but in that flat country we felt very exposed, and as yet vulnerable, and we were indeed a sitting target for land or air attack. I hurried round to the tail, anxious to see our gear unloaded, and within heard our Intelligence couple swearing like troopers as they worked their spanners in the confined space. Of a sudden there was a shout of blasphemy and pornography as they failed to synchronize the loosing of the last two bolts, and one side of the tail swung down, leaving the other fast to the fuselage, and the opening blocked.

We called for all hands to tear the tail loose and drag it aside, but, heave as we would, we failed. I was determined not to leave our jeep, and was relieved to see Longman run over to the hedge and return marching five apprehensive Germans before him. In the rear came a tall, shambling Dutch farmer, a sporting gun, rusty from hiding, under one arm, a bucket of apples in his hand, and a broad sash of orange worn bandoleer fashion, creased after secretion—probably under his mattress.

After much straining our international efforts succeeded, and the tail was pulled clear. While the unloading went on I checked from the map the route to the woodland rendezvous, a couple of miles away, then looked about to see how the rest of the force was faring. Belated gliders still came rustling and whispering down, and one, landing too far up the field, used a haystack at the end for a buffer. We sent our prisoners over to help, for the craft looked a little bent.

Within ten minutes we were away. The two Intelligence people were on their motor-cycles; the rest of us, nine in all, clung to the jeep and trailer. I drove out of the field into a minor road, and to the east, across a dead flat common, was the Reichwald about a mile away, its sombre shadows, bewitched as a scene from Grimm, concealing we knew not what. I learned that the General's immediate party had just gone ahead, and we waited a few minutes to collect the jeeps into a party. I felt as exposed as a man in one of those dreams where he finds himself walking unclothed in plain daylight in a populous place, for we were in clear view of Germany, for miles in other directions also, and from the air. The organization of a headquarters, excellent for office work, did not lend itself to quick military dispositions, and, without waiting for the last few stragglers, I got the majority of the party on the move.

A belated Signals officer roared past on a motor-cycle, anxious to get the General's communications working. Ahead of him, in full view across the road, the Americans had laid a string of mines, no doubt as a temporary anti-tank protection while they collected themselves after their drop. The Signals officer in his eagerness rode straight over one. A leg was blown off. We gave him a cigarette, and carried him into a house near by. He had a tickle between his shoulder-blades, and kept asking us to scratch it for him. We moved the mines, and within a few minutes turned up the track into a fairly thick wood, and found the nucleus of the headquarters.

It was a strange night we spent in the woods. To most of us the fog of war was impenetrable, and even the General and the BGS from their lofty altitude could only see the main features of the battle. Crumbs of news were dropped, and eagerly picked up. To the north, fifteen miles away, the first lift of the British First Airborne had come in west of Arnhem. The First Parachute Brigade had moved off in good order to seize and hold the bridge over the Lower Rhine. Behind them the Air Landing Brigade, glider-borne, had secured the landing-zones for the second lift and resupply next day. But wireless communication was not good, and few details reached us.

The 82nd American Airborne, in whose territory we ourselves were, were probing defensively towards the ominous Reichwald Forest, and offensively against fanatical resistance towards Nijmegen and its great road and rail bridges, four miles off, over the river Waal. Farther south still, it was believed that the 101st American Airborne had taken the bridge over the Maas, and were struggling to secure the route for advancing 30 Corps between Eindhoven and Grave. The Guards Armoured Division, leading the Corps, had fought against furious resistance to a point south of Eindhoven some ten miles from the American 101st. Meanwhile 8 Corps, who were to flank 30 Corps, had been and continued to be held up, and as a result 30 Corps were to be for the next vital days out ahead on their own with both flanks to defend, and the long lines of communication constantly cut by the thoroughly aroused Germans.

War is a selfish occupation, and most of us were concerned with our domestic arrangements. When very senior officers are personally conducting a battle from the midst of the fighting, themselves embroiled with the phonetic alphabet, codes, and radio procedure, there is little staff work for the juniors. Accordingly, I took a hand in the defence of our gipsy band. It was a thankless task. I located our glider-pilots, now formed into small platoons of ground troops, and strove to thicken their thin perimeter with some of our own spare men. But it was ever the same.

"Beg pardon, sir. I'm Colonel So-and-so's servant, sir. 'E told me to wait 'ere."

Once I saw a bonfire flaring into the night, as if it were to be a rallying-point for Germans.

"Put that bloody fire out!" I yelled.

But a resentful voice came back: "I'm cooking the Brigadier's 'ash, sir!"

I reckoned he might be.

Presently I saw that Longman had lit a small fire screened between our jeep trailer and a huge tree, and that some brew was cooking. By now I had been defeated by the passive resistance of our force, and ate Longman's concoction without comment. He then got out my sleeping-bag, and I loosened the laces of my boots and went to sleep.

At dawn our immediate plans were still obscure. I went off to gossip with Patrick Bush, and was in time to see him return from a walk with two prisoners. He was as plaintive as ever.

"Oh, dear!" he grumbled. "There's nowhere to send them, so I suppose they'll eat all my food."

During the morning the Germans issued forth from the Reichwald, played the hooligan about our abandoned gliders, and mortared our wood in a half-hearted sort of way.

At Arnhem the day was sterner. The 2nd Parachute Battalion had reached the town to find the rail bridge blown, and had pushed on to seize the northern end of the road bridge. Resistance had been stronger than was expected, and their numbers were already depleted. So swift was the German reaction that the remainder of the 1st Parachute Brigade were bogged down in a series of stiffening actions on their way to form a wider perimeter about the bridge. In the early afternoon the second lift came in, but these units too were committed to battle even as they landed, and our force ceased to dictate the course of events.

However, the Airborne task was done as had been commanded. It was now to be seen whether 30 Corps, then embroiled heavily round Eindhoven, and harassed surprisingly by heavy air attack, could cut their way through to Nijmegen, whose bridge was still untaken, and fight on across the island—

that is, the land between the Waal and the Lower Rhine—to Arnhem.

As we pondered our headquarters moved, still wondering, to a wood nearer Nijmegen. I was again without much to do, and asked the BGS if I might go and seek more transport to ease the work of our overloaded jeeps. He thought this a good idea. Longman and I drove through woodland tracks westward towards the open country through which the Guards Armoured were expected. We came to a railway line on which stood a derelict train, air-strafed. Germans lay dead about it, their loot of carpets, furniture, refrigerators, and even old clothes, unregarded within the box cars. On the fringe of the woods was the command post of one of the battalions of the 82nd Division, and squatting in the ditch beside it a number of prisoners awaiting disposal. Trailing past in the direction of the firing near by came some American parachutists. One of the Germans jumped up, and in good American cried to a lieutenant, "I been to the U.S.A.! I got a grandma in Milwaukee!"

The lieutenant glanced at him coldly, shifted his gum, and hit him a back-handed flip with his hand which knocked the ingratiating one arse over tip back into his ditch.

"Shurrup! You son of a bitch!" said the lieutenant without emotion.

There was no softness about the American Airborne men.

Longman and I came to open country, and reached the village of Malden, four miles south of Nijmegen. Armed bands of Dutchmen, their only uniform insignia of Orange, seemed in control, and were active in marshalling other Dutchmen or semi-Dutchmen whose record with the Germans had been friendly. We were the first British soldiers that the village had seen, and were received with a volubility not native to the staid Hollander, but as to the libations of wine and offerings of food, their absence was excused. The Dutch were on the edge of starvation, the penalty for the uncollaborative attitude which the nation as a whole had shown to Germany. The pathetic only gifts were apples, and I saw Longman passing these on covertly to the children.

The Burgomaster was in his office, holding a durbar with a changing stream of resistance men. He could give little help about transport, since the Germans had long since made away with all cars. As I went out I was followed by a youth wearing an orange armband. In good English, he told me that he knew of a car or two, for collaborationists had not been mulcted as were the rest. Outside my new acquaintance told me that his name was Jan, and from the crowd about the jeep called forth another youth, his brother.

We all of us drove to the Nijmegen end of the village, and there dismounted by some large houses in fine gardens. The Americans were fighting a small-arms battle. The Dutch boys were not perturbed, and took Longman off by covered ways. Behind a stone garden wall I found an American captain, and as representative of the elder, if not senior, branch of the Anglo-American family, asked kindly if all was well, and if I could help. The captain, before attending to me, gave some colloquial and unmilitary directions to an unidentifiable conglomeration of G.I.'s who filed unexcitedly away to line a hedge. As soon as he heard the deliberate firing of their carbines, the captain, a single-minded man, turned to me.

As so often happened, my ally was on another wave-band. Had he been British he would have welcomed me into the party as a rural sportsman gives a place to a strange but kindred spirit who comes upon him when ferreting. But now, somehow, our language was different in its intent.

"What was it you wanted?" he asked.

I said, with heavy levity and no originality, that I had only wondered if the battle was private or open to all-comers. The American weighed up this query very seriously, and finally said that he could not take responsibility of giving a job to a major, but that I could see the colonel back at the Command Post. By now the episode was as flat as a dilatory soufflé, and I disembarrassed our puzzled ally by following Longman.

Longman and the boys were in the house of a man whom they described as a Dutch Nazi. He was a middle-aged man with an important figure, a watch-chain, and multi-coloured shoes. The furnishings spoke of wealth, and the larder to which the Dutch boys led me was stocked in a manner possible only for a collaborator. A door from the hall led into a built-on garage, where a fine pale blue 1939 Studebaker was resting on wooden blocks, its wheels missing.

I told the owner that I proposed to requisition the car. He protested that it had not been on the road for four years, and that the Germans had taken the wheels and battery. The boys thereupon stated flatly that only two days before he had driven to Nijmegen to lunch with the Germans. The older man let this pass unchallenged, but reaffirmed that the Germans had the missing bits.

"I'll have a look round, sir," said Longman to me, "while the lads take you off to look at some more cars."

I went off—as I was meant to—and my guides, whom I now called Luke and John, found me three more cars in running order, two of them abandoned by the Germans, equipment still in them. We collected the cars in a sheltered lane, and I left Luke and John to watch them while I went to fetch Longman. I found him in the collaborator's garage fitting the last of the wheels.

"He had 'em down a well, sir," explained Longman. "But I can't no-how make him remember where he hid the battery. Reckon he's telling the truth about that. I'll have to leave the car for now, sir, but I'll get a battery somewhere and come back for it."

Our transport was much appreciated back in the wood. I gained a reputation for selflessness by declining to exercise finder's rights by keeping a car for myself. I explained that the need of others was greater, but that I would retain the next one I found. I relied confidently on Longman's prowess to provide a battery for the splendid Studebaker.

The situation round the wood in which we spent the second night was most confused. Odd parties of Americans and Germans stumbled about in the darkness, but our force of clerks by the grace of God was not molested. I am sure they regarded the training which they had had in Derbyshire, and the precautions which were urged on them in Holland, as the actions of a scaremonger. Yet the immunity which they had so far had was heavily against all probabilities.

I began to wish an odd German patrol would tumble over one of their typewriters, to remove the rather smug 'so this is the war they make so much fuss about' expression.

On the morning of the 19th word came that the Guards Armoured Division had passed through the territory of the 101st American Airborne, north of Eindhoven, and would soon be in touch with our own comrades, the 82nd, at Grave. General Boy Browning, with a small bodyguard, went off through the uncleared countryside in a jeep to meet them, and to make with them a quick plan to take Nijmegen bridge, so that help could get to Arnhem. Here such scraps of news as there were had an ominous ring to them.

The 2nd Parachute Battalion still defied all comers—infantry, artillery, tanks, and self-propelled guns—at the north end of the Arnhem road bridge. Few reinforcements had been able to fight through to them, and attempts to do so were leading to virtual annihilation of those taking part. To add local colour, if any were needed, it was somehow learned that Rory O'Brien had driven up to the bridge in his jeep, and was doubtless hurling defiance at the Germans.

Meanwhile the remnants of the rest of the Division were hemmed in, and were slowly being compressed into a pocket which the Germans were searching constantly with an increasing intensity of fire. The much-needed arrival of the Polish Parachute Brigade was still delayed, for the dropping-zone first planned just south of the bridge was not now secure. Furthermore, events had moved so quickly for the worse, and wireless communication between the 1st Airborne and ourselves was so erratic, that when the prearranged supply dropping-point fell into enemy hands the news was not received for some time. The resupply lift flew with the utmost resolution at the necessary low altitude through a storm of flak, many of the planes holding their course while burning, in order to drop their containers into hostile hands.

At Nijmegen, too, the German strength and speed of reaction had been surprising. The American 82nd Airborne, holding the great bridge over the Maas at Grave, and fighting off counter-attacks against both flanks of our narrow corridor, had not the strength left to do more than maintain a foothold in the outskirts of Nijmegen. And although the Guards tanks had rumbled over the Grave bridge on their way to join us, heavy fighting had broken out behind them, and they were, as our allies would have said, out on a limb.

Towards midday I asked the BGS whether I might go again to Malden, and this time Patrick Bush came too. We took food with us, wrapped in an English newspaper, and sat upon a stone coping beside the road as we heard the clatter of tank tracks nearing us. We spread Patrick's clean white handkerchief upon the wall, and on it laid our meagre lunch, supported by two bottles of lager. When the tanks came in sight we began to read each a piece of newspaper.

The cavalcade was impressive to the point of raising a lump in the throat. The tanks, travelling fast, had fought clear across three countries with little respite, and about them hung the apanage of war. They had battled sixty miles in the last two days to join up with the Airborne islands with no count of cost, and had the air of a crusade.

We felt that Grave was ours, Nijmegen soon would be with the aid of these steadfast soldiers, and after that Arnhem. Beyond the way lay clear into the North German Plain, and the prize for a break-through was Peace.

Patrick and I received startled stares from the leading Guardsmen, which changed to cheerful, if puzzled, salutations. A Staff car drew up for a moment, its roof rack laden with tank ammunition.

"What the hell are you doing here?" yelled a voice at Patrick, with the civility demanded from one Bombardier to another.

Patrick lowered his newspaper to reply with equal courtesy, in his high-pitched drawl, "Waiting for you idle, dozy people. Get along with you now to Nijmegen bridge."

The Division streamed past in all its pride and power, and we noticed that by a bold stroke medium artillery appeared early in its order of battle. Presently the units began to deploy as the leading squadrons came to a halt on the fringe of Nijmegen.

Longman appeared from the Studebaker's garage, and strolled over to a halted workshop unit, where he was well received by the Guardsmen's freemasonry. After he had drunk a large pannikin of tea I saw him return across the road carrying a battery. A few minutes later, evidently meeting with some technical difficulty, he whistled a couple of fitters over to the garage. Quite soon he came out looking pleased, and said to me: "Your car's all right now, sir. Best leave it where it is for the night until all these sharks have cleared off."

Back in our wood, we made a landing-strip in an open space, and before dark an Auster flew up the narrow corridor, looked at our handiwork, circled and looked again, then landed. This was our first physical contact with Headquarters 2nd Army, the superior formation of 30 Corps.

During the afternoon a combined Guards and Airborne attack was launched at the bridge, pressed all the more fiercely because of the hard scraps of news from Arnhem. But the thrust was blunted among the houses, and, despite the utmost determination, could make little headway.

After dark I went forward to the town. The night was black, but the streets were lit by the flames of burning buildings and the flash of gunfire. We were struggling to retain our foothold among the buildings, and the Germans were restlessly probing to loosen the foothold. From a shadowed doorway beside a garage, I was hailed in English. I peered within, a little nervy, for this was a strange night. A man showed an orange armband and said, "You are welcome. Please to take a drink with my family."

I followed up a stairway into a flat above the garage showroom, and met my host's wife, a daughter of about fourteen, and a son a couple of years older. In a few minutes the man put out two bottles of Pol Roger, and we drank, Continental fashion, a series of toasts until the champagne was gone.

"We hid those bottles against this day," said the wife.

She produced a photograph, and went on "My husband

has recently returned after six months' arrest by the Germans. This was how he looked before he was taken away."

There was little similarity between the full-faced, jovial man of the picture and my cadaverous host.

"They used to lock me in a room with a police dog, and watch me through a glass panel while I defended myself," he explained.

I believe he spoke the truth.

I made my way back to the wood in a strange state of melancholy. This campaign where I was present, but in which I had as yet little part, was weighing upon me. I missed intolerably the company of unit soldiers, where the minuses of individual fears add up to the plus of good courage. Certainly with no envy of their position, nevertheless I felt something of a renegade to be away from First Airborne, two rivers away. It was with these men that I had grown to military maturity, and imagination was able to picture them intimately and personally in their fight.

Throughout the next morning, the 20th of September, the tanks of the Irish Guards worked forward through the town, and by lunch-time commanded a stretch of the south bank of the Waal. Immediately that fine soldier General Gavin made ready a combat team from his 82nd Airborne, and, borrowing assault boats from the Guards, the Americans stormed across the wide, swift river and clawed a foothold on the opposite bank. These troops could ill be spared, for a heavy counter-attack had developed from the Reichwald. With a determination not surpassed during the War, the Americans broke out of their small lodgment, and against furious resistance fought their way to the north end of the rail bridge. The tanks then took the south end, and communication was made across the river.

At once the Bombardiers were ordered to rush the great road bridge, and to cross regardless of cost. The bridge was nearly a quarter of a mile long, with an equal length of high embankment at the far end off which tanks could not deploy. The whole stretch was covered at point-blank range by 88-mm. guns and by panzerfausts. By sheer dash sufficient tanks got over to secure the crossing, and to join up with the Americans on the rail bridge. From out of the chambers in the abutments of the huge structure about seventy Germans were captured, whose job it was to detonate the heavy charges which could have wrecked the bridge. It has never become known why they failed in their duty.

There was now but the Lower Rhine between the relieving forces and the men of the First Airborne at Arnhem. At Arnhem bridge Lieutenant-Colonel Frost, of the 2nd Parachute Battalion, had been badly wounded, and Rory O'Brien was in command. Few of the Airborne men were unwounded; food and ammunition were nearly gone. The houses from which they had denied the Germans recapture of the bridge had been burned down over them, and they fought on from slit-trenches scratched in the gardens, and from beneath the bridge itself. German tanks were able to stand off in the open and shell the defenders at will. Presently, still fighting, the remnant was literally overrun.

The rest of the Division, in little better case, was now hemmed in at Hartestein, six miles to the west. The Germans had taken the measure of the operation, and had ringed the Airborne perimeter with tanks, self-propelled guns, artillery, and mortars. The survivors of the great Division lived in holes in the ground, thirsty, hungry, and under a rain of explosives. To combat fear and the lethargy of exhaustion, they took refuge in aggression, and like men uplifted stalked and destroyed the machines of war arrayed against them, lightly armed though they were.

On the following day, the 21st, our tanks tried to crash their way through to the Lower Rhine, but the Island was impassable to vehicles if an enemy wished to deny the passage. The roads ran along embankments, surrounded by marsh, and it was impossible to deploy to outmanœuvre the enemy anti-tank guns. During the afternoon the Polish Parachute Brigade was dropped at Driel, close to the south bank of the Lower Rhine, and opposite the remains of the First Airborne, still fighting off all attacks in their woods across the river.

It became obvious that another plan must be made to relieve

the Airborne men, and accordingly 30 Corps passed the infantry of the 43rd Wessex Division through the tanks, and, preceded by patrols of the Household Cavalry in armoured cars, a junction was made with the Poles on the 22nd.

The situation was confused. The thin-stretched communications of 30 Corps were now being seriously attacked from both sides, and were constantly cut, once for over twenty-four hours. On the Island itself some German Tiger tanks, well disciplined, joined one of our own transport columns, and travelled up to Driel at the correct spacing. The Household Cavalry shot at and sank a tug and some barges on the Lower Rhine, reported their naval action, and were told to splice the mainbrace.

Against this giant, Faustian backcloth I played a humble walking-on part. The day that Nijmegen bridge was taken the BGS told me that the rest of the Headquarters were on their way by road, and that we must all find more suitable accommodation than a shrubbery. He suggested that I find a more permanent and weatherproof abode nearer to the town.

I took my jeep, and with Longman searched a prosperous-looking district south-east of the town. We found an avenue of good houses called the Sofiaweg, which led up to the highest point in Holland, Berg-en-Dal, from which one could look down on Germany, a few hundred yards to the east. As we drove slowly up the avenue, some one with evil intent put a burst of tracer across the bonnet. We swung among the trees, Longman as imperturbable as ever, and dismounted very quickly to skirmish. But the incident was typical of the hit-and-run confusion, for whoever it was had stolen silently away.

Later I was able to tell the BGS that the houses of the avenue were deserted, that three had been emptied of furniture, and that half a mile on towards Berg-en-Dal was a very large barracks, at present of uncertain ownership. That night we took over the three empty villas, and an operations room was set up in the one favoured by the General. I was sticking pins in a large wall map when Longman appeared with a mug of tea.

"I've put up the small tent in the garden, sir," he said.

"Your bed's made down. It'll be quieter than in here for you, sir."

He lingered after I had thanked him, then added:

"Don't you think we ought to take a look at the barracks up on the hill, sir? The seaborne tail may need it to-morrow if they get through."

Inspired by the looter's gleam in his eye, I agreed, and later managed to get away for a while. We stole up the road without lights, until presently we stopped on the wide gravel sweep before the main entrance. The place was vast, designed, probably, like Sandhurst for officer cadets. By the light of electric torches we went through the building room by room. The air of use and occupation, even to the burning kitchen fires, was eerie, and I, at any rate, was ready to jump at my own shadow, and more than once did so. We found our way at last to the top floor, and there in a series of long garrets was a tremendous quantity of stores. There was hair-oil, tooth-paste, soap, scent, clothing, and all the comforts of a Wehrmacht Naafi. At the far end was the greatest treasure of all. In the beam of our torches we saw cases of hock stacked high, sixty bottles to a case. There were a few cases of champagne, and untold gallons of Bols gin and rum in glass carboys, each holding twenty-five litres. Regardless of booby-traps or assault from the rear, we sampled here and there.

"I'll guard this," I said to Longman. "Go back and get the Camp Commandant to come up with a fifteen-hundredweight truck."

I heard the jeep crunch quietly across the gravel, and after a moment put off my torch, preferring darkness to the spotlight. Nijmegen was being heavily shelled, and the missiles were whispering overhead on their way from the Reichwald. An air attack developed on the bridge, the roar of bombs punctuated by the bark of our Bofors. About the no-man's-land in which the barracks stood was unexplained movement and sudden flurries of shots. With no unit purpose to guide me, I seemed to have lost military aplomb, so that the loneliness and uncertainty weighed upon me. I groped for an opened hock bottle and, although it was a rather sweet vintage, took comfort. I felt better by the time footsteps neared behind a beam of light.

"Well, well!" drawled the voice of Patrick Bush. "You look like a picture of Dutch courage."

I suppose I did, with an empty hock bottle in my left hand, a cocked automatic in the other.

Patrick had some men with him, and we ferried several truck-loads of liquid stores down to Sofiaweg. They were put in a secure place for distribution to the Americans and ourselves. When I felt my way out to my tent that night I brushed against the bush which overhung it, and a clink of glass sounded. I probed under the branches, and discovered that Longman had placed there for me a liberal offering of first fruits.

The next four days were shadowed by the disjointed news from Arnhem. About the bridge, once so staunchly taken and held, hung the silence of death. At Hartestein the survivors of the rest of the Airborne Division fought and died under a storm of shells, mortar-bombs, and bullets. General Urquhart, commanding, could rely but little on his few remaining wireless sets, and determined to try to send a representative to co-ordinate plans for evacuation with General Browning. The G1, accompanied by the CRE, got through by great good luck and that greater courage which tips the scale of fortune, and a plan was made.

By now the medium artillery of 30 Corps was able to give support to the Airborne men at extreme range. So effective and accurate was their fire that some time later the Pegasus flash of the Airborne Forces was presented to the 64th Medium Regiment RA to be worn on the right sleeve.

Attempts had been made to ferry over the Polish Parachute Brigade to thicken the decimated defenders of the Hartestein perimeter, but few could be transported over the fast-flowing Lower Rhine, contained as it was by soft, steep mud-banks, unsuitable for the launching of assault boats. There were few boats available, owing to the constant cutting of communications, and such as were at hand could not easily be got up the shell-swept road to Driel. Similarly, an essay with 'Ducks,' those large amphibious vehicles, failed utterly when the 43rd Wessex Division tried to put across the 4th Battalion of the Dorset Regiment. Not a duck could be got to the point of launching.

On the night of the 24th the Dorsets tried again, with orders to cover the Airborne evacuation timed for the next night. Machine-gun fire so reduced their numbers that only 350 men gained a foothold on the Hartestein bank. These fought their way to some high ground, held on to it all day, covered the withdrawal the next night, and for the most part died on their little hill.

On the night of the 25th survivors of the Airborne Division withdrew in full fighting order with their weapons to the river bank. All doctors and chaplains still alive had stayed behind with the wounded.

Sappers ferried the men across in assault boats, guided through the rain-swept blackness by tracer fired deliberately from Bofors guns. To relieve pressure on the boats, strong swimmers took to the water. Next morning 2200 men were received in a school at Nijmegen. The Division had begun its fight 10,095 strong.

Longman had brought up the Studebaker, and had parked it close to my tent. With it had come the two Dutch youths, Luke and John, who had announced that they wished to enter our service. I thought that they would be useful about the Headquarters, and arranged for them to eat and sleep.

The day after the return of First Airborne I took the Studebaker to the school where they were billeted. Most of the men had had twenty-four hours' sleep, and had afterwards cleaned themselves up for inspection by General Urquhart. Some of the exhaltation of their battle spirit still lingered with them, but there was a soberness about their eyes, part introspective, part the look of men who have a memory which they can share with no one living.

I asked for friends by name. "Dead" was the reply, or "Wounded," or "Missing." At last I learned that Dougal Pearson was returned, and presently he came out, no longer a boy but a grown man. We went back in the car to my tent and sat on my bed drinking rum, while Dougal told part of the story, much of his tale made up of unimportant impressions, irrelevant to the main theme of the plan which could have been a master-stroke to end the War. He recalled German infantry marching up a road singing songs, only to be shot down at point-blank range, followed by successive parties who, attempting no concealment, were killed as they stepped over the heaping bodies of their comrades. He told of Ian McMillan and George Field, gay and inseparable as I remembered them in life, still inseparable as they fell side by side in death. Rory had somehow reached the bridge, had continued the impudent defence with a handful of fit men to help him, the encouragement of the wounded, and the spirits of the dead. No more had been heard of Rory after the fourth day.

The story, told in the dark, and spoken as if memory were the subconscious narrator, held more glory than any epic writing could ever give it.

Two days later the First Airborne Division was flown home, and was soon followed by Corps Headquarters. The 82nd and 101st American Airborne Divisions passed under command of 30 Corps, and another G2, Dennis Dodge, and myself were left behind to act as liaison officers, between the Americans and their new superior formation.

Dennis Dodge and I, now left alone, moved into the nicest of the three houses vacated by Corps Headquarters. The choice was influenced by a fine reception room with a parquet floor, which Dennis said would polish up well for dances. Our two servants were there to look after us, and Luke and John to look after them. Longman became a major-domo, and stocked our cellar from liquor caches in the woods. We were not left immobile, for Dennis and I had each a jeep, there was the Studebaker for social occasions, and at our disposal on a good air-strip close by was a flight of Auster aircraft.

Dennis used these flying-machines voluntarily. I never did so unless ordered.

I was once so commanded. We took off without incident from our very long air-strip and flew at tree level following the road south to Helmond, where the pilot set the thing with brilliant precision in a double tennis court. Almost I persuaded myself that this was a legitimate means of travel. Unfortunately, on the return each of us thought the other was reading the sign-posts, and only discovered this assumption to be in error when we were shot at from the ground by small arms. One man even seemed to be throwing stones at us. We went quickly away, and the pilot and I developed a warm argument about our position. To prove his contention that we had wandered over 's Hertogenbosch, the pilot flew back for another look, in spite of my readily conceding his point.

As we neared Nijmegen again a Messerschmidt 262 came and took an interest in us. My pilot wound in and out of the roadside trees, and assured me that the German moved too fast to hit us. However, I think my conductor was a little upset, for when the time came he made three attempts to land, and at last touched down two-thirds of the way up our ample air-strip, and ran into the wood at the far end.

The days wore a mask of tragi-comedy. Close by was a large house used as a hospital by the American 82nd Airborne, who were holding off the German threat from the east. Their outposts at Berg-en-Dal were a few hundred yards from the Sofiaweg, and from the hill one looked down on Germany below. A little farther south was the Reichwald, perhaps five miles from us, but here the threat was more serious, for constant armoured counter-attacks sallied from the dark alleys of the wood. Thus the hospital down the road was busy, and the Americans buried their dead on a waste patch next to our garden. The plain white crosses sprouted in orderly lines, row upon row, to mark the fruit of war.

The Germans were shelling Nijmegen by day and night from the direction of the Reichwald. The shells whispered and murmured over the house in the Sofiaweg, save for a few which grew tired and came to earth too soon, so that little by little the street and its avenue of trees tumbled about us.

It was incongruous, therefore, when Longman said of a morning, "Will you use the Studebaker or the jeep to-day, sir?" and then:

"About dinner, sir. There are eight guests. Should you want me to borrow a radiogram, sir?"

I never became used to driving off after a comfortable breakfast, to return at night for a bath, a change, drinks, and a dinner party, as if I were a business-man alternating between my place of work and my country home. For the interval during the day was remote from the journey between the City and Surrey. The 101st American Airborne were now forward on the Island, cheek by jowl with the very active Germans. The way to them lay through Nijmegen, where the citizens were busy about their affairs, often picking their way through the fresh debris of shelling. The great bridge to the Island continued to have the earnest attention of the Germans, and the crossing of it was not encouraged by them. The steelwork was scarred by shell and bomb splinters. Downstream the rail bridge so daringly captured by the Americans lay collapsed, a span destroyed by German frogmen, who had on the same night nearly succeeded in blowing the road bridge. As a result of the hostile endeavours the river was closed by a boom, patrolled by boat, and its banks lined by Bofor guns which were fired by their happy crews at every piece of floating wreckage.

The Island was flooded, bleak, and miserable, and the tenure of unhappy life was short. Whenever we could, Dennis and I invited officers of the 101st and of the 82nd, who were in foxholes facing the Reichwald, to spend an evening with us. These particular Americans were cool and resolute men, and they always came to our villa clean in person and restrained in war-talk, and ready for a few hours to accept for what it was worth the contrast of comfortable hospitality to the holes in the ground awaiting their return. Neither were they wolves in soldiers' clothing, and the respectable daughters of the Dutch whom we invited to meet them could with safety to their virtue forget their resistance days.

Letters from Tessa were now beginning to arrive, and I learned that she had from some source been given a circumstantial account of my death, which was said to have taken place within forty-eight hours of landing. I pointed out to her that, as Mark Twain had remarked in similar circumstances, the report was exaggerated. But happily married men in war-time become distracted soldiers during the long intervals between the stimuli of action, and as I read from time to time of the prodigies being performed by the infant Louise I began to feel home-sick.

Almost at once 30 Corps told Dennis and I that it was time for us to go back to England. On this Dennis arranged a monster farewell party, and on our last night we retired to bed heedless of the shelling, which was heavier than usual. But some time near dawn a violent concussion shook the house. Upon our agitated appearance on the landing, Longman, however, informed us that the domestic boiler had exploded. He added that it was fortunate that this catastrophe had been withheld until the last day.

After breakfast Dennis left in his jeep for Brussels to arrange an airlift for ourselves and two vehicles to England. He was not prepared to accept any sort of passage. He himself wished to be put down in the south, and I was determined that I should be dropped in Tessa's lap in Lincolnshire.

Meanwhile I drove the Studebaker, followed by Longman with the jeep and trailer and the two Dutch boys, to an Ironside battalion near Grave which was commanded by my former company commander, Barry Martin. I exchanged the car for a crate of champagne, and handed over Luke and John to the Mess Sergeant. They both felt that they would now soon find themselves on German soil, and I left them arguing whether Berlin, Munich, or Berchtesgarten would be the preferable goal.

We drove off in the jeep to pay final respects to 30 Corps. As we drew near the roads were lined with Military Police, and immediately about the Headquarters was an air of expectancy. Longman took all this for granted, but I felt that there was a possibility of mistaken identity. This feeling was confirmed when our arrival was closely followed by the King in a Humber Staff car, and Field-Marshal Montgomery in a Rolls Royce.

The small, quiet figure of the King held a significance then, in war, which to some is obscured in times of peace. In his person we saw more than the supreme warrior to whom all

British fighting-men owe their final allegiance. We saw him as the emblem of a cause and the inspiration of a creed, as the bearer of a talisman which had been handed down through the centuries, and which, so worthily and proudly carried now, would be handed untarnished into the future.

Through the afternoon and early evening Longman and I drove south to Brussels, following the signs laid by 30 Corps on their drive to join us at Nijmegen. The sign was the Ace of Clubs, and from the debris by the wayside we could see that the carving of Club Route had been a grim and costly task.

Dennis was awaiting us at a prearranged hotel, and whisked me off at once to a party. Just before going with him I delved under the tarpaulin of the jeep trailer to secure some kit. The ten-hundredweight trailer was filled with jars of rum and gin.

"Longman!" I exclaimed. "What's all this?"

"It seemed a pity to leave it behind, sir," answered Longman, and quickly lashed down the cover over his cargo.

Next morning Dennis and I drove out to the airfield, where he had already made a friend. At that time American Dakotas were ferrying across medical supplies, and to beg a lift back for ourselves and servants was easy, but to persuade the plane crews to take our jeeps and trailers was another matter. There were no loading ramps at the airfield, nor were the interiors of the Dakotas equipped with wheel troughs or strong points for lashing down.

As the day wore on we began to despair, more especially as a surprisingly high percentage of the pilots who landed were teetotallers. But in the early afternoon we found two jovial Americans whose eyes lit at the promise of gin. From hutments and hangars our friends mustered a strong-arm gang who lifted our vehicles bodily into two Dakotas. In a few minutes we were airborne.

My jeep was tethered by a piece of knotted string, but Dennis's party the night before had excelled all his previous entertainments, and, careless of being run over, I bedded down on a heap of unpacked parachutes.

By tea-time we had landed in Lincolnshire. Longman took

train to London, and I drove off to Tessa. For once, she showed some surprise when the jeep and trailer stopped at the door of our friends' house. When we had all calmed down a little our hosts produced a bottle of gin which had seen better days, and for whose small content they made apology—good spirits were just then difficult to come by. I remembered Longman's foresight, and went out to the jeep to fetch a glass jar which contained four gallons of best Bols.

CHAPTER XIII

AN EXPERIMENT WITH TROOPS

Before we flew to Holland there had been much of interest in the work at Airborne Corps Headquarters. After our return we missed the very alarms and changes of plan about which we had formerly grumbled. In a bold moment I told the BGS this. He remarked that if I did not like paper work he was not one to blame me, and added that, although much money had been spent in an attempt to turn me into a Staff officer, he would see if he could not find me a more congenial job.

In the Service, just when one has become lulled into quiescence, events impinge suddenly upon one, as shots startle the unwary traveller who wanders into an ambuscade. Within a couple of days the BGS sent for me, and presented me to another brigadier who was in his office. The visitor was the Commander Airborne Establishments, known as CAE—in order to conform to the Army custom of initialling everything, and possibly for brevity, too.

CAE was the standard brigadier size, middle height and stocky. I have always wondered from where major-generals are recruited, since they are long and lanky. They may, of course, be examples of the stature growing with the job.

CAE, who was in charge of a variety of static Airborne units, told me that he was forming a second Parachute Regiment Infantry Training Centre, and that its Commanding Officer was to be Colonel Andrew Pollock. He said that he was prepared to accept me as second-in-command. I expressed much gratitude, and dissembled my ignorance of this particular stage in a soldier's training, since as Andrew Pollock was an officer whose bravery and martial flair had been recognized by a D.S.O. and three bars and a Military Cross I knew I should have no lack of guidance in my new job.

I told Longman all about the coming change, and was glad when he expressed his intention of going with me. I went along to see Patrick Bush about his posting.

"Oh, dear!" drawled Patrick plaintively. "I'll be sorry to see two Guardsmen leave. Though why I'm sure I don't know. Guardsmen are such a trouble to me. They're not peaceful like other people. They're always wanting things."

The new unit was being formed at Shorncliffe Camp, near Folkestone. When Longman and I arrived there we found the barracks perched on the edge of an escarpment which fell to the English Channel, half a mile away. The place had been built by Sir John Moore, and he had housed and trained there those light regiments which had so bemused the French pursuers during the masterly retreat to Corunna. But if these old traditions lingered, so did the ancient amenities and sanitary arrangements.

In the Officers' Mess I found an Airborne company commander named Atkins, from whom I had the first clear story of what was happening. Our Airborne unit was taking over in stages from a Primary Training Centre, or PTC. A PTC is the unit where a civilian has his hair and clothes removed, and a beret and battle-dress issued in lieu. Here too he first hears those threatening words "Pay attention! What we're going on with now is the rifle. It's going to be your best friend. This is a rifle!"

The budding soldier unfolded his petals for six weeks at a PTC, then passed on to an Infantry Training Centre, or ITC, for another eight weeks, after which he was said to be fit to join the Training Battalion of his regiment.

In the case of our new Airborne ITC, Atkins told me that the course was to be twelve weeks instead of the usual eight, as additional physical training and tests were superimposed on the usual syllabus. As the PTC companies successively finished their time they would go away to ordinary ITC's, and one by one would be replaced by Airborne men.

In the anteroom before dinner I found some forty officers.

There was none of that atmosphere of bonhomie which had been so marked in Ironside and Airborne messes, and nobody had a drink in his hand, which lack made the members seem improperly dressed. At five minutes to the dinner-hour the PTC Commanding Officer came in. He shook hands, apologized for being away earlier, and offered me a whisky, for which I was grateful.

Dinner was a gloomy and over-formal meal, at which conversation was initiated from the head of the table, and the general contribution was non-committal acquiescence. Afterwards the officers drifted away, as if furtively, in the direction of Sandgate and Folkestone.

Next morning the Commanding Officer drove me round the various ranges and training areas, showed me something of the barracks, which were a maze of buildings and improvisations too illogically planned to memorize, then took me into his office. On the wall behind his desk was pinned a huge sheet of paper. He pointed to it.

"That's my training chart," he said. "You'll need one twice as big for a twelve weeks' course. I can tell from this just what any of my platoons are doing at any moment. Unless, of course," he admitted, "there's a hitch. Then I sometimes have to recast the whole thing."

The chart was quite two yards square, was typed in symbols and abbreviations, squared in many colours like a Chinese chequer-board, and held as much detail as a Bradshaw Guide.

"I never get to bed before two in the morning," said the Commanding Officer. "Now you can see why."

Quite early next day he sent for me, made me sign for some papers in a little black box, said good-bye, and drove away. I was left standing in the office, afraid to approach closely the desk invested with the magic of command. Through the windows I saw squads of men hurtling to and fro on unguessed occasions, and was certain that at any moment the machinery of the unit would run down, and I without knowledge of how to repair and restart it. I felt as if I were in a monster aeroplane, and had been called to the control cabin to hear the pilot say, "It's all yours now, I'm baling out."

The telephone rang, and I had no option but to answer. The caller was Colonel Pollock, whose accent, thick as Highland porridge, conspired with a bad long-distance line to be unintelligible. He opened with a phrase which sounded like "Omsk, Tomsk, and Tobolsk," and followed up with digressions into Balkan vernacular. It was some minutes before I understood that he was not after all going to take over the unit, and had retired over the Border, the better to conduct negotiations for another appointment.

Almost at once CAE followed on the wire.

"All going well?" he asked. "Any difficulties?"

I replied 'yes' and 'no,' and hoped he would connect the right question and answer.

"Good!" said CAE brightly. "Colonel Pollock will not now be taking over. We have no successor immediately in view, so you will carry on as second-in-command in command."

Thus christened, as by a stuttering godfather, I was left to control two thousand men, when my previous experience had not gone beyond forty odd.

My first reaction to this problem was to share it, for there were certainly some senior officers in the unit whose advice would have been sound. Then I remembered that authority is weakened if those who wield it show open bewilderment.

Lance-Sergeant Smartly used to say, "If you don't know what to do, and have got to think something out, don't do it in front of the men. Get away out of sight, and when you come back do something, even if it's wrong."

No doubt he spoke from the level of the Sergeants' Mess, but the moral was equally axiomatic for field marshals.

The Staff College opened up a new, if more cautious, line of thought.

"If you're overwhelmed," they had said, "stand back and get your breath. Lots of problems sort themselves out if you don't meddle with them."

These two directives, though rather contradictory on the face of it, were really complementary. A man can tackle at once the things he understands, and by the time this work is done other puzzles will either have solved themselves or become more understandable.

Finally, Rory O'Brien had always maintained that a fish rots from the head. To avoid the body of the creature becoming contaminated, he commanded his officers rather than his men, following the dictum that there are no bad men, but only bad officers.

It seemed, then, best to see to the Officers' Mess first. It was not difficult to introduce the Ironside club atmosphere, where respect for seniority springs from manners rather than duty. On top of this I superimposed an Airborne innovation, which was a small, bright bar, in which respectable women were welcome in the evening.

The immediate result of humanizing the Mess was that the members began to use it, and thus to know each other better, thereby beginning to build the sort of intimate comradeship which had been so marked in Rory's Squadron.

Of course, this unbridled licence went to the heads of a few unbalanced young men. I did not want to prune their activities myself, for our off-duty morale remained a delicate growth for some time, and the company commanders were prompted to direct excess spirits into the proper channels, so that when the mess furniture was from time to time broken up and burnt the fire was kept under control, and the damage debited discreetly to the mess-bills of the incendiaries.

I had expected that Airborne officers would be posted to us as the new companies arrived, but CAE rang up to say that so great was the shortage we must be content with an occasional one. For the majority, we must transform the ex-PTC officers. Some few of these were too old to follow the hard training of our hand-picked recruits, and others did not seem to have either the knowledge to instruct them nor the personality to lead them. These were posted back to their various regiments. The residue were good fellows, and when a few of them had gone away to take various courses, the better to fit them for their new work, we clapped red berets on their heads and called them Airborne.

Within a few weeks the change-over to Airborne men was

complete, and the unit was two thousand four hundred strong. Each of the five training companies had ten platoons, and I found myself working late into the night, as my predecessor had foretold, to draw up a monster chart which co-ordinated the work of fifty platoons, in varying stages of advancement, for forty-four periods a week for three months. I kept telling myself that this was just the work for which the Staff College fitted a man, but either I had been a particularly stupid pupil or their instruction had been indifferent—an unlikely explanation—for I failed utterly. At last I formed a Brains Trust to work on it, and we did manage to fill in all the squares of the chart. When completed it looked masterly. Unfortunately it was like a mathematical sum, which, though beautifully set out, arrives at a conclusion at variance with the answer in the back of the book. The thing just would not work out in practice.

I, and other headquarters officers connected directly with training, found ourselves always hurrying from one place to another to improvise solutions to problems for which our paper robot could not cater.

One day, after I had found two companies on one range, a company with haversack rations eating in addition hot dinners in containers, and another company with no dinners at all, I knew for a while black despair, and longed for the Operations Room again.

It came to me suddenly that the Staff College had only taught us to write lengthy and full orders on paper so that we should have a basis for giving verbal ones direct. With much the same sort of feeling which Julius Cæsar must have had as the waters of the Rubicon lapped cold about his stomach, I tore the chart off the wall. The Imp of the unit was at once exorcized.

In place of the malevolent sheet of paper there was a weekly Order Group to plan the coming week's work. The company commanders knew from the War Office syllabus the lessons to be given in each of the twelve weeks of an intake, and at our meeting, taking turns for first call, they indented for what they required. They fixed their times for ranges and training areas; for transport, meals out of barracks, issues of maps or compasses, haircuts, baths, padre's hour, clothing issues, football grounds, medical inspections, and every activity. The various headquarters officers booked requirements on the spot and if necessary amended them.

This was the ultimate decentralization, and there was never again any trouble over our complicated arrangements.

In Europe the War was drawing to a close. Sixth Airborne had flown over our very heads, as we gazed up from the barracks at Shorncliffe, to make good the bridgehead over the Rhine. This was the first large-scale tactical Airborne landing of the War, for the troops were dropped on the objectives which they were required to seize and hold. As during the night before D-Day in Normandy, when gliders had dived down to within yards of the bridges over the Caen Canal and the river Orne, *coup de main* parties were again used to capture the bridges over the river Issel, securing a route which opened the way to Berlin itself.

Unlike the operations in Holland, ground troops forced the Rhine to join up with the Airborne men within twenty-four hours. Even so, within that short period Airborne casualties had reached 15 per cent.

The individual ever burrows about his affairs under the weight of great events, like a heaving ant, I thought now that I should be left for a while where I was, for the Far East was remote in all our thoughts, and I found rooms for Tessa within a half-mile of the barracks.

She drifted down from London, the infant Louise in a kind of box, and settled herself in with her most disembodied air, as if an eastern guru had taught her the lack of significance of place and space, and that to be was all. The evening and week-end social life of the Mess had developed to an extent, and Tessa's arrival was of interest to the dear enemies who formed our close-knit company of *vivandières*. Seniority was abolished off-duty among the males, but lingered among their wives, and Tessa hurled confusion among their established customs of precedence by being quite unconscious that she was the second-in-command in command's lady, and being unable in any event to remember to which officer each wife was attached. This unconscious impartiality earned her a reputation for democracy, and the senior wives were left with no privilege of condescension to castigate sweetly the junior.

A little while before Victory Day CAE rang up to say that a Commanding Officer had at last been appointed, an ex-Chindit who had parachuted mules into the jungle. No one arrived, and I carried on as before. One day a strange lieutenant-colonel wandered into my office, and we chatted sociably for some time, I having no idea who he was or what he wanted. At last he said that he was the new commanding officer. I made motions to vacate the desk, until he stopped me, saying that he had been living amid swamps and leeches for what seemed in retrospect most of his life, that he was returning that day to London to arrange his wedding, and that he was going to take one of the longest leaves in the history of the War, even if he was to be sent before a court martial at the end of it.

I was on my own, therefore, when Victory Day burst on us with a report like a damp squib, rumour having blown hot and cold for a day or two, so that the uninspired announcement was robbed of drama. While we had been waiting to hear this news the Adjutant had been worried about its effects on our high-spirited young soldiers. It seemed probable that they would inflict on Folkestone more scars on the first night of peace than the town had received in five years of war. I thought it unfair and impracticable to confine the unit to barracks, but thought that we might well lure the majority to remain.

Accordingly we organized a dance and a monster bonfire. Coastal areas were still forbidden to break the black-out, but there was no rule about collecting materials for a fire. The bulk of our combustibles was a pile of forty-gallon drums of oil, which had for years been perched on the white cliffs to set the sea alight and give to an invader the traditional warm welcome. The fire was lit accidentally, and must have put to shame those beacons which flashed the tale of the Spanish Armada from Beachy Head to the North.

However, if these measures kept our men in order on Victory night the future could not consist of a series of conflagrations, and I wondered how we could hold enthusiasm at a pitch of intensity without the stimulus of battle as a goal.

Parents well understand that if they have lively, healthy, and intelligent children they must expect them also to be more mischievous and less easy to keep fully occupied than the dull, starch-fed sort of child. Our large family at Shorncliffe were all lively, healthy, and intelligent. They were volunteers; they were a degree fitter than the best physical category A; and, being young, and as yet untried, felt that as budding birdmen they must acquire and maintain a reputation for intrepidity.

At this time of doubt there was posted to me a new Regimental Sergeant-Major. Regimental Sergeant-Major J. Christ was a regular Bombardier Guardsman, who had joined the original Airborne Division in the very early days. He had been wounded and taken prisoner by the Germans at Arnhem. When his Stalag was overrun next spring by the Guards Armoured Division the Sergeant-Major's parachutists were found to be mounting guard, turned out as if for an inspection, and their captors were peeling potatoes and cleaning the latrines.

Christ had the detailed book experience which I lacked. Within a few days any loose strings of administration were tight, weak non-commissioned officers were smartened or purged, and any possibility of aimlessness vanished, for military duty taught by an expert is as much an object in barracks as on the battlefield.

Sixth Airborne was again being brought up to strength after its jump across the Rhine, and the subsequent impromptu, irrepressible dash across North Germany, for the Division was shortly to go to Palestine. It was worrying, therefore, to find that wastage of recruits was on the increase. There was always some wastage due to unsuitability or to physical breakdown, but now large numbers requested transfer to other regiments. We wanted no pressed men, and did as we were asked. Indeed, there was no option. Until a parachutist does the final jump of his course he can elect not to go on.

The causes for this new defection were varied. The major one was that there is a risk in parachuting, however remote, and that many good men who were prepared to accept it in war felt differently in peace. For now there was peace in the East, too. Again, demobilization was taking away our experienced instructors, whose personalities had buoyed up the novices. Then there was the unsettling effect of the move to the Airborne Forces Depot for the final hardening, and the move to Ringway airfield for the jumping course under Royal Air Force supervision.

To make up for these losses by the wayside, Airborne recruiting teams tended to paint a picture as rosy as the red beret, and some recruits of the wrong type came to us. One aggrieved man, applying for a transfer, told me indignantly that he had thought he would be issued with double rations, and another that he understood he would not be required to march. I made representations to CAE that the recruiting people should offer only blood, tears, and sweat, and, for reward, the heritage of glory won at such bloody cost over the first five years of the new formation's life. The good man is more attracted by such a promise than by that of a featherbed.

Thus we continued to receive plenty of volunteers, but of a better type, who did not quit.

We found that after the mid-course seven days' privilege leave there was a spate of applications to be posted away. It was obvious that home influence was working against us. However much we sympathized with anxious relatives, our job was to counter their wishes.

The red beret was precious to our young men, and we now awarded it as formally as a decoration, after a parade on the day before leave. The glamour of the new headgear carried the wearers through the distractions of their week at home, and had a surprisingly steadying effect.

Then, again, before an intake left for the Depot there was a passing-out parade, at which our departing pupils were inspected by a notability, and marched past a saluting base with all the pageantry which we could command. The soldier, however much he grumbles at the extra work, loves to show himself off, and this rousing final day, which included a dance in the evening, did much to give momentum to the purpose of the men at the Depot and Ringway.

The Commanding Officer returned from his leave, and during the early summer I had much less work to do. My own demobilization was due in October, and Tessa and I often talked of the future. I, at any rate, regarded release with mixed feelings, for there had been pleasure and a small feeling of achievement in the Service. I had no pre-war life to go back to, and no plans for a new civilian one. It was hard to imagine a return to the humdrum, and both of us were inclined to settle overseas. Yet it was clear that for a time, at least, it would be difficult to transport ourselves abroad, and, as an added complication, Tessa said that she would not be surprised if she were going to have another baby.

The Commanding Officer departed on a parachute course. Hardly had he returned, intact, than he called me in to say that he had been offered command of a battalion in Sixth Airborne, and would be going at once to take over before leaving for Palestine.

I moved into the big office again.

I was sitting at the desk wondering who would succeed our departed Commanding Officer, hoping that the new man would be as charming as the last, and praying that he would create no tiresome upheaval, when CAE rang up, with his genius for chipping in on one's thoughts by telephone.

"That you, Tom?" he asked. "You will take over command as a lieutenant-colonel. If you feel like signing on for another year I've another job for you later on."

I went to our lodgings to see whether Tessa would stand for an extra twelve months as a camp-follower. She was prepared to, for by now she had decided firmly that she would have another baby, and was therefore against the emigrant ship. I signed on that day.

It was a fortnight before Tessa said, "Longman's getting very careless. I've noticed several times lately that he's got the crown on your shoulder mixed up with those things you had when you were a captain."

I was surprised that I felt so differently about the unit now that it was my own, and that I was no longer keeping the chair warm for some one else. It was a satisfactory feeling, as if one had paid the final instalment on a motor-car, and the machine at last really belonged to one. During my long spell as that half-creature second-in-command in command I had not felt at liberty to monkey with the system, but only to try to be a good steward who administered according to the letter of the law on behalf of the absent master.

Now, however, there was a second-in-command as steward of the Regulations, and I was free to monkey.

I remembered so well the System during my recruit days. It had been the enemy of humanity, and, had it but known it, of proper discipline, because it destroyed goodwill. Just as at a school the strict master can unbend with the young fellows of his class to an extent which would be disastrous to a weak master, so, in a unit whose discipline is absolute, liberties may be taken with the System.

It may be remembered that the System demands that the soldier should receive nothing beyond the letter of the regulations, and that those in authority are paid to see that he gets it.

As a first assault on this ancient citadel of bigotry, I formed a Commanding Officer's committee. There were several members from each company and department, and the committee met fortnightly. The ostensible purpose was to bring up matters of welfare and amenities, but more important was the opportunity to keep a finger on the pulse of the unit. Often some routine order, thoughtlessly worded, creates hardship and discontent out of all proportion to its necessity. At my committee I learned exactly what was the impact on the individual in the barrack-room of promulgations issued from the comfort of the Orderly Room. Similarly, the representatives could learn from me the reasons for such orders.

I never found that the meeting was in any danger of becoming a soviet, but, on the contrary, that when soldiers understood that there was a purpose behind an order they were more amenable to a discipline which they could understand than to one whose workings were a mystery to them.

There was leisure now to study the refinements of man-management. I had noticed, throughout my time in the Army, that the soldier slept whenever he could. He slept in railway carriages, on platform benches, in canteens, in lorries, and when standing in queues. He slept during lectures, at the start line for an assault, while awaiting counter-attack, and even during battle.

Many units fixed reveille at six o'clock in the morning, and first parade at nine. The men thus had three hours in which to shave, tidy barrack-rooms, breakfast, visit the latrines, and put on equipment. Two hours is ample for these manœuvres. At Shorncliffe our numbers were such that we had to serve meals in two sittings. But there was no necessity for the late sitting to get out of bed at the same time as the early. By alternating weekly, companies had an extra hour in bed when on late meals. To the layman it will seem obvious common sense to arrange reveille as late as is reasonable. But the layman would be surprised how rarely the more rigid type of military mind can see the obvious.

Regimental Sergeant-Major Christ put on full ceremony for daily Orders. He was that very best type of warrant-officer whose inflexibility went with absolute fairness. Quite often he would speak up in favour of a criminal, though sometimes he would expose a man's character as a dentist's drill uncovers a quivering nerve. Now and again his remarks impaired the gravity of the occasion.

There was one cunning paratrooper to whom I had granted forty-eight hours' compassionate leave so that he might marry with the lady of his choice. He had, I knew, recently been on ten days' privilege leave, and could well have had the ceremony performed then, but had told me that his mind had not been made up. I gave him the benefit of his doubts, and let him go, to every one's annoyance.

However, on the second day of his forty-eight hours his company commander produced at Orders a telegram from him. "Request extension further forty-eight hours," it said. "Marriage not yet consummated."

I sat silent, staring at this human document.

"Permission to speak, sir?" asked the Sergeant-Major, and, without waiting for it, said, "Don't see why he wants forty-eight hours for a five-minute job, sir."

Following Ironside custom, I tried to make Orders a time to praise as well as to blame. A man may pretend to be angry because he must clean up before being marched in, but just the same he is delighted to have official recognition of a worthy deed.

I had always been against niggling punishments for wrong-doers, many of those laid down being as petty as stopping a child's jam at tea. If grown men are treated as boys they often come to act childishly. I began more and more to admonish the good soldier who had fallen into some small fault, but to sentence the consistently bad one to the maximum of my power. There is no excuse for being a bad soldier. Most are good ones, so virtue cannot be difficult to achieve.

Towards the end of the victory year demobilization began to take such a heavy toll of our instructors that we became nearly a hundred and fifty short. Replacements were few. CAE agreed to us retaining the pick of our recruits for a month after the end of their course, in order to train them as potential non-commissioned officers. The Sergeant-Major came into his own, and at the end of their four weeks the youngsters were trained in bearing and duties to a standard fully equal to that in the Brigade of Guards. When those picked recruits returned to us from jumping at Ringway they brought back with them freshness, vigour, and ambition, so that the daily routine took fresh momentum.

The work of training this cadre became too much for Sergeant-Major Christ, and he delegated some of it to an excellent Bombardier Guards sergeant. One day the Sergeant-Major said, "We need a drill sergeant, sir!"

I pointed out that only the Brigade had such provision on their establishment. The Sergeant-Major was not impressed by difficulties with the War Office, and was so importunate that for the sake of peace I wrote a Staff College type memorandum to higher authority, with such effect that we were told to promote our Bombardier sergeant to warrant-officer, surplus to establishment. Sergeant-Major Christ was delighted, and twirled his moustache and flourished his pace-stick more magnificently than ever.

Surprisingly, we sometimes had difficulty in filling vacancies in our young corporals' cadre.

It is not easy to get some men, however suitable, to take that first step out of the ranks signified by one stripe on the arm. Its significance should be explained to them. The gulf between a lance-corporal and a field-marshal is narrower than that between him and his old comrades, for both are commanders with all the weight and power of Military Law and King's Regulations to wield. Yet the man with one stripe must maintain the gulf between himself and the private soldier while still sleeping in a common barrack-room, using the same canteen, and rubbing shoulders with him at every turn. He takes an added responsibility, with its greater capacity for getting him into trouble; he must give up to some extent his old friends, yet until he enters the Corporals' or Sergeants' Mess he cannot make new ones; and, now that leadership is his, he can no longer relax in times of crisis, with the comfortable conviction that it does not concern him, and that some one in authority will come along to wave a magic wand.

The best way to overcome reluctance was, I found, to explain the chain of command. The Field-Marshal commands but two or three Army Commanders, who in turn command four or five Corps Commanders, who command two or three Divisional Commanders, who command three Brigadiers, who command three Lieutenant-Colonels, who command six Company Commanders, who command three Platoon Commanders, who command three Section Sergeants.

If the section sergeant is sick, wounded, killed, or absent the acting lance-corporal will have to command ten men to the field-marshal's three or four, and will not be paid for the job. A good man is put on his mettle by the comparison, and feels at once the weight of a baton in his knapsack.

Sergeant-Major Christ's smartening effect on our men was such that the unit was often asked to provide detachments for functions at various of the Cinque ports. This privilege injured a little the pride of an arm of another Service, whose depot looked on the provision of guards of honour as their own right. Perhaps to teach us a lesson, this unit challenged us to a boxing-match. Our rivalry, though active, was really very friendly, and our officers and wives were invited to return to our opponents' Mess for a party after the battle.

There was such interest in the coming match that bets were freely made throughout the district, and when word spread abroad senior officers from other Commands decided to be present.

The unit was nervous of the outcome, for our enemies could draw upon more men than we could, and had also a strong boxing tradition. However, one of our P.T. instructors was welter-weight champion of the Imperial Services, and he took our team into training for a fortnight. They were struck off all duties, and before the night were all given a forty-eight-hour pass. I told them that if they finished the battle inside the scheduled time they would be able to catch the last train to London.

The team must have been eager for leave, because they caught the train with time to spare, victorious by nine bouts to four, and winners of the milling contest too.

During the evening Tessa was sitting among the officers of the other side. She was chatting happily to them, but they, I thought, looked unresponsive. At last, as one of our young men brought yet another bout to an abrupt end, I heard her say, "It's a pity the parachutists aren't fitter. Of course, they're very young, you know, or they'd do better."

I went hot and cold as I saw our hosts squirm, and tried to signal Tessa to be silent. She took my signs as approval, and apologized again as another of our opponents bit the dust, and the referee once more cried "Green the winner!"

It was not till I got her alone that I found Tessa had identified the red corner with our red berets, and had out of mistaken politeness apologized throughout the evening for the wrong team.

That peace of a limited nature had indeed come was brought home to us when a little petrol was allowed on the ration. I dug out Arabella, the old green Bentley, from the hen-house where she had roosted six years long since her return from France on the first day of war. She was in a sorry state.

I had some excellent fitters in the MT workshops, and these stripped and rebuilt the old car in off-duty hours, working for love of fine machinery as much as a wage. Soon I was once more delighted by the sound and feel of the sprightly old lady. Tessa, who had to negotiate the awkward near-side door, said that Arabella was jealous of the unborn child, but I think the exercise was beneficial, for the infant was unusually lusty when it arrived, some weeks before its time.

Before Christmas CAE rang up to say that I was to take command of the Airborne Depot in the near future. He also told me that there would be general leave over the holiday.

It is always an unpleasant task to detail men for an unwelcome job, and I worried for a long time how best to pick the skeleton staff who must remain on duty over the first peace-time Christmas. At first I thought it better to keep back unmarried men, but suddenly remembered our many Scots. When asked, these volunteered in a body, and took their leave at Hogmanay, preferring 'first-footing' to Father Christmas.

CHAPTER XIV

FULL CIRCLE

LONGMAN had just been demobilized, and I was feeling a sense of loss without him; the second-in-command was on leave; and Tessa's baby, prompted to impetuosity by Arabella, was likely at any moment to face the world, when CAE rang up.

"Get off to the Depot at once," he said. "The Commandant has to leave immediately to a new appointment."

I drove up to Chesterfield in Arabella next day. Although I had by now had a little practice in command, I felt again some of the diffidence I had experienced when I was on my way to the ITC, nearly a year before. The Depot had been formed in its present place, and was deeply rooted. The Commandant from whom I was to take over had been in command for a long time, and the unit was coloured by his marked personality. A temporary soldier must always feel a little at a loss when he is to step into the shoes of a capable Regular.

The last stretch of the journey was through begrimed country, the pit-head gear of coal-mines fingering the low, drab clouds. The Depot was surrounded by a high wire fence inside which were acres of brick hutments which nestled like chicks about huge dining-halls and gymnasiums. The fears and doubts of the departed thousands who had passed through on their way to parachute at Ringway seemed to linger in the air.

I had only once stayed at the Depot, years before, and remembered the lively rowdiness of B Mess, where hard young officers lived while they did synthetic jumping training, mingled with voluble foreigners of different nationalities and even sexes, who were preparing to fly by night over occupied Europe, and to jump into a darkness out of which often they never came again into the light.

Now, I made my way to A Mess. There was a farewell dinner that night for the Commandant, who was going overseas. Despite the cheerfulness of the evening, I felt a touch of sadness. I envied the Commandant his continuing Service career, stepping as he was from one circle of comradeship into another, while we temporary soldiers must walk out into the loneliness of a world with whose comforts we had lost touch. Again, on the Commandant's behalf I felt vicariously his twinge of sorrow at giving into the hands of another person a unit which he had done much to build.

Next morning the hand-over took place, and I was told that very shortly I should have to move the Depot to a new home in the Isle of Wight.

The very first day on which I took the chair in my new office I received a sharp reminder that here I should not find all the soldiers willing. As I looked out of the window I was startled to see a file of men go past, handcuffed two by two and escorted by Regimental Police. I rang for the Adjutant, and indicated the chain-gang. The Adjutant explained that this circumscription of activity was authorized, and, indeed, essential. He said that one of the many functions of the Depot was to detain the really wild and bad men, in some cases absentees for years from Airborne units, who were from time to time apprehended. Further, it was our business to collect evidence of absence or desertion and to prepare the cases for courts-martial. Many of these individuals were criminals of the worst type. To illustrate this, the Adjutant in his turn indicated the window. Looking out, I saw a wildly running figure closely pursued by another individual with a bayonet raised to stab. Before the pair moved beyond the range of vision, the pursuer, who was very fleet of foot, closed the range and struck his quarry a blow in the right shoulder.

"You see, sir!" said the Adjutant, with the pride of a man whose cause is proved just. "We have to keep some restraint on them."

During the first few days I tried to get the feel of the Depot, for the atmosphere was different from that of an ordinary unit. The Parachute Training Company was moving permanently to work with the Royal Air Force at Ringway, and the Demonstration Company which would replace it was not yet formed. Thus we were without much sense of military purpose, for our remaining tasks were to redistribute the Regular soldiers posted to us, and hold the others until demobilization.

There was also the problem of a mixed unit, which was to me a new one, for a large number of ATS were employed in the offices, transport lines, and dining-halls. Their officer used our Mess, and embarrassed me by standing up whenever she saw me, and by refusing to accept the normal courtesies, such as precedence through a doorway. Life must be very difficult for women in a Mess where they are a weak minority, for Service language and conversation are robust, and the men are constantly catching themselves up in the midst of unfit remarks. Thus the females feel themselves to be a nuisance, and the men reflect on the coarseness of their own masculine minds.

Similarly with the ATS Other Ranks—to be saluted by them was at conflict with Western custom, and they soon guessed my feelings, for they seemed to go out of their way to ambush me, saluting very smartly, mouth prim, but a giggle in the eyes.

These personal embarrassments, however, could have been borne, had it not been obvious that the dug-in old sweats on the permanent staff of the Depot, like students at a co-educational college, thought less of work than dates, and less of comradeship than cutting out a friend. One often stumbled upon tense mixed groups enacting their eternal triangles in out-of-the-way corners of the camp during working hours.

In the end I arranged to leave our ATS behind when we made our move to the Isle of Wight. Their loss was most difficult to replace, for at their particular jobs the girls were often more reliable and sensible than men. However, when we found ourselves without them the emotional cross-currents ceased to eddy and swirl through the unit, and the men's energies were directed again in a strong tide to soldiering.

We were in the midst of preparing advance and rear parties for our move, handing in accommodation stores, and performing nameless expedients to avoid being billed for barrack damages, when Tessa had her baby. I had been daily expecting the news, and the duty officer had instructions to wake me if word came at night. Word came in the early hours, and—perhaps because of some past experience—the Duty Officer shrank from rousing me for fear of retribution. He was now visited with retribution for letting me sleep, and saw no justice in it. However, when I had spurred Arabella down the Great North Road, through the shocked traffic of London, and urged the old car, game to the last, along the flying stretches of the Dover road, I received my own retribution for being late, and saw no justice there either.

Tessa was sitting up, drinking gin with the matron of the nursing-home.

"I can relax to-night," said the matron, accepting another glass, "our next maternity case isn't due for a couple of days."

The malevolent infant to which she referred decided, however, to arrive in a rush that night, and Matron later regretted her little party.

Tessa's new daughter was unusually ugly, and I could only hope that she would have enough brains to make a career. But the child's transformation over the next few months was almost magical, and in a short time I was able to look at the blonde and blue-eyed baby and say to myself that she would succeed even with no brains at all.

Some of the officers from the ITC came in to see my augmented family, and to drink the gin. Now that the war-tide of blood was only just on the ebb, this merry-making at a birth was indeed an example of the chronic optimism of man.

Our new home on the Isle of Wight was pleasant enough. Part of the barracks was brick-built, and as insanitary as had been Sir John Moore's camp at Shorncliffe, and part was modern—well-equipped hutments in the shape known as a Spider. The authorities, however, cannot leave well alone, and had catered for more contingencies than usual by putting a prison on one side of us, a mental home on the other, and a Borstal Institution behind.

I now had a dual rôle, for as well as being Commandant of the Depot I was Garrison Commander of the Island. A Garrison Adjutant lived in barracks to help look after the other scattered units. He was a man who took his duties seriously, for he conducted me on many tours of inspection, which included visits to civilian notabilities whose goodwill might, he thought, ease the position of the military. For now that war was over for a time the soldier was regarded as a nuisance who still retained some training ground on which to maintain his skill against the next call upon it, and who took up passenger-space in buses, trains, and ferries. The Island was hospitable, and during these little trips we ran largely on alcohol at very few miles to the pint.

As I went about I kept an eye open for lodgings for Tessa and her two daughters. It was tantalizing to see in barracks a good Commandant's house, which I as a non-Regular soldier was barred from using. Some time after my demobilization I was gazetted in the Regular Army Reserve of Officers, but I am still uncertain whether I shall be allowed a married quarter next war. As I searched for a temporary home I saw clearly the difficulties which a soldier must face as he moves from station to station. If he has a house elsewhere, and lets it, the rent is taxed as income, but the rent which he pays out at his new station qualifies for no relief. Tessa and I, desperate for somewhere to live temporarily when I was released, had by now bought a tall old-fashioned house in Chelsea, whose inconvenience had frightened away others. We learned full well the injustices of taxation as they afflict the soldier.

I began to despair of finding lodgings. One of the few places which might have suited my family was infested by a lady brigand who demanded a payment in excess of my total pay and allowances. I nearly sealed the bargain, thinking her weekly quotation was for the month. However, one day the Garrison Adjutant took me by chance to see a Dutch-Canadian farmer and his wife. Since Tessa is partly Dutch, I Canadian-born, and our newest daughter named Johanna, these kind people took us in.

Work within the Depot was not congenial. I was not dealing now with young hand-picked recruits who had in front of them the goal of their parachute course, and behind them the inspiration bought at such lavish cost by their earlier comrades of the red beret. Instead, most of the men we handled were old sweats, whose goal was civilian life, and whose affectation it often was to debunk an inspiration to which they had themselves contributed.

The goal of release, though desired, was viewed with mixed feelings, for these men had fought in battles which had been epic, and had swept on to their victories on waves whose crests had not easily been attained. Yet at home they found little of the exultation which they had expected to follow conquest, little resurgence of hope and the determination to build anew, and, disillusioned, many of them slipped from the crest of the wave to the trough.

It was one of my jobs to interview all men before release, and I saw a hundred or two every month. The object was to help solve any final problems, and to assess the men's military character on a printed form. The excellent demobilization scheme was weakened by its failure to publicize the value of an official military character as a guide to employment. These chits were completed after much searching of documents and study of the men. Yet, even if an employer troubled to glance at one he would no doubt have been pleased to read the assessment 'good.' A soldier need be but indifferent to rate 'good,' and too often his comrade with 'exemplary' would be on the same start-line in civilian life.

However, the fate of the men was less worrying than the fate of the officers, for a large proportion of these were unable easily to find a niche for themselves when release came. In the democratic Army to which they had belonged promotion to commissioned rank had come more by merit than influence, and many competent officers had worked their way up from a background similar to that of the Other Ranks whom they had commanded. It was quite natural that, having improved their position by their own efforts, they should feel frustrated at returning to the social and economic level from which they had begun their ascent.

Also, from the national point of view, it was a loss to discount the qualities of versatility and leadership which these officers had discovered in themselves. The desperate history of many such after demobilization can be traced through the books of labour exchanges, and the personal columns of the Press.

For a long time after the War most Commanding Officers heard from time to time from these unwanted men. Usually there would be enclosed in the letters printed forms from some business concern or other, listing qualities on which a confidential opinion was asked. One did one's best to answer the queries honestly, but the results often failed to give a picture of the merits of the men concerned, because on the forms there were rarely to be found the right spaces to describe the intelligence, devotion, and bravery of the men in the stress of battle.

Perhaps if one had described how such qualities stood out in the great test of life or death those who read would not have understood or cared. They might have felt that such virtues were not applicable to the door-to-door sale of insurance or toilet articles.

However, life was not always grim. The unit had its own sailing club, where a couple of whalers, a couple of dinghies, and some dangerous canoes made from seaplane pontoons lay on a hard by an attractive inn kept by an ancient mariner. The first time I took out a dinghy, skippered by another of our officers dignified by the name of Commodore, we were upset a hundred yards from shore by a prowling wind-gust which swooped at us through a gap in the rising ground behind.

We hung on to the gunwale, and propelled the craft ashore like frogs learning to swim. The ancient mariner met us on the shingle, bearing tumblers of hot rum.

"I went in to warm 'un up so soon as I see'd ye shove off," he said, and we felt that no more comment was needed.

These nautical expeditions must, however, have attracted

outside attention, for I was made an honorary member of the Royal Yacht Squadron for my term as Garrison Commander. During Cowes week I took Tessa to tea on the famous lawn. She was not particularly interested in the racing, but was delighted to see runner beans growing against the boundary fence, and scraggy ones at that.

She remarked that war was a great leveller.

During that summer I felt that political influence was affecting the Army. Whether it came from Right, Left, or Centre did not matter, for the soldier should serve no master but his monarch. Sections of the Press often took up a soldier's case, arguing against King's Regulations and Military Law, safeguards of justice which had always been enough for the good soldier. It seemed a pity that the bad soldier should so easily be allowed to run unchecked to the shelter of his Member of Parliament, and to gain undeserved sympathy from uninstructed newspaper publicity.

Some newspapers were indeed uninstructed on military matters, perhaps remaining so wilfully. One of the rôles of the Depot was to co-operate with the police in the event of an escape from our neighbouring civil prison. An individual gained his freedom soon after we arrived in the Island, and, after he had committed an act of violence during a burglary to obtain food and clothing, we were asked to help.

Our Demonstration Company was now doing intensive training, and I thought that if they were to be employed on a man-hunt they might as well work as if on a military operation, gaining practice of wireless communication and map-reading, and for fitness' sake carrying all weapons.

My friends on the mainland later made many caustic remarks to me after they had read Press accounts of the intensive man-hunt made by two thousand parachutists, who took no chances against their solitary enemy, but moved always by platoons, fully armed.

Towards the end of my extra year of service I found difficulty in training young officers who came as replacements for the older ones now being demobilized.

These had, admittedly, a difficult task to impress their

authority upon the hardened veterans who now came under their command, but their difficulties were not caused all by inexperience. Britain was without doubt scraping the very bottom of the barrel of manhood. The percentage of indifferent officers in these late intakes was high. Too often the type was wrong.

A good officer springs from one of two sources. Either he must have been as an Other Rank outstanding in personality and technical ability or he must be a cadet of a family whose background and tradition is leadership. A worthy commission may spring from either premise. The text-book runs neck and neck with the stud-book.

No fault may be found with either source of supply, but every fault may be found with the young officer who has neither the knowledge of the text-book nor the instinctive know-how conferred by the stud-book. A soldier will follow his traditional social superior, as their respective ancestors have followed and led back through the pages of history. And a soldier will follow his social equal who has a stronger personality, and greater technical ability. But a soldier will not follow his social equal who has neither personality nor ability.

While at the Depot I was instructed to attend a Posbee. A POSB is a Parachute Officer Selection Board. Here for three days some twenty or thirty young officers, newly commissioned, were segregated in the depths of the country, anonymous in numbered overalls, while a battery of professional and amateur psychiatrists bombarded them with verbal and physical tests. One Airborne Commanding Officer was co-opted on to each board, and was allowed to have his own say about the selection.

I arrived at the proving ground at tea-time on the day the candidates were to assemble, and was directed to the Mess of the permanent staff. The Commandant was a full colonel, and under him were several assistants, one of whom was a psychiatrist. All these officers were perfectly reasonable people, and gave not the least impression of being cranks—not even the psychiatrist. They were most interested in their work, and talked instructive shop as if they enjoyed putting me in the picture.

After dinner we all of us went along to the students' ante-room to mingle with the youths and drink beer with them in an atmosphere of conscious bonhomie. The board claimed, and rightly, that any outstanding personalities, for better or worse, would impinge on one before the end of the evening.

The candidates fell naturally into four classes. The first sort were bright and confident, like star salesmen, ready to listen with deference to the opinion of their seniors, but swift to follow with their own, lest they be thought 'yes-men.' Mentally and physically, this type crowded the other groups away from the forefront of the chit-chat. Second, also confident, but not so ready of tongue, were a few capable-looking fellows, probably rankers commissioned after long service. These were not quite at ease, not yet having found their feet in the Officers' Mess. The third party was an amorphous blob of nonentities, acutely uneasy, and doomed to do duty officer for the term of their service. The fourth lot was made up of a few quiet young subalterns who seemed to view the proceedings with polite distaste. These last resented, I felt, the way some of their comrades were mentally jumping through hoops like sagacious performing animals, and were determined that, even though they themselves should fail to be picked for parachute service, they would not force their attentions upon the selectors. As a result, they overdid their reserve, and sulked in a corner.

Alcohol is the great revealer. Before long the first type became tiresome, the second began to cap each other's tales of war experience, the third started to interpolate a few gauche remarks, and the fourth came out of isolation and were amusing.

The next day two circuses went on at once.

In the one the psychiatrist was ring-master, and the candidates, divided into squads, waited in parties outside his office. One by one they disappeared within, like clients to a clairvoyant, and emerged after a long time with an introspective and unhappy air. Later the psychiatrist showed me how he probed into the inner recesses of the subconscious. They say that the most religiously inclined virgin often teaches the staff of the operating theatre quite a lot when drunk with ether. Just so, the subconscious of the ordinary non-perverted man seems to be a foul pit which crawls with evil and distorted fixations, tendencies, and potentialities, any one of which may slither at any moment over the coping to the freedom of corruption.

After the psychiatrist's little lecture I felt like a man in whom an evil cancer festers and poisons, and declined an offer to try the tests for myself, lest I became conscious of the horrors within me.

Just the same, the tests tallied closely with the individual impressions one had formed in the bar the night before. This man was diffident, that one not too truthful, the other had wife-trouble. Diffidence and prevarication had been obvious the previous evening, and even the wife trouble would have been confided then had the unfortunate been pressed to a large whisky on top of his beer.

The other circus was not mental but physical. Laid out round the camp was a kind of assault course, but its obstacles were not straightforward hurdles to be conquered by courage and agility. Instead each posed a problem not unlike that which faced the countryman who wished to transport three geese and a fox across a river in a rowing-boat whose capacity was limited to himself and one goose and/or fox.

The idea was that the squad, brought up short by one of these constructed conundrums, would mill about in an eager pack like hounds at a check until old Tranter, in the shape of a natural leader, surfaced from the mob and instinctively co-ordinated all activity to his plan of action. The system worked all right. The brighter candidates kept their self-conscious excitement in check, found a quick solution, and got their comrades going as a team to carry it out. But, perversely, I could not much like these budding generals. They were too prefectorial. There was too much youth-leader stuff, like:

"Right, chaps! Quiet a minute! I see how we must do it. Do you, Merrilees, place the barrel within stepping distance of the bank. Hungerford! Swarm up the rope, there's a good fellow. Carpenter and you-at-the-back-there! Lie in the mud.

That's capital! Now, I will swing across the gulf on the rope, with the ring of the grenade in my teeth."

I should have liked to have seen any of them make the late McEntee lie in the mud.

However, there was no doubt at all that the private cards of us spectators tallied to a remarkable degree at the end of the time. I had been told that I must try to let at least half a dozen of the candidates succeed, for the deficiency in Airborne officers was serious, and so, with misgiving, six were passed for parachuting.

The criticism which I had of the selection procedure was that any experienced regimental officer could have picked the outstanding candidates, almost in order of merit, in the Mess the night before.

The Wosbees, or War Office Selection Boards which choose promising rankers for training at OCTU's as potential officers, use much the same procedure as did our Posbee. These Boards test for nearly all the qualities which an officer should have, save the one without which all others are useless. For they have no machinery which discovers whether, should the candidate be commissioned, Other Ranks will follow him willingly, and not because orders say they must.

It would be better to take all potential officers away from their units, name them cadets, issue them with a special badge of rank, and attach them to a strange unit as cadet platoon commanders under instruction. A cadet who took his place in the Officers' Mess, and who showed that he could handle the platoon of which he was supernumerary commander, would well repay OCTU training. Many of those sent forward by the present trick method of selection do not repay training, although in the letter of their job they may be word-perfect.

One day, when the time of my release was very near, CAE rang up to tell me that a film of the Arnhem battle, to be called *Theirs was the Glory*, had been completed. It was to have a première in London where notabilities would be present, for whom the Depot was to provide a guard of honour.

We picked the guard in good time, nearly all of them men who had fought at Arnhem, and practised them in their duties, so that no dishonour might be done to the memory of the 1st Airborne Division. Towards the end of the practice parades the guard commander came to see me. He said that the men felt strongly that, representing their dead comrades, they should not be called upon to pay respects to certain of the notabilities whom rumour said would be present, since in some cases the record over two wars of some of these persons had been either pacifist or downright subversive.

I had a long talk with the guard, for I felt that this was one of those occasions where an explanation would carry more weight than an order. In the end the men saw clearly enough that they must do what was required of them, and that the reputation of the dead stood too high to be fouled by earthly bickering.

Tessa and I were given two cheap tickets to view the film. We arrived early, for I was still a little nervous that the guard would do something to mark their displeasure towards certain individuals, should they be present. However, we were both hustled to our seats fairly quickly, though I did protest to one soft white official that it might be as well if I kept an eye on the guard.

The programme began with a long showing of the Victory procession. I was stirred by the cross-section of armed might, the grandeur of each succeeding detachment swelling the emotions until one was unconscious of self. But this was military jingo, the jingo which follows a regimental band. The grandeur was set in its frame by the humble tail of the procession, in which the soldier could well sink his pride. For it was the parties of firemen, nurses, voluntary workers, and, above all, the tired, worried housewives which put into perspective the marching infantry, the tanks, and the guns.

I saw demonstrated how through those years we had been, not just an armed nation, but a nation in arms, and had put out a war-effort which transcended that of any of our foes or allies. The unconquerable spirit was not in the Forces only, for the spirit belonged to the country, to the men, women, and children who lived in these islands.

At last one saw that war serves a purpose, as devouring fire tempers and purifies, for in the past years our people had been practised a few steps up the stairway to the angels, and had for a while been unified by common purpose and sacrifice.

When the tail of the procession passed off the screen, there was left behind a vacuum into which poured the forces of disunion and selfishness.

The film of Arnhem, faithfully done, was to the soldier dramatic, to the civilian unsensational.

The soldier does not at the time of action realize that he is doing more than his duty, and that duty may be construed as heroism. His view, too, is limited to his own deeds, and he has not the view of the larger picture, painted by the many brushes of his comrades, which may in its entirety be an epic. Thus the battle of Arnhem, which the facile camera could build from disjointed bits into a mosaic, surprised in its drama many who had taken part.

The story was not acted, and there were in it no actors. The tale was retold by survivors of those who had drifted down into the wooded country west of Arnhem on that pleasant autumn Sunday two years before. Almost gauche, they showed again the intolerable conditions under which they had fought so long, grasping in their hands the key to an earlier victory, to relinquish it only when it was prised from their paralysed fingers.

Rory appeared in the film, returned safely, as might have been expected of that indestructible man. He was to be seen stumbling among the exposed wounded about the great bridge itself.

When big demands are made upon it the human spirit pours forth prodigal courage, as from a cruse which never empties. Yet always tradition gives depth to the cruse. The tradition of the Airborne men in this Arnhem battle, in the merciless winter fighting in Tunisia, on the wild night flight to Sicily, and while guarding the Allied left flank in Normandy, had been but short. They had gone to war in an unaccustomed way, lightly armed and equipped with no real support of armour or artillery, and with no centuries-old tale of battle honours to uphold them. Their spirit of devotion to their duty came from the men themselves, and the only inspiration was from the recent dead.

The film was unsensational to the civilian, who expected desperate charges, dramatic orders, selfless sacrifice consciously made, and a clear pattern of advance and retreat. War does not clearly show such things. At its most intense moments the mind takes refuge in schoolboy humour, and in the devil-may-care of the village cricket-match, as if unconsciously to play down the tensity of the menacing moment. The soldier does not wail over the dead, not at the time, for a turn may come for everybody. Pervading all is the miasma of confusion, so that a man knows little of what is happening to either side of him, and, worse still, behind.

It was curious that a film should epitomize for me the half-formed philosophy of soldiering which was in my mind. It was not an especially good film, and the fact that it told of a particularly heroic battle was immaterial. Perhaps its power was in its true portrayal of men under the shadow of fear and strain, blasphemous, joking, debunking themselves, and bound together by comradeship.

As Tessa and I went home that night I knew that it was this comradeship and singleness of purpose which the demobilized soldier would miss, as he would miss no other experience in life. And, if Peace can be said to bring tragedy, there is tragedy in the death of the spirit of a disbanded unit. For such spirit is built indeed by blood, tears, and sweat, and its living entity starves when the men who have served it are scattered.

It was at a farewell party in the Sergeants' Mess that I heard a member of the guard of honour chatting to Tessa.

"We were sorry you and the Commandant didn't come up the red carpet," he said.

Tessa explained that this entrance was reserved for those who had ten-guinea seats.

"Politicians and film stars!" exclaimed the Sergeant. "What does the likes of that lot know of fighting? They did ought to've sent some of the Arnhem officers up the middle."

"You forget the title of the film, Sergeant," said Tessa. "'Theirs *was* the Glory.'"

I packed my kit at the Depot, and made ready to hand over to my successor. The six-year term was done. Things built or botched were to be left to other hands to preserve or reconstruct.

I came out of the demobilization centre in uniform, a card-board box of corner-boy's clothes under my arm, and looked at the world to see whether I could recognize it. For the shape of an object varies with the viewpoint of the beholder, and this was a viewpoint on which I had not before stood.

I remembered how, when I had written my book about my farming life in Wales, I had written of the vision of a proud return when war was done. Now I knew that there was no pride in the soldier returning to civilian life, only disquiet and a sense of loss.

I joined Tessa and the children that same evening. Tessa looked at the garments given me, and made no remarks, save that she thought the raincoat would fit her.

Louise was toying with the badge in my beret, and Tessa watched her for a moment.

"I'll have that silver star made into a brooch," she said.